A GUIDE TO SANDWICH GLASS

WHALE OIL LAMPS AND ACCESSORIES

RAYMOND E. BARLOW
JOAN E. KAISER

PHOTOGRAPHS BY
  FORWARD'S COLOR PRODUCTIONS, INC.
  LEN LORETTE
  HUGO G. POISSON

EDITED BY LLOYD C. NICKERSON

BARLOW–KAISER PUBLISHING COMPANY, INC.

OTHER BOOKS BY RAYMOND E. BARLOW AND JOAN E. KAISER

The Glass Industry in Sandwich Volume 2
The Glass Industry in Sandwich Volume 3
The Glass Industry in Sandwich Volume 4
A Guide to Sandwich Glass Kerosene Lamps and Accessories
A Guide to Sandwich Glass Vases, Colognes and Stoppers
A Guide to Sandwich Glass Witch Balls, Containers and Toys
A Guide to Sandwich Glass Candlesticks, Late Blown and Threaded Ware
Barlow-Kaiser Sandwich Glass Price Guide

FORTHCOMING BOOKS BY RAYMOND E. BARLOW AND JOAN E. KAISER

The Glass Industry in Sandwich Volume 1
Future guides will contain:
    Cup plates
    Lacy glass
    Blown molded glass
    Free-blown glass
    Pressed pattern tableware
    Salts
    Household items
    Cut, etched and engraved glass
    Bottles and pungents

A GUIDE TO SANDWICH GLASS
WHALE OIL LAMPS AND ACCESSORIES
First Edition

Copyright © 1989 by Raymond E. Barlow and Joan E. Kaiser

All correspondence and inquiries should be directed to
Barlow–Kaiser Publishing Company, Inc.
P. O. Box 265
Windham, NH 03087

in conjunction with

Schiffer Publishing Ltd.
1469 Morstein Road
West Chester, PA 19380

This book may be purchased from the publisher.

Try your bookstore first.

First Printing

Library of Congress Catalog Number 88-64002
International Standard Book Number 0-88740-171-6

Front cover: Photo 2020 Bulb lamp with square base, whale oil burner, c. 1830.
Back cover: Photo 2068 Globe lamps with quatrefoil base, whale oil burner, c. 1840. Photo 2101 Three-Printie Block lamps with octagonal standard and square base, c. 1850. Photo 2114 Circle and Ellipse lamps with hexagonal base, c. 1850. Photo 2135 Wooden pickwicks, c. 1850.

For assistance in locating any of these products or to place an order, please ask a bookseller.

Guide to Sandwich Glass: Kerosene Lamps and Accessories, Vol. 2
Raymond Barlow, Joan Kaiser(Editor)
1st ed

Store Price: $24.95
Antiques/Coll, GLASS, Antiques/Collectibles, Glass

Paperback , 132 pages
Schiffer Publishing, Ltd.
07/28/2007
Product # 9780887401725

B & N Sales Rank: 0

✗ **Not in store**

✔ **In Stock**
(See a bookseller to order this item)

Store Delivery:
4-5 business days
Home Delivery:
Express (Members):
Orders arrive in 3-4 business days
Standard (non-Members):
Orders arrive in 3-7 business days

About This Item

From the Publisher
The lure of Sandwich glass still exists for collectors, almost one hundred years after it was last manufactured. With this guidebook, containing 322 full color photos, as well as diagrams like the Dolphin candlestick, those who enjoy American glass will be greatly helped in their effort to identify that which was made in Sandwich. A price guide is available and will be updated regularly. It represents a unique contribution to the complete identification and evaluation of Sandwich glass.

Customers Also Recommend

Publisher Information

Schiffer Publishing, Ltd.
77 Lower Valley Road
Route 372
ATGLEN, PA 19310

610-593-1777

Thank you for shopping at Barnes & Noble

INTRODUCTION

The most important tool you can have to authoritatively identify Sandwich glass is a comprehensive and painstakingly researched guide. This book is such, as well as the other books in the series. It describes every type of glass that was produced in Sandwich, Massachusetts, and all of its photos are made from original plates appearing in Volume 2 of *The Glass Industry in Sandwich*. The identification numbers are the same as those in the larger edition, which allows easy cross-reference. (Guide books with photos from Volumes 3 and 4 are available. Volume 1 is in preparation.)

The photos from the large edition, Volume 2, have been divided into two smaller guides. This one contains the complete chapters on earlier lighting devices (whale oil, burning fluid, etc.), and lamp shades and globes. Another guide, available now, contains later lighting devices (kerosene, etc.), Overlay lighting devices, suspension lamps and lanterns, smoke shades and bells, gas lighting devices and electric lighting.

The extensive categorization and illustration of Sandwich glass should make this guide valuable for field use. The prices in this guide reflect the market at the time of publication. They will be periodically updated in a separate price guide available from the publishers.

WHAT IS SANDWICH GLASS?

It is simple to define Sandwich glass. It was all glass that was produced within Sandwich, Massachusetts, a town on Cape Cod that was founded in 1637.

Glass production came to Sandwich in 1825, when Deming Jarves built and operated an enterprise that became world famous. He called it the Sandwich Glass Manufactory. It was incorporated as the Boston and Sandwich Glass Company in 1826. During the sixty-three years it was active, the factory produced an average of 100,000 pounds of glass per week. Yet this production was only *part* of the glass that should be attributed to Sandwich factories.

In 1859, the Cape Cod Glass Works was established and began to manufacture glass. For ten years, this second factory produced 75,000 pounds of finished glassware each week in competition with the Boston and Sandwich Glass Company. When this company closed, production once again started up in 1883 under the name of the Vasa Murrhina Art Glass Company. Because of manufacturing difficulties, very little of their spangle and spatter glass reached the market. However, the pieces that can be documented should be given Sandwich attribution.

There were several later attempts to manufacture glass in Sandwich after the closing of the Boston and Sandwich Glass Company factory in 1888. In that year, a group of glassworkers built a small glass works and called themselves the Sandwich Co-operative Glass Company. This venture lasted only three years, but its products are recognized as Sandwich glass.

Still another company, the Electrical Glass Corporation, started production in 1890, followed by the Boston and Sandwich Glass Company II, the Boston and Sandwich Glass Company III, and the Sandwich Glass Company. The Alton Manufacturing Company was the last to produce glass on this site. Its most notable product resembled Tiffany glass and was called Trevaise. Like its predecessors, the Alton Manufacturing Company was short-lived, and in 1908, glass was no longer manufactured in Sandwich. *But the glass made by all of these small companies are recognized as Sandwich glass because of their geographical source.*

There were several other companies in Sandwich that worked on glass but did not make it. They cut it, etched it, engraved it, decorated it, and assembled it. The glass that they worked on, called *blanks*, was brought to Sandwich from factories in Pennsylvania. Regardless of what was done to the surface of this Pennsylvania product, *it cannot be called Sandwich glass*. Only glass that has been shaped while hot can be attributed to a particular factory.

This book deals only with the glass that was manufactured in Sandwich and is therefore entitled to be called Sandwich glass.

INVENTORY OF SANDWICH GLASS

No.	Description	Condition	Date Purchased	Amount	Date Sold	Amount

LIGHTING DEVICES

1825–1870

The manufacture of lighting devices by the Boston and Sandwich Glass Company was, by its very nature, specifically suited to Deming Jarves and his people. The method of producing light was one area in which Jarves involved himself directly.

By 1825, when Jarves' Sandwich Glass Manufactory opened its doors, the general public was demanding something better than candles to illuminate their homes and workplaces at an affordable price. The glass industry as a whole responded to this demand. We ask our readers to keep in mind that the darkness of today is not the darkness that was known to them in their time. Darkness in the early 1800's was total. There was no city glow, no reflection from the sky. When clouds covered the moon, blackness covered the earth like a blanket. Your eyes, opened or closed, mentally made no change. Even a match illuminated this type of darkness to a startling degree. So a small night lamp set beside a sick youngster's bed was a tranquil pleasure for an anxious mother. A single flame near a dangerous stairwell guarded the footsteps of the elderly. A small lighting device placed on a windowsill or a shelf in a fanlight acted as a beacon to bring home a family across the prairies of the West. Only the size of a match flame, the glow could be seen for miles.

As you study the evolution of lighting as it related to the glass industry, remember that parallel changes took place in the manufacture of lamps in other mediums as well, particularly pewter, tin and porcelain. When one takes an overview, one realizes that the part played by the Boston and Sandwich Glass Company was limited. Yet, lighting played a major part in the history of Sandwich's glass industry.

Jarves' familiarity with the marketing of lighting devices extended back to 1813, when, in his early twenties, he was listed in the Boston City Directory as a merchant of dry goods at 11 Cornhill. He continued in this direction after forming a partnership with Joseph B. Henshaw on April 4, 1814. At this time, the Boston Porcelain and Glass Company was formed in East Cambridge, Massachusetts. Jarves served as clerk. In November 1817, after repeated failures, the porcelain and glass manufactory was sold at public auction to a group of men that included Jarves. They incorporated as the New England Glass Company on February 16, 1818, with Jarves as agent.

Jarves' involvement in the New England Glass Company's lighting devices stemmed from his great interest in streamlining production and gearing it to the mass market. On February 2, 1822, he patented an improvement in the tin drop burner that was used on glass lamps to burn whale oil. The original concept of a vertical wick tube in the center of a supporting disk is sometimes credited to Benjamin Franklin, who experimented with wicks while working in his father's chandlery. However, it was John Miles of Birmingham, England, who patented a vertical wick tube with a flanged disk in 1787. The Miles patent disk worked well on an enclosed metal font because pressure of the flange against the metal neck of the font assured a tight fit. But pressure applied to the neck of a glass font would crack it. The drop burner based on Miles' principle that was used on glass lamps had the simple tin disk that rested loosely on a neckless font, but if the lamp were tipped over, the whale oil spilled out. To insure a tight fit on glass, brass or plated metal collars were cemented to the necks of glass fonts, threaded to accept a threaded burner. However, the cost of the metal collars plus the cost of labor to cement them led Jarves to look for a way to obtain the same result at less expense to the buyer.

Jarves surrounded the tube that held the wick with a cork stopper.[1] The cork stopper fit snugly into the neck of a glass font. If the lamp fell over, the oil did not spill, and the fire that normally followed a spill was averted. According to the writings of Charles Cotesworth Pinckney Waterman, who worked closely with Jarves from 1825 until the late 1860's, Jarves sold the patent to Boston lamp manufacturer William Carleton[2] for $100. Carleton saw the ultimate potential of this new idea. The cork tube whale oil burner became the beginning of a long procession of improvements that Carleton had his hand in and from which he accumulated great wealth.

PROGRESS IN LIGHTING TECHNOLOGY

	BURNER DESIGN	FUEL	LAMP DESIGN
1700's	drop tube loose cap	whale oil colza oil	
1787	flanged cap (John Miles)		
early 1800's	threaded cap metal collar		blown font blown base
1822	cork tube (Deming Jarves)		blown font wafer shallow pressed base
1830	tube above cap tapered tube (Isaiah Jennings)	burning fluid (Isaiah Jennings)	blown font wafer pressed base and standard
1836	safety case (Isaiah Jennings)		blown molded pattern font wafer pressed base and standard
early 1840's		lard	pressed font wafer pressed base and standard
1846		crude kerosene (Abraham Gesner)	
1852	improved safety burner and case (John Newell, Eben Horsford and James Nichols)	kerosene (coal oil, petroleum)	glass font metal cup metal standard marble base
late 1850's	deflector thumbwheel		
1860			glass font metal connector pressed glass base and standard

Black'fish (-fĭsh), n. **1.** (Zoöl.) A small kind of whale, of the genus *Globicephalus*, of several species. The most common is *G. melas*. Also some-

Blackfish (*Globicephalus melas*).

times applied to other whales of larger size.
2. (Zoöl.) The tautog of New England (*Tautoga*).
3. (Zoöl.) The black sea bass (*Centropristis atrarius*) of the Atlantic coast. It is an excellent food fish; — locally called also *black Harry*.
4. (Zoöl.) A fish of southern Europe (*Centrolophus pompilus*) of the Mackerel family.
5. (Zoöl.) The female salmon in the spawning season.
☞ The name is locally applied to other fishes.

Cach'a-lot (kăsh'á-lŏt), n. [F. *cachalot*.] (Zoöl.) The sperm whale (*Physeter macrocephalus*). It has in the top of its head a large cavity, containing an oily fluid, which, after death, concretes into a whitish crystalline substance called *spermaceti*. See SPERM WHALE.

Sperm' whale' (spĕrm' hwāl'). (Zoöl.) A very large toothed whale (*Physeter macrocephalus*), having a head of enormous size. The upper jaw is destitute of teeth. In the upper part of the head, above the skull, there is a large cavity, or case, filled with oil and spermaceti. This whale sometimes grows to the length of more than eighty feet. It is found in the warmer parts of all the oceans. Called also *cachalot*, and *spermaceti whale*.

Sperm Whale.

Pygmy sperm whale (*Zoöl.*), a small whale (*Kogia breviceps*), seldom twenty feet long, native of tropical seas, but occasionally found on the American coast. Called also *snub-nosed cachalot*. — **Sperm-whale porpoise** (*Zoöl.*), a toothed cetacean (*Hyperoödon bidens*), found on both sides of the Atlantic and valued for its oil. The adult becomes about twenty-five feet long, and its head is very large and thick. Called also *bottle-nosed whale*.

Sperm-whale Porpoise.

Sea' el'e-phant (sē' ĕl'ê-fant). (Zoöl.) A very large seal (*Macrorhinus proboscideus*) of the Antarctic seas, much hunted for its oil. It sometimes attains a length of thirty feet, and is remarkable for the prolongation of the nose of the adult male into an erectile elastic proboscis, about a foot in length. Another species of smaller size (*M. angustirostris*) occurs on the coast of Lower California, but is now nearly extinct.

Sea Elephant (*M. proboscideus*).

Wal'rus (wŏl'rŭs; 277), n. [D. *walrus*; of Scand. origin; cf. Dan. *valros*, Sw. *vallross*, Norw. *hvalros*; literally, whale horse; akin to Icel. *hrosshvalr*, AS. *horshwæl*. See WHALE, and HORSE.] (Zoöl.) A very large marine mammal (*Trichecus rosmarus*) of the Seal family, native of the Arctic Ocean. The male has long and powerful tusks descending from the upper jaw. It uses these in procuring food and in fighting. It is hunted for its oil, ivory, and skin. It feeds largely on mollusks. Called also *morse*.

Walrus (*Trichecus rosmarus*). Male.

☞ The walrus of the North Pacific and Behring Strait (*Trichecus obesus*) is regarded by some as a distinct species, by others as a variety of the common walrus.

Burn'ing, n. The act of consuming by fire or heat, or of subjecting to the effect of fire or heat; the state of being on fire or excessively heated.
Burning fluid, any volatile illuminating oil, as the lighter petroleums (naphtha, benzine), or oil of turpentine (camphine), but esp. a mixture of the latter with alcohol. — **Burning glass**, a convex lens of considerable size, used for producing an intense heat by converging the sun's rays to a focus. — **Burning house** (*Metal.*), the furnace in which tin ores are calcined, to sublime the sulphur and arsenic from the pyrites. *Weale*. — **Burning mirror**, a concave mirror, or a combination of plane mirrors, used for the same purpose as a burning glass.
Syn. — Combustion; fire; conflagration; flame; blaze.

Cam'phene (kăm'fēn or kăm-fēn'), n. (Chem.) One of a series of substances, $C_{10}H_{16}$, resembling camphor, regarded as modified terpenes.
Cam-phine' (kăm-fēn' or kăm'fĭn), n. [From CAMPHOR.] Rectified oil of turpentine, used for burning in lamps, and as a common solvent in varnishes.
☞ The name is also applied to a mixture of this substance with three times its volume of alcohol and sometimes a little ether, used as an illuminant.

Lard (lärd), n. [F., bacon, pig's fat, L. *lardum*, *laridum*; cf. Gr. λαρινός fattened, fat.] **1.** Bacon; the flesh of swine. [*Obs.*]   *Dryden*.
2. The fat of swine, esp. the internal fat of the abdomen; also, this fat melted and strained.
Lard oil, an illuminating and lubricating oil expressed from lard. — **Leaf lard**, the internal fat of the hog, separated in leaves or masses from the kidneys, etc.; also, the same melted.

Gas (găs), n.; pl. GASES (-ĕz). [Invented by the chemist Van Helmont of Brussels, who died in 1644.]
1. An aëriform fluid; — a term used at first by chemists as synonymous with *air*, but since restricted to fluids supposed to be permanently elastic, as oxygen, hydrogen, etc., in distinction from vapors, as steam, which become liquid on a reduction of temperature. In present usage, since all of the supposed permanent gases have been liquefied by cold and pressure, the term has resumed nearly its original signification, and is applied to any substance in the elastic or aëriform state.
2. (*Popular Usage*) (*a*) A complex mixture of gases, of which the most important constituents are marsh gas, olefiant gas, and hydrogen, artificially produced by the destructive distillation of gas coal, or sometimes of peat, wood, oil, resin, etc. It gives a brilliant light when burned, and is the common gas used for illuminating purposes. (*b*) Laughing gas. (*c*) Any irrespirable aëriform fluid.
☞ *Gas* is often used adjectively or in combination; as, *gas* fitter or gasfitter; *gas* meter or *gas*-meter, etc.

Ker'o-sene' (kĕr'ṓ-sēn'), n. [Gr. κηρός wax.] An oil used for illuminating purposes, formerly obtained from the distillation of mineral wax, bituminous shale, etc., and hence called also *coal oil*. It is now produced in immense quantities, chiefly by the distillation and purification of petroleum. It consists chiefly of several hydrocarbons of the methane series.

In'can-des'cent (-sent), a. [L. *incandescens*, *-entis*, p. pr. of *incandescere* to become warm or hot; pref. *in-* in + *candescere* to become of a glittering whiteness, to become red hot, incho. fr. *candere* to be of a glittering whiteness: cf. F. *incandescent*. See CANDLE.] White, glowing, or luminous, with intense heat; as, *incandescent* carbon or platinum; hence, clear; shining; brilliant.
Holy Scripture become resplendent; or, as one might say, *incandescent* throughout.   *I. Taylor*.
Incandescent lamp or **light** (*Elec.*), a kind of lamp in which the light is produced by a thin filament of conducting material, usually carbon, contained in a vacuum, and heated to incandescence by an electric current, as in the Edison lamp; — called also *incandescence lamp*, and *glowlamp*.

Jarves continued in his capacity as agent of the New England Glass Company until he began production of glass in his own Sandwich Glass Manufactory on July 4, 1825. Lighting devices immediately became an integral part of the production line. An account book of the glass produced weekly, called the *sloar book*, shows that in the first week of manufacture thirty-five smoke shades and hundreds of peg lamps were made. During the week of August 1, 1825, over nine hundred pounds of glass were worked in the shops. Included were 135 high stem lamps and 132 chamber lamps (i.e., bedroom lamps). Eighty small Mallory lamp glasses were made the week of August 13 as well as a quantity of Liverpool lamp glasses. By the early part of September, 275 small round foot lamps, seventy-two high foot lamps, sixty-three low foot lamps and many button stem lamps were a regular part of production.

All of these early lamps were sent out with burners, which were purchased in Boston and fitted to the lamps prior to shipping. There is no indication that the machine shop at the Sandwich factory site was equipped to manufacture burners at any time. Letters written by Deming Jarves in Boston to his brother-in-law William Stutson at the factory as early as November 23, 1825, mention the three types of whale oil burners commonly in use: "common tubes", meaning the 1822 cork tubes, "plated caps", referring to wick tubes that were inserted through plated metal or pewter disks that were threaded to be screwed to threaded collars, and "brass caps", which were threaded brass disks through which wick tubes were inserted. In a letter dated June 14, 1826, Jarves mentioned rose foot cylinder lamps with brass caps. His letter to Stutson on October 17, 1827, complained that many of the tin caps had rusted from being packed in damp straw.

As this book was being written, the Sandwich Glass Museum acquired an important collection of factory correspondence to add to their files. A letter dated November 23, 1827, documents the Boston and Sandwich Glass Company's purchase of threaded lamp caps from William Carleton, the lamp manufacturer to whom Jarves had sold his cork tube patent. William T. Mayo wrote from the Boston office to Jarves, who was in Sandwich, the following:

"Mr. Carl(e)ton has made about 200 plated lamp caps, believe he will sell them 25¢ each. They are not inferior to Schulz' in appearance. Shall I send them?"

It is evident that at this time the burners were attached to the lamps at the Sandwich facility. However, on March 28, 1828, Jarves stated that he was having lamp tops cemented on at the Boston store because it was cheaper than paying lamp capper Wheeler in Sandwich.

Beyond simple lamp capping, there is no indication in the records that lamp assembly businesses handling glass lamps in quantity had begun to flourish in the Boston area. William Carleton was listed at various times in the City Directory as a tinman and lamp manufacturer, but most documented Carleton lamps were metal sinumbra and solar types. Only the shades were glass. Glass lamps at that time required no assembly. The lamp font stored fuel and the lamp burned with an open flame as does a candle.

Glass lamps that had lamp glasses (Editor's note: The term *lamp glass* referred to the article we now call a "globe".) surrounding the flame were supplied with threaded burners with a coronet that secured the lamp glass with a set screw. On July 20, 1829, Deming Jarves was granted a patent that is now designated as No. 5577X for "affixing glass chimneys". The details of his patent are not known.

The first of many chemically produced lighting fuels was introduced in the United States by patentee Isaiah Jennings on October 16, 1830. Jennings had perfected a method of combining alcohol and turpentine. On May 11, 1831, the *Barnstable Patriot and Commercial Advertiser* informed Cape Cod readers about the new lighting fuel.

A new liquid has been discovered by Isaiah Jennings of New York which he uses as a substitute for Oil in Lamps. It is described as a species of alcohol, and the advantages it possesses over oil are said to consist of its cheapness, and the fact that it never chills, and that no smoke issues from it. It is transparent. It never burns the wick, and is less dangerous, as no sparks have ever been known to originate therefrom. There is no dripping below the burner, and no choke in the tubes. It is not injurious to the eyes, there is no grease and is much sooner lighted.

Alcohol was a name given to any product that was highly refined or distilled from another substance. For example, the burning fluid known as camphene qualified as alcohol because it was distilled from spirits of turpentine. Some statements in the article turned out to be untrue—one in particular: alcohol, naphtha, camphene, gasoline, and most subsequent mixtures that came under the heading of burning fluid proved to be the most dangerous fuels ever handled by man for the purpose of lighting. Thousands of deaths and injuries were directly attributed to the explosive nature of these fuels.

The Boston and Sandwich Glass Company became directly involved with Isaiah Jennings on November 22, 1833, when a special Board of Directors meeting was called, presided over by the director who had held his seat the longest, Deming Jarves. A gentleman named George G. Channing claimed to have a patent for the burning of his alcohol mixture in a lamp that had been patented by Isaiah Jennings. He proposed to sell one quarter of the patent to the Boston and Sandwich Glass Company for $1500. The patent would be owned, divided into four parts, by the Boston and Sandwich Glass Company, the New England Glass Company, George G. Channing and William Carleton. The arrangement was to be for the manufacture and sale of Jennings' lamp and the sale of the alcohol mixture.[3]

By this time, the friction match had been invented. Although it made lighting the lamps easier, it increased the fire hazard. The first of the friction matches was called "loco foco", and was advertised as a new device that burst into flame when rubbed against any hard surface. The new convenience made it possible for children to light lamps without supervision. If the lamp held one of the new combustible burning fluids and the match was struck too close to the fumes, the lamp or the nearby container that held fuel to fill the lamp exploded. Newspapers published

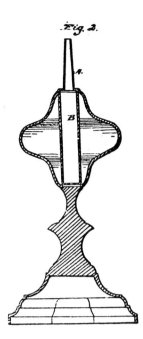

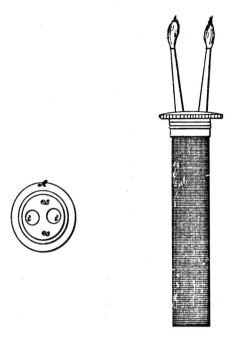

Figure 2 of Isaiah Jenning's patent No. 29 illustrated the safety tube on his alcohol and turpentine lamp. The metal tube was to be perforated with small holes or perforated with large holes and covered with wire gauze. A similar tube was to be inserted into the spout of the fuel filler can. "The object of the insertion of such tubes is to prevent the running out of the liquid except in minute quantities should the lamp, or other vessel be upset, and also to prevent the passage of flame from the outside to the fluid contained within the lamp, or other vessel." The patent was dated September 22, 1836. The burner has only one tapered tube, although the lamp appears to be larger than a night lamp.

On October 4, 1853, John Newell of Boston took out patent No. 10,099 for a camphene lamp burner with a similar metal safety tube. Newell claimed as his improvement the silvering of the perforated tubes and the wire gauze, or mesh, and the addition of tiny vent holes in the burner cap. He suggested that the tubes could be constructed entirely of wire gauze.

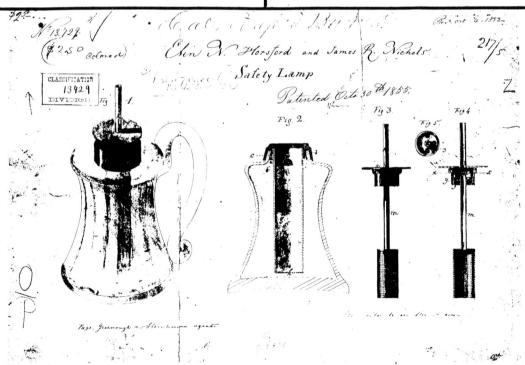

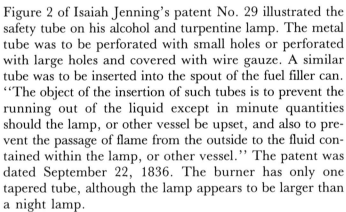

The United States Patent Office received this application from Eben N. Horsford and James R. Nichols on October 4, 1852, as noted in the upper right corner. However, the patent No. 13,729 was not issued until October 30, 1855, three years later. Horsford and Nichols extended the narrow wick tube to the bottom of the font and surrounded it with the safety tube, called a "safety case" on the patent. Safety tubes as illustrated on all three patents have been found on Sandwich lamps.

throughout the burning fluid era told of terrible disasters that followed explosions—the loss of homes and barns and the maiming and death of children were common news items in almost every issue. Many of the cellar holes that can be seen on the back roads of New England are the direct result of burning fluid disasters. The *Barnstable Patriot* of August 17, 1852, reported an accident in the home of glassmaker and preacher Joseph Marsh.

> On Sunday evening last, a very serious accident occurred at Sandwich, from the ignition of burning fluid. Three of the daughters of the Reverend Joseph Mash (sic) were very badly burned, and it is thought that two of them may not survive. The accident occurred by filling the lamp from the can, in the evening, while the lamp was burning.

From the late 1700's on, Patent Office records show continued efforts to experiment with new burners and lamps or improve existing designs. Isaiah Jennings alone was granted nineteen patents prior to 1830. But the new fuel now being burned in lamps manufactured by an ever expanding glass industry resulted in accelerated attempts to increase the candlepower and decrease the danger. The fluid burner that came into common use was still the simple tubes that supported a round wick, but the tubes extended upward from a threaded disk and did not descend downward into the font to cause a heat buildup. A two-tube fluid burner had tubes that angled outward above the disk and were tapered to provide a tight fit where the wicks emerged. The slots that had been in the sides of the cylindrical whale oil tubes that allowed the insertion of a pick to raise the wick were eliminated. Little caps that hung from a fine-link chain covered the tubes when the lamp was not in use, preventing evaporation and eliminating offensive odor. As these inventions took place and the customer had his choice of fuels and burners, Jarves' cork tube burner was used less and less because a lamp purchased with the cork tube had no metal collar to which a fluid burner could be screwed.

It is not the intention of the authors to provide a detailed study of burners because they were not manufactured at Sandwich glass factories. Records prove that burner and collar designs cannot be used as a means of documenting the origin of lamps. But a knowledge of burner designs that are most frequently found on Sandwich lamps and in which Sandwich glass companies had a legal interest will help you date Sandwich lamps, bearing in mind that styles changed drastically between 1825 and the early 1900's, when our study ends. Also, management had a very real concern regarding advancements in man-made fuel. At the same time the public accepted it for its brighter glow and manageable consistency, it was being warned against using it in glass lamps, especially in small glass lamps with handles that were carried through the dark to light the way to a bedchamber. A fall over an object inadvertently left in a darkened hallway not only led to a broken bone, but to burns as well. "Use metal lamps only!" was the cry of the newspapers protecting their readers. "Would the market for glass lamps decrease?" was the worry of the Boston and Sandwich Glass Company. In an effort to protect their stockholders, the Board

of Directors constantly glorified the use of glass lamps with all fuels.

On September 22, 1836, Isaiah Jennings of New York, New York, was granted patent No. 29 for a safety lamp that burned alcohol and turpentine compounds in which the fluid wick in the font was surrounded by a perforated metal tube that extended to the bottom of the font. The tube measured about ½'' in diameter. Jennings suggested that if the tube was perforated with large holes, it should be surrounded by several thicknesses of wire gauze, or mesh. The patent also called for a similar guard to be placed inside the spout of the vessel that supplied the lamp with fluid. Jennings' principle of preventing the flame from following the fumes back to their source had been invented by Sir Humphrey Davy in 1816. Using a tube to separate the air from the fluid had some value, because the Davy principle and subsequent improvements over the next twenty years can be found on Sandwich lamps in obvious well-used condition. Boston's John Newell was issued patent No. 10,099 on October 4, 1853, for silvering the mesh to prevent corrosion. He added tiny vent holes in the burner cap to alleviate pressure that built up in the font. According to Dr. Edward A. Rushford in an article written for the August 1936 issue of *American Collector*, although Newell's burner had two cylinders, one inside the other, small lamps were made with only one cylinder. Patent No. 13,729 was issued on October 30, 1855, to Eben N. Horsford and James R. Nichols for the further improvement of a narrow inner tube surrounding the wick that in the patent is illustrated as an extension of the narrow wick tube to the bottom of the font. It would appear from Dr. Rushford's article that both the Newell and the Horsford and Nichols safety lamps were on the market by 1852. Newell advertised his lamp in the *Scientific American* on December 18, 1852. The December 18 issue carried a complimentary editorial that resulted in a controversy over whether Newell's was a modern inovation or only a modification of Jennings' 1836 patent. The quibbling correspondent turned out to be James R. Nichols, who had already registered the Horsford and Nichols patent on October 4, 1852.

As previously stated, improvements came rapidly in the 1830's. Closely following the heels of the 1836 safety tube patent was Samuel Rust's patent lamp, described in the *Yarmouth Register and Barnstable County Advertiser* of January 4, 1838, as being a lamp of common form that had a burner with a flat wick that could be adjusted by means of a brass nut. This is the first indication found by the authors of a flat wick that could have been used in the Sandwich area. Bear in mind that Rust's flat wick preceded the use of kerosene by ten years.

The *Yarmouth Register and Barnstable County Advertiser* of December 20, 1838, contained an article noting that Boston and Sandwich Glass Company plates, preserve dishes, bottoms of lamps and similarly shaped articles were pressed in iron molds. The writer made a point of mentioning *bottoms* of lamps. From this statement we can deduce that the tops, or *fonts*, were blown into molds or were free-blown separately, to be attached to the pressed bases by the use of a wafer-shaped piece of hot glass that was about the diameter and thickness of a quarter. The units

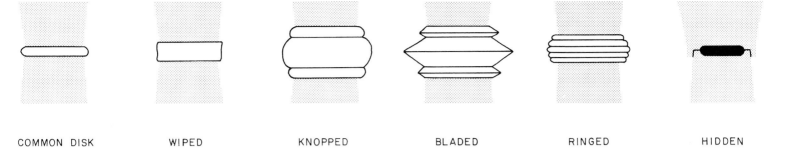

| COMMON DISK | WIPED | KNOPPED | BLADED | RINGED | HIDDEN |

Fig. 4   Types of wafers used in Sandwich. The disk was the most common. The wiped wafer was made by smoothing the common disk to conform to the shape of the units it connected. The knopped wafer was sometimes reworked into the bladed configuration. The ringed wafer was often used to join a free-blown font to its base. The number of rings varied. Two units were occasionally joined by a wafer that cannot be seen on the outside of a completed lamp. Wafers do not have mold marks because they were shaped by hand. The size of each type can vary on a matched pair of lamps.

were joined by holding the base in an upright position, placing a hot wafer-shaped glob of glass on top of it, then placing the font on the wafer until it adhered without support. When three units were needed to make a tall lamp—a pressed base, a blown knop center, and a font—two wafers were needed to join the units to each other. Even after the Boston and Sandwich Glass Company factory had completely converted to coal to heat the glass, and larger pieces could be pressed and blown, the wafer method of construction continued to be used. A variety of bases were "mixed and matched" with an unlimited number of fonts, providing the customer with many styles of lamps from which to choose.

As you study the styles of bases and fonts that can be documented without question as having been made in Sandwich, study also the types of wafers that were used between the units of each lamp in addition to the common disk wafer. Free-blown globe and bulb fonts were often joined with ringed wafers, as shown in the accompanying illustration. A knopped wafer was used, which was sometimes reworked to resemble a series of blades. An occasional wiped wafer is found, which is the common disk flattened to conform to the shape of the units it connected. Be aware that the wafer was sometimes hidden, particularly when joining two blown units. All of these wafer shapes joined to lamp units were dug in sufficient quantities at the factory sites to guarantee Sandwich production. Construction methods should always be open to review because the future may uncover added production methods that were not available for study at the time of this publication. *Separate lamp units joined without the use of a wafer were not dug at the factory site by the authors.* Many beautiful lamps in patterns that were used at Sandwich can be found on the antiques marketplace that do not have wafers.[4] Buy them because they are beautiful, but not because they are Sandwich.

When considering an all-glass lamp for purchase, examine each unit of the lamp independently. Only in this manner will you be able to identify a purchased lamp as Sandwich. Learn the forms and patterns of the fonts, the forms of blown center units, the forms and patterns of the bases, and the types of wafers used to connect the units.

The financial panic of 1837 brought a halt to the steady and continual growth of the Boston and Sandwich Glass Company. It was impossible to maintain a workforce because glass did not sell at any price. Yet while the nation's economy ground to a standstill, three major changes took place in the decade between 1835 and 1845 that affected the glass lamp industry and therefore are important to Sandwich glass collectors because the changes help to date lamps.

In 1836, the factory began to heat their furnaces with coal instead of wood. Coal burned at a higher temperature than wood, so the liquid glass in the pots was heated beyond the molasses consistency it attained from a wood fire. Glass placed into molds to be pressed flowed more easily into crevices, so larger pieces could be made—bases with taller standards, fonts with extensions. As a result, by 1840, a better quality product was being manufactured. Fewer underfilled articles were turned out of molds, a characteristic the authors find appealing, but one that places some primitive pieces in the category of folk art.

Second, even though management was considering the closing of the factory in 1840, they realized that to continue and remain competitive meant major style changes in their products. Molds were purchased in which glass fonts were pressed because it took less time to teach a glassworker how much glass to drop into a pressing mold than it did to train a glass blower to make free-blown fonts or to blow the correct size bubble into a patterned mold. By 1844, when a furnace was constructed specifically for manufacture of colored glass, the Boston and Sandwich Glass Company was well on its way to increased production of lamps, vases, candlesticks and tableware in a variety of beautiful colors and patterns. Therefore, 1840–1870 is generally the date given for the manufacture of those articles. Examples of lamps would be Star and Punty, Circle and Ellipse, Loop, and Waffle and Thumbprint.

The third major change in lamp production was the elimination of long, narrow fonts on stand lamps. They allowed the last bit of whale oil to be wicked up but contributed to the explosive power of burning fluid. An almost empty elongated font with a small diameter lower extremity contained too much air that was heating and expanding, inviting explosions. So fonts were shortened so that the lamps were suitable for both whale oil and burning fluid, depending upon the burner selected by the customer. Free-blown bulb fonts were phased out. Two pressed patterns that were just recently being manufactured but which had limited use were Loop, shown in photo 2018, and Four-Printie Block, shown in photo 2104. Although Four-Printie Block vases were made over a long period, such lamp designs were abandoned in favor of the shorter Three-Printie Block pattern, which continued to be produced heavily for at least another ten years. Patterns that came into prominence as the change in style took place were Tulip, Acanthus Leaf, and Prism and Crescent.

Throughout the early 1840's, the factory limped sluggishly along in parallel with the economy. The situation became so bad that in 1844 Board members were still considering ''winding down the business''. Only through Jarves' super-human effort and his personal finances was the corporation able to muddle through this period in history and make plans for new furnaces and new showrooms to be in operation and style changes to be in production to take advantage of an upturn in world finances that surely was just around the corner.

An example of Jarves' thinking, as he realized that the bulk of future production would be to satisfy the demands of the ever-expanding lighting industry in the United States, was recorded in the minutes of a June 17, 1844, Board meeting. Jarves had personally purchased half of the patent rights of a lamp cap for $750 with the understanding that the Boston and Sandwich Glass Company would reimburse him for it when financial conditions improved. The patent was for a single tube and double tube whale oil cap that had a double chamber ''to catch and hold the drip & prevent from running out in case the lamp is in horizontal or inclined position''. It had been granted as No. 3582 to Robert H. Eddy[5] of Boston on May 10, 1844.

The Board of Directors decided they could now purchase the patent rights from Jarves and pay him interest on his money from the time of purchase. The Board agreed to sell back to Jarves the use of the cap. He could pay the Boston and Sandwich Glass Company a royalty of one cent per cap if he wanted to use them on something other than glass lamps.

This decision by the Board was an interesting one. Deming Jarves at this time sold glass and other dry goods privately in Boston. He also owned the Mount Washington Glass Manufactory in South Boston. The Board decided that Jarves would be allowed to use the Eddy patent whale oil cap on lamps, which he purchased from other sources to sell privately, but under no circumstances would he be allowed to use the cap on glass lamps manufactured at his Mount Washington works. The June 17 meeting began by Jarves attempting to force the Board to do his bidding under threat of his resignation as agent of the company. Heated arguments may have ensued throughout the whole meeting as Jarves maneuvered to control Board decisions, but he finally lost the right to use the whale oil burner on Mount Washington lamps.

As the country came out of the deep depression in 1845, so did the Boston and Sandwich Glass Company. By this time, the demand for lighting devices with their many improvements gave a lift to the company that brightened its financial picture and the morale of its workers. By 1847, the factory returned to full production.

The reason for this rapid comeback was the expansion westward of the United States. Up until this time, the population was concentrated along the Eastern Seaboard. With new growth in the West came new homebuilding and the concomitant demand for glass. The Boston and Sandwich Glass Company had to take advantage of this

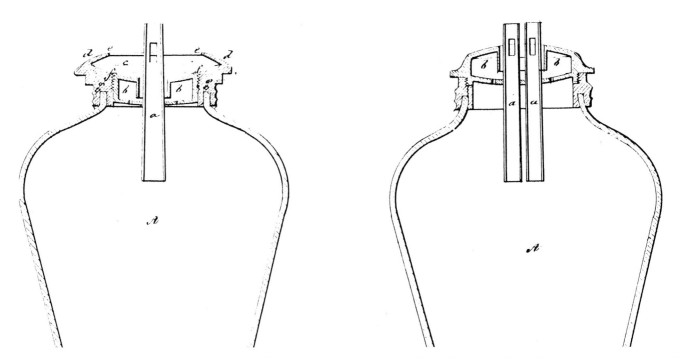

Deming Jarves' patent attorney Robert H. Eddy was granted patent No. 3582 on May 10, 1844. It was for a whale oil burner that had a double chamber to catch the oil and prevent it from spilling out if the lamp fell or was carried in an inclined position. Jarves had purchased half of the patent rights with the intention of selling his interest to the Boston and Sandwich Glass Company.

need in order to fully utilize the freight service provided by the new railroad coming to Sandwich. Raw materials had to be delivered in larger quantities and sufficient orders had to be on the books to fill freight cars. The new source of high quality glass sand in the Berkshire Mountains of Massachusetts almost guaranteed a ready market.

Lamps manufactured in the mid–1840's burned sperm oil, whale oil, lard and the ever increasing variety of man-made substances. The invention of a new fuel source did not mean automatic obsolescence of an old one. Free whale oil often came ashore on Cape Cod. The *Sandwich Observer* on August 28, 1847, reported that a herd of black-fish had come ashore at Truro, and the whole of Cape Cod showed up. Blackfish were small whales about twenty feet long. They were expected to yield a barrel of oil each, so a beaching of this number would light the Cape for a long time at no cost other than the manpower needed for the rendering. All those who worked took home their share with the exception of the ministers in the towns where the whales came ashore. The coming ashore of a large pod, the correct name for a "herd", was considered to be an act of God. The minister was given all of the oil from the largest whale so that he might light the church and his home until the whales came ashore again.

On January 23, 1847, an advertisement in the *Sandwich Observer* advised that the following lighting devices could be purchased by seeing Charles H. Chapouil at the Boston and Sandwich Glass Company ware room.

No. 1 and 2 Solar Lamps
Britannia Lamps
Lanterns
Reading Lamps

A year later, the ad was expanded. In addition to metal teapots, castor frames and table cutlery, the previous list of lighting devices was enlarged to include:

Sewing Lamps
Cornelius' Patent Lard Lamps for burning cheap oil
Hanging and Side Solar Lamps for lighting Stores, Meeting Houses or Halls
Solar Wicks
Solar Chimneys

These lamps were made from metal. They were purchased from other sources to be sold at the factory for the convenience of Sandwich citizens. However, the glass globes and chimneys were made at the factory. Globes, shades and chimneys for metal fixtures comprised a large percentage of the factory's production until the last fire was extinguished in 1908. This does not mean that the manufacture of colognes, vases and tableware was curtailed, but every flint glass factory depended heavily on the needs of the lighting industry.

Late in 1847, a new fuel for lighting was beginning to find its way into the market. Canadian geologist Abraham Gesner discovered how to produce crude lamp oil from coal in 1846. This product that later became known as *kerosene* was introduced to the English lighting industry by James Young of Glasgow, Scotland. As methods for distilling it were perfected, it invaded the market and eventually changed the lighting industry.

In the meantime, a satellite business developed for the cutting and shaping of marble bases. On December 25, 1847, it had been reported that Colonel E. Chamberlain, who was employed by the Boston and Sandwich Glass Company in the manufacture of marble stands for lamps,

A pod of blackfish ashore on Cape Cod. The small whales provided lamp oil that was rationed out to the people who helped render the blubber.

had made a stand with a highly polished surface in the shape of a monument, "which we should suppose would cause the rich glass to be in great demand". The marble standards soon gave way to brass standards. The brass standard required a brass cup into which the peg beneath a glass font could be cemented. This transition took place during the 1850's. Lamps made during this time period were used with whale oil burners, fluid burners, and the completely different style of burner designed to provide the proper draft for the new kerosene.

The year 1853 saw the coming of still another fuel for lighting—sea-elephant oil, which was obtained from wal-

Tuesday, FEBRUARY 10, 1885.   Copyright, 1885, by HARPER & BROTHERS. $2.00 PER YEAR, IN ADVANCE.

Whale fishing off Long Island, New York, as illustrated on the cover page of *Young People An Illustrated Weekly*. This February 10, 1885, issue shows how the blubber was cut and boiled on the seashore.

rus. It was capable of burning as clean and clear as sperm oil, but was cheaper. The acceptance of this oil devastated the walrus population in southern waters. Within five years, the price of sea-elephant oil skyrocketed and it became too expensive to burn. A variety of fuels continued to be advertised by general stores, including inexpensive rosin oil. But kerosene was gradually taking over the market. On April 20, 1858, the *Barnstable Patriot* heralded the arrival of a "Patent Kerosene Lamp".

> Mr. Robert Tobey of Sandwich has disposed of a large number of these lamps to our citizens during the past week, and they have, on trial, been found all they are presented to be, and we advise all who would have a good light without smoke, and that too at a cost of but ½ cent an hour, to purchase one of these lamps of Mr. Tobey, who is now visiting the Cape towns.

Thus began the kerosene era that was to bring success and good fortune to all who were connected to the Boston and Sandwich Glass Company and the new Cape Cod Glass Works in the 1860's.

THESE SIMPLE HINTS WILL HELP YOU IDENTIFY SANDWICH LIGHTING DEVICES

The Boston and Sandwich Glass Company used one or more wafers to combine the units of stand lamps. A like item molded in one piece is not Sandwich.

Learn the forms and patterns of the fonts, the center units and the bases. Accept any combination providing all units can be documented as Sandwich.

Make sure the documented Sandwich units were joined to each other by one or more of the styles of wafers documented as Sandwich.

Do not use burners, metal fittings and metal bases as a means of identifying the glass.

Identify by association. Study other articles that have documented Sandwich patterns such as colognes, vases, candlestick bases, finials and tableware.

For in-depth study of a particular method of manufacture, refer to other chapters in *The Glass Industry in Sandwich*. For example, detailed information can be found on blown glass, Lacy glass and pressed pattern tableware.

NOTES TO CHAPTER 2

1. United States Department of Commerce Office of Patent and Trademark Services documents the issue of a patent for "improvement in the tubes for glass lamps" to Deming Jarves on February 2, 1822. The patent is not available for study because a fire at the Patent Office on December 17, 1836, destroyed the records and many of the patents. Restored patents were reindexed and given new numbers followed by an "X", as were patents that were resubmitted. So far, every X-patent requested by the authors was buried deep in the Archives or could not be identified as having been resubmitted after the fire. However, the 1822 patent is the only one indexed that relates to tubes for glass lamps.

2. Charles C. P. Waterman wrote the following sentence in his 1875 history notes that were to be placed in the Town of Sandwich Centennial box. "While connected with the New England Glass Co. Mr. Jarves invented the cork tubes for lamps which he sold to William Carleton for one hundred dollars which was probably the stepping stone over which Mr. Carleton passed to the great fortune he amassed and with which he in his life time did so much good." Boston City Directories list Carleton's address as 30 Beach. Deming Jarves lived at 6 Beach as early as 1796, when he was six years old, and they may have grown to manhood together.

3. This information, as recorded in minutes of Boston and Sandwich Glass Company Board of Directors meetings, is in conflict with the article that appeared on May 11, 1831, in the *Barnstable Patriot and Commercial Advertiser*. The Patent Office cannot find a patent issued to George G. Channing. However, this date precedes the fire at the Patent Office. It is possible that Jennings sold his patent to Channing, in which case there would be no patent record in Channing's name. Or Channing might merely have been a spokesman for Jennings at the Board meeting and his presence or correspondence was misinterpreted by the clerk who recorded the minutes.

4. Patrick F. Slane, who established the American Flint Glass Works in South Boston, and John Golding were granted patent No. 3892 on January 23, 1845, for "a new and useful improvement in the arrangement of the mechanical means or molding apparatus used in the process of cementing or connecting the bowl of a glass lamp to the foot or standard of the same". According to Slane and Golding, in order to produce a stand lamp as a single unit, the combined foot and standard had to be pressed and placed in an upright position while still in the mold. A second mold for the "bowl of the lamp" had to be positioned directly over the standard, into which molten glass was placed and blown, "the glass in the two molds cementing itself by being in a state of fusion. The two molds must then be very carefully opened in order to deliver the lamp. The inconvenience of this method will be apparent when it is stated that the upper mold has to be applied and adjusted to the lower one for each and every lamp that is made, which application and adjustment not only require considerable time and care, but greatly enhance the liability of forming imperfect lamps. The above method has been tried and abandoned for the reasons above stated." The patent illustrates a metal stand with a shelf that supported the upper mold and a vertical rod that served as a hinge pin for the two halves of the upper mold. Even so, lamp production by this method was considerably more laborious than Jarves' method of pressing the combined foot and standard, separately pressing or blowing the font, and quickly joining the units by means of a hot glass wafer.

5. Robert H. Eddy was Jarves' patent attorney. He drew up the specifications for Jarves' patents. The *Barnstable Patriot* of May 6, 1862, carried an advertisement for Eddy's services as a patent attorney. However, patent No. 3582 was presented to the Patent Office as his own.

INVENTORY OF SANDWICH GLASS

No.	Description	Condition	Date Purchased	Amount	Date Sold	Amount

2001 FREE-BLOWN CONICAL LAMP WITH PLAIN FOOT, WHALE OIL BURNER

4⅞" H. x 2½" Dia. 1825–1828

Very little time was expended in the making of this lamp. It is glass in its simplest form, constructed by blowing the font, shaping it, and drawing the five knops of the stem from the same gather of glass. The plain foot was spun separately on the end of a blowpipe, then attached to the knop stem by a crude wafer. Unmelted sand can be seen in the center of the font, approximately one half way from the bottom. This sand is forever locked in the glass and its presence does not detract from its value today. Management accepted that as much as 10 percent of the finished product might have to be sold at trade sales (auctions) as seconds. Single tube whale oil burners gave off less than half the light given off by burners with two tubes. In a letter dated October 31, 1827, agent Deming Jarves wrote to William Stutson, "Stamford makes cylinder night lamps broad at top. Make a lot." Jarves illustrated this font attached directly to a circular base. So be aware that this lamp can be found with no stem. *Courtesy, Sandwich Glass Museum, Sandwich Historical Society*

2002 FREE-BLOWN GLOBE LOW FOOT LAMP, WHALE OIL BURNER

3¾" H. x 4" Dia. 1825–1828

Early lighting devices made of glass were simple in form. A round bubble served as a font, its opening drawn and smoothed out to give it a finished surface to accept the cork tube burner. The bottom of the font was permanently adhered to the free-blown saucer, which has a rim that was turned upward and folded under for strength. The saucer is larger in diameter than the font to catch any oil that spilled during refilling. Note how far the heat tubes penetrate into the font. Whale oil thickened as the temperature dropped. Within minutes after the lamp was lit, the tubes began to heat up. The heat was transferred first to the flat disk, then downward into the font, heating and liquifying the oil so that it was easily drawn up the wicks. *The Bennington Museum, Bennington, Vermont*

2003 FREE-BLOWN GLOBE PETTICOAT LAMP, WHALE OIL BURNER

4⅞" H. x 3½" Dia. 1825–1828

For the most part, this lamp is the same as the one shown previously, but the center of the saucer foot was drawn up 3½" to give it height. This resulted in virtually eliminating the area reserved for oil spills. Although the globe font and the skirt-like base were each blown separately, the units were joined while still hot without the use of the disk of glass we refer to as a *wafer*. The Boston and Sandwich Glass Company sloar book records the making of 170 petticoat chamber lamps during the week of March 9, 1828, in the shop headed by Samuel Kern. The lamp was produced in blue, and in a blue and clear combination. It is also attributed to the New England Glass Company and could have been made by other flint glass factories working during this time period.

2004 FREE-BLOWN GLOBE PETTICOAT LAMP, WHALE OIL BURNER

7⅞'' H. x 4½'' Dia. 1825–1828

The upper and lower units of this lamp repeat the style of the lamps shown previously, with height added by attaching them to a stem that was formed by combining three knops with a short button stem above which is a poorly executed wafer. Note the amateurish way in which the lower unit was attached to the stem. In his letters to William Stutson, Jarves continually admonished the workers to keep the glass light. Lamps such as these were turned out rapidly and were inexpensive; their only purpose was to provide a light at the proper level for the customer's need. These manufacturing "defects" do not detract from the value in today's market. Each lamp had its own individual character that is sought after by collectors, though that was not the intent of the glassworker. *The Bennington Museum, Bennington, Vermont*

2005 FREE-BLOWN CONICAL PETTICOAT LAMP, WHALE OIL BURNER

9⅜'' H. x 5⅜'' Dia. 1825–1828

Even if you find this lamp with a threaded cap, its long, narrow font tells you it should carry a whale oil burner. Explosive fuels produced in the 1830's did not do well in deep fonts, so the fonts were made shorter in proportion to their width. The font is connected to the high foot by a button stem. The saucer rim is wide enough to catch spilled whale oil, and is folded under for strength. Although such folding was left to the discretion of its maker, most were folded under so that spilled oil could be easily cleaned up. *Courtesy, Sandwich Glass Museum, Sandwich Historical Society*

2006 BLOWN MOLDED FLUTE LAMP WITH FREE-BLOWN LOW FOOT, WHALE OIL BURNER

8'' H. x 5'' Dia. 1825–1828

This is the earliest lamp we have found that was made by blowing glass into a one-piece, patterned dip mold. There are twelve flutes extending half-way up the font, with a pronounced rib between each flute. Several glass factories in the Boston area used this pattern. Although the font was small, it was extensively reworked after it was removed from the mold. The four knops and button that make up the stem were fastened to the font and saucer base by wafers. The rim of the base was folded to the outside and lifted to make the saucer shape commonly seen on lamps made from metal as well as from glass during this time period. This lamp was also made without the dome in the center of the saucer. Jarves illustrated it on an order that accompanied his June 10, 1828, letter to Superintendent Stutson. The order was for "2 doz. low Knob & B. S. Lamps". Knob and button stem lamps were also made with free-blown unpatterned globe fonts.

Jarves' drawing of a "low Knob & B(utton) S(tem) Lamp" that accompanied an order from Gregory and Bain for two dozen. The order was enclosed with a letter dated June 10, 1828. *Courtesy, Sandwich Glass Museum, Sandwich Historical Society*

2007 FREE-BLOWN BEEHIVE PETTICOAT LAMP

6¾'' H. x 4½'' Dia. 1829–1835

Glass that was blown and tooled into the Beehive configuration is much sought after by Sandwich glass collectors because it has never been proven that it was made at any other glass works. It is documented that William E. Kern made a Beehive sugar bowl as a wedding gift for his sister Catherine, who married Frederick Eaton on January 28, 1830. The lamp shown here is in the private collection of Hiram Dillaway's descendants. The foot, which follows the lines of plain free-blown pieces, and the font were made separately and joined by a solid knop stem. Because Beehive pieces were hand tooled, no two are exactly alike. The number of rings can vary according to the consistency of the molten glass and the whim of the maker. Letters written by Deming Jarves prove that brass collars were used as early as June 1826. In later years, this font was blown molded into a pattern that was known as *Ring*. The Ring pattern has vertical mold marks and each font is identical. Look for the mold marks and you will not mistake it for this early free-blown Beehive.

2008 FREE-BLOWN BEEHIVE LAMP WITH PRESSED HEXAGONAL BASE

7½'' H. x 2¾'' Dia. font, 5⅛'' Dia. base 1835–1840

Eight concentric rings make up the font. The ninth "ring" is not a part of the font, but is a large wafer that holds the free-blown font to the pressed base. The hexagonal base is a sturdy one often seen on vases, candlesticks and other lamps. The brass collar is threaded to receive a threaded burner. Beehive pieces are very, very rare on today's antiques market. Keep in mind that the burners required a soft braided wick that extended through the tubes and down to the bottom of the font, in order to use all the available fuel. *Courtesy, Sandwich Glass Museum, Sandwich Historical Society*

2009 FREE-BLOWN LAMP FILLER

2'' H. x 3½'' Dia. 1825–1835

One could walk right by a glass lamp filler at an antiques show without recognizing it as a lighting accessory. Most households used a lamp filler made of tin that resembled a can or small coffee pot with a curved spout at the bottom. The spout was often supported by a length of tin that extended from the pouring end back to the can. The large opening at the top of this glass one allowed it to be filled with lighting fuel without spilling. The examples examined by the authors had flared rims to capture fuel that missed the wide neck and drain it down into the body. When originally constructed, the spouts were elongated into slender forms that were beautiful. Unfortunately, they were easily damaged from the abuse of constantly being inserted into necks and collars of small lamp fonts. After such damage, they were often cut back and machined, as was the spout in this photo. As with every applied glass handle, examine carefully when purchasing. A lamp filler with a damaged spout or handle has little value. *Courtesy, Sandwich Glass Museum, Sandwich Historical Society*

2010 FREE-BLOWN TOY HAND LAMP, WHALE OIL BURNER

1½'' H. 1825–1835

The dimensions of the font, the little handle and the size of the cork tube whale oil burner tell us that this lamp was meant for a child. Ignore the crimped trailing end of the applied handle and study just the portion that is held. The handle that would easily slip out of an adult hand would be comfortable between the thumb and fingers of a child. The tube is only $^{13}⁄_{16}$'' long with an outside diameter of $^{3}⁄_{32}$''. The tube has the tiniest slot for the needle-like pick-wick used to raise the wick. Original factory documents prove that toy lamps were made in abundance and sold readily. Larger handled lamps for adults were called *chamber lamps*. We have no evidence in factory records of lamps specifically designed to be ''courting'' or ''sparking'' lamps. The lack of a straight-sided opening indicates that this lamp could properly be used with a corkless drop burner. *The Bennington Museum, Bennington, Vermont*

2011 BLOWN MOLDED RIBBED TOY HAND LAMP, WHALE OIL BURNER

McKearin GI-7 1⅛'' H. x 2¼'' Dia. 1825–1835

Early hand lamps made for children can be distinguished from small night lamps by the size of the handle. If the hole will not take an adult finger, the lamp was made for a child. The amount of whale oil that this lamp would hold is limited. The glass was blown into a ribbed ball stopper mold, and reworked to form a melon font. This type of tube burner with cork was perfected by Deming Jarves in 1822, when he was agent for the New England Glass Company. The tube is held in place by the pressure of a cork stopper against the rim. According to writings of C. P. Waterman dated April 27, 1865, ''Mr. Jarves invented the cork tubes for lamps which he sold to William Carleton (owner of a Boston lamp manufacturing business and a director of the Boston and Sandwich Glass Company) for $100.'' The tin cap through which the tube passes is marked ''PATENT''. There is another tin disk beneath the cork. *Courtesy, Sandwich Glass Museum, Sandwich Historical Society*

2012 BLOWN MOLDED TOY HAND LAMP, WHALE OIL BURNER

(a) Matching stopper 3⅜" H. x 2½" Dia.
(b) Toy hand lamp 2" H. 1828–1835
Toy lamps were often made from the same molds that were used to make decanter stoppers. The rayed pattern that is on the top of this stopper became the rayed base of the lamp. The glass that would have formed the plug of the stopper was sheared off, leaving a rim that was the right diameter for a tiny whale oil burner. When considering the purchase of a handled piece, whether it be a pitcher, custard, lemonade or lamp, examine the applied handle carefully. Applied handles with tails that were crimped are often damaged, and the damage may be difficult to see. Make sure there are no cracks through the handle or the crimps, and that the end of the tail is not chipped off. Damaged handles seriously affect value, so take care of the perfect pieces in your collection. The Bennington Museum also has a candlestick made from a stopper mold, which can be seen in photo 4001. *The Bennington Museum, Bennington, Vermont*

2013 BLOWN MOLDED DIAMOND DIAPER TOY LAMP, WHALE OIL BURNER

McKearin GII–18 2" H. x 1⅞" Dia. 1825–1826
This tiny lamp originated in a mold that had a band of diamond diapering around the center with bands of vertical ribs above and below. After the glass was removed from the mold, the piece was crimped below the diapered band to form the ribbed foot and drawn in at the top to form a rim to fit the tin whale oil burner. Sixteen diamonds in a circle form the base pattern. Blown molded pieces that can be identified as toys from factory records command higher prices than their adult-size counterparts. *The Bennington Museum, Bennington, Vermont*

2014 BLOWN MOLDED DIAMOND DIAPER PEG LAMP, WHALE OIL BURNER

McKearin GII–19 3¾" H. x 2" Dia. 1825–1830
This peg lamp was blown into a mold that had a band of diamond diapering around the center with a band of vertical ribs below. Not clearly seen in the photo is an upper band of diagonal ribbing to the left that surrounds the shoulder of the lamp. It is interesting to note that the lamp had once been sold by McKearin's Antiques. George S. McKearin and his daughter Helen McKearin established the system by which we identify blown molded patterns today. This lamp has a smooth-surfaced peg so that it could be inserted into a brass, pewter or glass candle socket. The small amount of fuel it held indicates that it was used for momentary light or heat: walking through a dark hallway, reading a note, melting wax to seal an envelope. The single tube whale oil burner is original to the lamp. Blown molded lighting devices such as this seldom come on the antiques market. When they do, they command a high price. *Courtesy of Richard A. Bourne Co., Inc.*

2015 FREE-BLOWN LAMP WITH HAND PRESSED SQUARE ROSE FOOT BASE

10¾'' H. x 3'' Dia. font, 3⅛'' Sq. base 1825–1828

The base of this lamp is crude and is one of the earliest pressed in Sandwich. The plunger, called a *core* when the pressing of glass was in its infancy, was shaped like a rosette with a pattern of rounded ribs that can be seen beneath the base. Present day collectors call this base a "lemon squeezer base". In discussing the correspondence of Deming Jarves, Sandwich Glass Museum Director Barbara Bishop and Historian Martha Hassell noted that, "It is tempting to apply the term *rose foot* to lamps with blown fonts and hand pressed bases that appear to resemble petaled flowers". Authors Barlow and Kaiser agree in light of the fact that under the word *rose*, Webster's 1847 Dictionary refers the reader to *rosette*, which is defined as "in architecture, an ornament in the form of a rose, much used in decorations". The simple one-piece mold that formed the smooth outer surface of the base was referred to as a *receiver*. Excess glass was primitively forced out at the corners and was machined away until the lamp stood vertically. A wafer placed atop the base connected the hollow standard. Jarves called the hollow center unit a *bulb*. "Let the bulb be taller & fount not over large. Keep the bulb and fount light," he wrote to Stutson on July 2, 1827. A second wafer connected the font to the hollow standard. The stamped brass collar is a later replacement. In a letter written to Deming Jarves on September 26, 1826, Salesman William T. Mayo ordered for Nathaniel Bassett of Newburyport, Massachusetts, "2 pr Globe plated Cap R. F. Lamps" and "6 pr Globe Cork Tube R. F. Lamps", so be aware that both the cork and threaded types of whale oil burners are correct for this time period. *Courtesy, Sandwich Glass Museum, Sandwich Historical Society*

2016 FREE-BLOWN CUT LAMP WITH HAND PRESSED SQUARE ROSE FOOT BASE

11'' H. x 3'' Dia. font, 3¼'' Sq. base 1825–1828

The constant use of this shape font is testimony to its popularity throughout this period, as is the design of cut acorns, but take the time to study the pressed base carefully. It was made very early in pressed glass history. "Tall rose feet lamps" were advertised for sale in the *Old Colony Memorial and Plymouth County Advertiser* on May 6, 1826. The smooth outer surface was shaped by a very crudely made mold receiver. Its plain lines were relieved by a complicated pattern of ribs alternating with inverted ribs on a very shallow plunger. The shaped wafer attached to the base slants to the right. The center unit is a blown standard composed of a short, wide center knop with a smaller knop above and below it. This is an early configuration. The authors suspect the glass blower intended the standard to have the same shape above and below the large center knop. Failing this, he added a small disk wafer above the standard, on top of which he placed a large shaped wafer, into which he forced the font. The entire assembly leans 5 degrees. Normally, this would have been corrected by grinding the base until the lamp stood straight, but for some reason the base was not leveled and the lamp was left with a delightful tilt. *Courtesy, Sandwich Glass Museum, Sandwich Historical Society*

2017 FREE-BLOWN CONICAL LAMPS WITH PRESSED BEAR PAW RECTANGULAR BASE

(a) Large lamp 12¼'' H. x 3¼'' Dia. font, 3½'' x 4½'' rectangular base
(b) Shade 5¼'' H. x 6'' Dia.
(c) Combined size 20¼'' H.
(d) Small lamp 11'' H. x 2¾'' Dia. font, 3½'' x 4½'' rectangular base 1828–1835

Two large paws, each with five claws, cover a rectangular platform. The paws are back to back, each one facing the shorter sides of the platform. An opening pressed beneath the base extends upward between the paws. A star is molded into the center of this opening, which can be seen through the glass from the outside. From the top of the pressed base upward, the lamps take on individuality, each glassworker blowing the form to his own liking. Note that the large hollow center knop on lamp A has a completely different configuration than lamp B, making accurate dimensions irrelevant. Lamp A was fitted with a roughed and cut shade, prisms and metal fittings when it was altered for electrification.

2018 FREE-BLOWN CONICAL LAMP WITH PRESSED BEAR PAW RECTANGULAR BASE

11'' H. x 2¾'' Dia. font, 3½'' x 4½'' rectangular base 1828–1835

Here is the smaller of the lamps shown previously with matching fragments of the bear paw base that were dug at the factory site. All of the early Sandwich lamps were made at the original Sandwich Glass Manufactory/Boston and Sandwich Glass Company site. Deming Jarves left this company to build the Cape Cod Glass Works at a second site in 1858. Note the unique shaped wafers that connect the hollow standard to the font and the base. Several styles of wafers were used in Sandwich as well as in other glass factories.

2019 FREE-BLOWN CYLINDER LAMP WITH PRESSED SQUARE BASE

7⅜'' H. x 2¼'' Dia. font, 3'' Sq. base 1830–1835

Contrary to many accounts, very few pieces of glass dug from the Boston and Sandwich Glass Company factory site are perfect. This lamp is perfect in form, but was thrown away because the entire surface lost its sheen in the annealing leer. There is no design of any kind on the font and no collar had ever been attached. The lamp was dug by Francis (Bill) Wynn in 1954. To date, the authors have not located a lamp combining the cylinder font with this base. There are two square steps that are quite high for their width. The three segments that make up the standard are square with rounded sides. There is a platform above the standard that was molded as part of the base. A wafer was placed on the platform and the font was adhered to the wafer. The plunger was designed to penetrate the base through the square steps and two of the rounded ones.

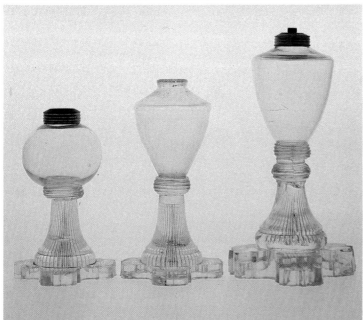

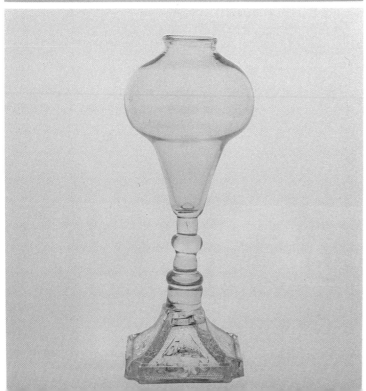

2020 FREE-BLOWN BULB LAMPS WITH PRESSED SQUARE BASE, WHALE OIL BURNER

8¾" H. x 3" Dia. font, 3⅛" Sq. base 1828–1835

Not often do the authors write about the rarity of a piece of glass, but this photo shows one of the most beautiful, closely matched pairs of this time period. The original cork tube burners, marked "PATENT" on the disks, are in mint condition. If they had seen much use, they would be scorched and the lamp fonts would be stained inside. Blue was the earliest color used in Sandwich. The lamps match perfectly in color, as well as in the pressing of the simple stepped bases. The ringed wafers accentuate the fine lines of the fonts and the bases. Keep in mind that these early lamps might also be found with threaded collars and whale oil burners. When pricing lamps, remember that a pair is worth more than the value of two singles, and that a perfectly executed, originally matched pair is worth more than a pair of lamps that were purchased singly and mated by the collector.

2021 FREE-BLOWN LAMPS WITH CROSSBAR BASE

(a) Small, globe font 6⅜" H. x 3" Dia. font, 3⅜" Sq. base
(b) Medium 7½" H. x 3" Dia. font, 3⅜" Sq. base
(c) Large 9¼" H. x 3⅛" Dia. font, 4¼" Sq. base
    1828–1835

This is an interesting series of lamps when you realize that all three held the same amount of fuel. The vertical lines pressed into the inside surface of the bases were on the plunger. Note how an increase in the size of only one unit changed the height of the burner. Lamp A is 1¼" shorter than lamp B. Both bases are the same size; the change in the font accounts for the added height of lamp B. The plunger of base B did not penetrate as deeply into the mold. There is no pattern of prisms beneath the ringed wafer. Although base B is hollow, there is no longer an opening. It was completely closed by a glob of glass that was attached to hold the base on a pontil rod while the font was joined to it. The four arms of bases A and B have a pattern of beads beneath that can be seen on the candlestick in photo 4006. Height was added to lamp C by combining the font with a larger base, made by using a larger amount of glass to give it weight. Each arm has a prism pattern beneath it.

2022 FREE-BLOWN LAMP WITH PRESSED LACY SQUARE BASE

7¾" H. x 2⅞" Dia. font, 2¾" Sq. base 1828–1835

It is possible to find this lamp well made and proportioned correctly. The lamp shown here dates very early, and is probably one of the first attempts to attach a font to a mechanically pressed base. The workmanship is quite poor. Note where the hot glass ran over the edge of the base in the forefront of the photo. The font does not stand straight on the stem, nor is the stem straight to the base, caused by overheating in the annealing leer. This imperfection does not deter from its value. The square base with cut-out corners has a fan-like pattern on two opposite sides and a crosshatched pattern on the other two sides. The background was stippled to hide defects and make the glass appear more brilliant. Pressed glass with stippled backgrounds and a delicate tracery of patterns is known as *Lacy glass. Courtesy, Sandwich Glass Museum, Sandwich Historical Society*

2023 FREE-BLOWN BULB LAMPS WITH PRESSED LACY SQUARE BASE, WHALE OIL BURNER

7" H. x 2¾" Dia. font, 2¾" Sq. base 1828–1835

Both of these Lacy bases came out of the same mold. Note that the bands of perpendicular lines across the front of each base are narrower on the left side, showing that the defect in the mold was constant. The free-blown font was held to the base by a ringed wafer. The cork tube burners are correct for the time of manufacture, but nonetheless, the lamps would maintain their value if the burners were replaced by a later improvement. The burners should have wicks that extend from the tubes to the bottom of the fonts. *Courtesy, Sandwich Glass Museum, Sandwich Historical Society*

2024 FREE-BLOWN BULB LAMPS WITH PRESSED LACY SQUARE BASE

6¼" H. x 2⅝" Dia. font, 2⅜" Sq. base 1828–1835

Shallow Lacy bases were pressed early at the Boston and Sandwich Glass Company. They were easy to press and could be turned out in quantity. The stippled pattern was on the plunger. A simple pattern with leaves on each corner was in the receiver, so it is on the upper, outer surface of the finished base. A double wafer was used to attach each base to its free-blown bulb font. The peg that is used for a stubby stem is often shorter on one lamp than on the other. This is caused by too much pressure in applying the font while the glass was hot. This does not deter from the value of an otherwise matched pair. *Courtesy, Sandwich Glass Museum, Sandwich Historical Society*

2025 FREE-BLOWN GLOBE LAMP WITH PRESSED TRIANGULAR SCROLLED STANDARD AND PAW FOOT BASE

8¼" H. x 3" Dia. font, 4½" each side of base 1827–1835

The simple form of a blown sphere was combined with one of the most intricate bases made at Sandwich. Three vertical C-scrolls rest on a triangle with curved sides and blunted, thick-walled corners. A five-toed paw protrudes from each corner. Each toe has several claws that grip a section of glass that holds the triangle up off the table. There is a flat platform above the base that looks like a wafer but was actually molded with the base. A ringed wafer was placed on this platform and the blown font was attached. If these types of lamps became too hot in the annealing leer, and tilted to one side as this one did, only the little paw feet had to be machined to level the lamp.

2026 FREE-BLOWN BULB LAMP WITH PRESSED TRIANGULAR SCROLLED STANDARD AND BEADED CIRCULAR BASE, WHALE OIL BURNER

11¼" H. x 2¾" Dia. font, 5" Dia. base 1827–1835

Here is an excellent example of combining several motifs to make a mold. The C-scroll standard, usually combined with a paw foot base, is shown here above a circular foot that has concentric bands of beads and prisms beneath. (To study the breakpoint between the standard and the base, study the photo of the wooden pattern that follows.) A ringed wafer, placed on the bottom of the font, was then adhered to the pressed knop above the C-scroll, and a permanent bond was made. The unusually long neck guaranteed a tight fit for the cork surrounding the tubes of the burner. *Courtesy, Sandwich Glass Museum, Sandwich Historical Society*

2027 WOODEN PATTERN FOR TRIANGULAR SCROLLED STANDARD

1827–1835

Molds were made by using a wooden pattern as a model. Once the desired form was established in wood, it was made into a sectioned mold or combined with a choice of other wooden patterns to make an intricate mold. This triangular C-scroll pattern was combined with the triangular paw foot base as well as the beaded circular base. The patterns were stored at the factory. When a mold became worn and needed to be replaced, the pattern was sent to a commercial mold maker, who cast a new mold at a foundry. The wooden patterns acquired a dark brown or black patina because they were soaked in oil before being encased in plaster of Paris as the next step in making a mold. The oil prevented the plaster from adhering to the wood. *Courtesy of Richard A. Bourne Co., Inc.*

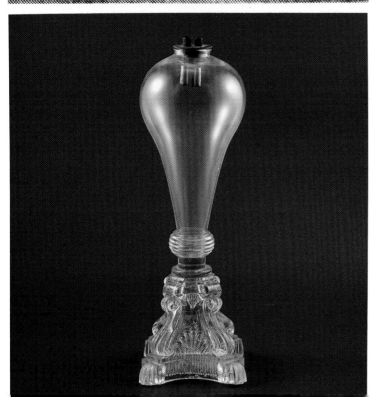

2028 FREE-BLOWN BULB LAMP WITH PRESSED SQUARE SCROLLED STANDARD AND PAW FOOT (LION HEAD) BASE, WHALE OIL BURNER

12" H. x 3¾" Dia. font, 3⅞" Sq. base 1827–1835

Several different bases with scrolls and paw feet were dug at Sandwich, but when the dug fragments are small, it is difficult to relate them to a particular base. This base with its four vertical S-scrolls, curved sides and flattened corners is strongly related to Corinthian architecture, as is the similar triangular base. There is a shell between each scroll, and, above each shell, the poorly-defined head of a lion. The four paws are stylized; they have no detail and no claws. Beneath each paw is a button of glass that could be machined to level the lamp. A band of prisms can be seen between the paws, pressed into the inside of the base. This is an extremely large, heavy lamp that held a many days' supply of fuel. The 1" Dia. peg below the ringed wafer was molded in one piece with the base, despite the fact that it appears to be a continuation of the font.

2029 FREE-BLOWN GLOBE LAMP WITH PRESSED SQUARE SCROLLED STANDARD AND PAW FOOT (LION HEAD) BASE

8¾" H. x 3⅝" Dia. font, 4" Sq. base 1827–1835

The font of this lamp, although blown, is exceptionally heavy. The bottom of the font can be as thick as ½". This helps us date the lamp. Glass heated in earlier wood-fired furnaces had the consistency of window putty, so the finished product often weighed more than the gaffer intended. This problem was corrected when the factory began to use coal in 1836. The head of an animal appears on the base between the upper ends of the S-scrolls. The head is poorly formed, making it easy to understand why it was referred to as a lion head in factory records. The sloar book for the week of September 22, 1827, recorded that the shop headed by Benjamin Haines made seventy Lion Head lamps in move No. 6 and forty-three in move No. 8. The lamp base shown in this photo is the only one made in this time period that fits the description in the records. It is the opinion of the authors that the base shown in photo 2076 with its well-defined lion heads was not in production in 1827. *Courtesy, Sandwich Glass Museum, Sandwich Historical Society*

2030 FREE-BLOWN GLOBE LAMPS WITH PRESSED SQUARE SCROLLED STANDARD AND PAW FOOT (LION HEAD) BASE, FLUID BURNER

12½" H. 1827–1835

Here is a beautifully executed pair of lamps built upon the same Lion Head base shown previously. An unpatterned plunger was used, so there is no prism band inside the base. A shaped wafer above the base peg holds a very large hollow knop, or "bulb", according to Deming Jarves. On very rare occasions, the glassworker inserted a coin or a small doll into the knop before he attached it to the other units. Another reworked wafer holds the font. Fluid burners screw into the collars. They are also correct for the time period. The first chemically produced fuel was patented on October 16, 1830. Burning fluid was very explosive, more so if used in the previously shown lamp with the elongated bulb font. If the bulb font lamp was left lit until the fluid level was low, the amount of fumes that developed in the almost empty chamber spelled potential disaster. *Courtesy of The Toledo Museum of Art (Acc. No. 67.97 A&B)*

2031 FREE-BLOWN CONICAL LAMP WITH PRESSED CUP PLATE BASE, WHALE OIL BURNER

Lee-Rose 10

6½" H. x 2⅜" Dia. font, 3¼" Dia. base 1828–1835

This is a beautifully shaped lamp. The font was tapered by flattening the sidewalls while the unit was turned on the end of a pontil rod. A wafer and a button stem connects the font to a very thick cup plate base. The thickness indicates early vintage. A pattern of concentric rings is on the upper surface of the base, and a rayed pattern is on the underside. Examination of dug fragments shows that, when cup plates were warped or of uneven thickness, they were set aside to be used for lamp bases. The warp was compensated for by attaching the stem at a slight angle. As their popularity increased, cup plate lamps became a standard line item. This two tube cork burner is marked "PATENT" on the metal disk. *The Bennington Museum, Bennington, Vermont*

2032 FREE-BLOWN TOY LAMP WITH PRESSED DIAMOND CHECK TOY PLATE BASE, WHALE OIL BURNER

4⅛" H. x 2⅜" Dia. 1828–1835

This is the child's version of the adult cup plate lamp shown in the previous photo. The base of this lamp was pressed in the 2⅛" Dia. Diamond Check toy plate mold. Note its thickness, indicating early manufacture. The solid knopped standard was free-blown as part of the font and applied to the center of the bottom of the plate. All early lamps with plate bases have a rough pontil mark underneath, on what would be the smooth upper surface of the plate. Cork tube whale oil burners are still often found on their lamps. *The Bennington Museum, Bennington, Vermont*

2033 FREE-BLOWN TOY HAND LAMP WITH PRESSED DIAMOND CHECK TOY PLATE BASE, WHALE OIL BURNER AND MALLORY LAMP GLASS

(a) Lamp 3⅞" H. x 2¼" Dia. 1828–1835
(b) Mallory lamp glass (chimney) 2½" H. x
    1⅛" Dia. at fitter 1825–1835
(c) Combined size 6¼" H.

Here is the same lamp shown in the previous photo with the addition of an applied handle. The ringed collar was permanently fastened to the rim of the font. This was one of several early threaded collars used at Sandwich. A threaded whale oil burner was fitted to it, providing more stability than a cork tube burner. The burner and the blown cylindrical chimney predates the toy plate base lamp and was illustrated by Deming Jarves in a letter dated November 23, 1825. It was called a *Mallory lamp glass* and is nothing more than a cylinder with a flared bottom rim that fits under the set screw of the burner. Today we would not allow a child to play with fire, but if children did not learn to handle open flame, they would be left with no light at all. They learned to respect fire at an early age, but reports of death due to accidents when handling lamps were common. Do not hold hand lamps or tableware pieces by their applied handles unless you support the base. Old glass is brittle and the weight will crack the handle. *Courtesy, Sandwich Glass Museum, Sandwich Historical Society*

2034 FREE-BLOWN GLOBE LAMP WITH PRESSED CUP PLATE BASE

Lee-Rose 15

(a) Cup plate ½" H. x 3" Dia.
(b) Lamp 5½" H. x 2¾" Dia. font, 3" Dia. base
    1828–1835

The quickest form for a glass blower to make was a sphere. Here we see the simplicity of that effort. The font was attached to a button stem, which was nothing more than a plain stem with a flat button-shaped knop in its center. Note the concentric rings in the center of matching cup plate A. They disappeared when the plate was reheated to attach the stem. When these plain-rimmed little plates, whether attached to a lamp or not, show broken bubbles or machining around the rim to remove excess glass, consider it to be part of the manufacturing process. This does not deter from their value. Some cup plates are thicker on one side than on the other, another early production problem that does not affect value. There was no way to control thickness in the first primitive molds. It depended on the amount of glass dropped into the mold.

2035 FREE-BLOWN BULB LAMP WITH PRESSED CUP PLATE BASE, WHALE OIL BURNER

Lee-Rose 31

7⅜'' H. x 2¾'' Dia. font, 3½'' Dia. base 1827-1830

This lamp is by far the rarest of the cup plate lamps. Note the depth of the plate, almost deep enough to be called a nappie. According to Ruth Webb Lee and James H. Rose in their book *American Glass Cup Plates*, the plate without the lamp is rare, even in clear glass. Lee and Rose believe it was made only briefly because the deep shape may have been impractical. The combination of a rare cup plate, and a button stem lamp with a bulb font adds significantly to value. The neck of the font was made to accept a drop tube or a cork tube burner. There is not enough neck on which to cement a metal collar.

2036 BLOWN MOLDED TWISTED RIB LAMP WITH PRESSED CUP PLATE BASE

Lee-Rose 43

6½'' H. 1828-1835

This is a beautifully made conical font that should have a whale oil burner. The short blue stem was fastened to a base that was made at the Boston and Sandwich Glass Company and the New England Glass Company. Underneath the base is a pontil mark. This was the point at which a pontil rod was attached to hold the base when it was joined to the stem. A fine diamond point pattern covers the fifteen scallops, delineated by a rope pattern. Twisted rib fonts were made in Sandwich by 1828. The base was manufactured using an early pressing technique.
Courtesy of Richard A. Bourne Co., Inc.

2037 FREE-BLOWN CONICAL LAMP WITH PRESSED CUP PLATE BASE

Lee-Rose 51

(a) Fragment ½'' H. x 3¾'' Dia.
(b) Lamp 6½'' H. x 2⅝'' Dia. font, 3¾'' Dia. base 1828-1835

This lamp has a tapered font combined with the cup plate identified as Number 51 in *American Glass Cup Plates* by Ruth Webb Lee and James H. Rose. A different method —a ringed wafer with a short stem—was used to attach the font to the plate. A sheaf of wheat alternates with a tiny heart on the rim. Many different cup plates used as lamp bases were dug at the Boston and Sandwich Glass Company site. They appear to have a pontil mark on both sides, but that is not the case. A pontil mark is on the underside only, caused by holding the plate while attaching the stem and upper unit. The scar on the upper surface was where the stem broke away and the base was discarded. A true pressed cup plate not intended for use as a lamp base does not have a pontil mark because it was not reworked after it was removed from the mold in which it was pressed.

2038 BLOWN MOLDED TWISTED RIB LAMPS WITH PRESSED CUP PLATE BASE, WHALE OIL BURNER

Lee-Rose 54
7'' H. x 3⅜'' Dia. 1828–1835
Soon after mechanical pressing began, molds that were used to press small plates were also used to make pressed bases for lamps and candlesticks. After the plates were made, they were turned upside down and button stems were attached to the patterned side of the plates. The fonts were fastened to the stems with clear glass wafers. Note that, although the lamps are the same height, the blue font on the right is longer and the clear stem is shorter. Pairs with so much hand work seldom matched exactly, but these variations do not affect value. On January 20, 1829, Jarves wrote to Stutson, ''The Twisted Lamps sell very well. When the metal is seedy or corded, make them well twisted. The straight ribbed is not so much liked.'' Accompanying the letter was Jarves' drawing of a 7½'' high blown candlestick with a 5'' plate foot, and the directive to make seven or eight dozen candlesticks with the 4½'' to 5'' plate foot. See *Barlow-Kaiser Sandwich Glass Price Guide* for difference in value between clear and colored cup plate lamps.

2039 FREE-BLOWN BULB LAMPS WITH PRESSED LACY ACANTHUS LEAF CIRCULAR BASE, WHALE OIL BURNER

(a) Large 8'' H. x 2⅜'' Dia. font, 4½'' Dia. base
(b) Medium 7⅜'' H. x 3½'' Dia. font, 3⅜'' Dia. base
(c) Dug fragment of small base 1⅛'' H. x 3⅛'' Dia.
1828–1835
While digging in the northeast corner of the Boston and Sandwich Glass Company factory yard in the summer of 1972, author Ray Barlow uncovered base C. Before the day's dig was over, more than sixty fragments of this lamp were unearthed. Three of the fragments showed destruction that occurred in the leer at the time of annealing, proving that this pattern was manufactured in Sandwich. Documentation of this find was sent to several museums to help them authenticate this pattern as Sandwich. Note the corrugated rim on all of the bases. Similar lamps with smooth rims have not been documented as Sandwich.
Courtesy, Sandwich Glass Museum, Sandwich Historical Society

2040 FREE-BLOWN BULB LAMPS WITH PRESSED LACY ACANTHUS LEAF CIRCULAR BASE

10½'' H. 1828–1835
It is sometimes believed that the mold used to make the cover of an Acanthus Leaf sugar bowl was adapted to manufacture this lamp base at Sandwich. This is not true. The proof lies in the edge of the lamp base. It is corrugated. The outer edge of the cover of a sugar bowl is smooth. In the fragments found at Sandwich, all Acanthus Leaf circular lamp bases had corrugated edges. If you find this lamp with a smooth edge and have determined that it was not machined to remove chips, purchase it as a good New England area lamp, but not a Sandwich one. Remember that there were other flint glass factories in Boston, South Boston and Providence that were producing the same types of lamps and tableware. The production lines of these other factories have not been fully documented.
Courtesy of Richard A. Bourne Co., Inc.

2041 FREE-BLOWN BULB LAMP WITH PRESSED LACY ACANTHUS LEAF OCTAGONAL BASE

8¾'' H. x 3'' Dia. font, 4⅛'' Dia. base 1830–1840
This most interesting base may be the "8 square and Leaf foot" referred to in 1829 correspondence. Its Lacy motif of stippling and leaves was pressed beneath the base. The plain eight-sided rim turns upward to act as a reservoir to catch spilled oil. Ribbed knops were poorly applied to the top of the base. A ringed wafer above the knops fastened the bulb font to the base. The overall effect would be pleasing if the workmanship had reached higher standards. These poorly-made pieces are sought after by collectors because they show attempts to advance the state of the art. The Boston and Sandwich Glass Company made candlesticks with this base as shown in photo 4007 in Volume 4. A variant of the Lacy socket Number 2 shown in photo 4007 has a pattern of grapes on the upper surface. The metal collar in this lamp photo is a much later addition.
Courtesy, Sandwich Glass Museum, Sandwich Historical Society

2042 PRESSED LACY ACANTHUS LEAF BASE OF ABOVE LAMP

Here is a lamp placed on its side so that you can study the pattern beneath the base. All of the pattern, including the background stippling, is on the underside. A single leaf with four scrolls extending from it is repeated four times, each leaf motif covering two panels of the octagonal base. A border of beads surrounds the leaf pattern. Note the slight discoloration around the center. This is a sharp, jagged edge where a pontil rod held the base while the wafer was applied to attach the base to the bulb font. This is a manufacturing fact of life—the base is not chipped and value is not affected.

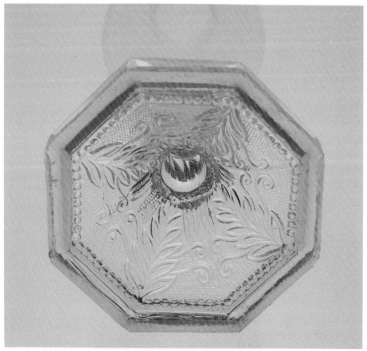

2043 BLOWN MOLDED RIBBED LAMP WITH PRESSED LACY ACANTHUS LEAF OCTAGONAL BASE

McKearin GI-7
8³⁄₁₆'' H. 1830–1835
Deming Jarves discussed "straight ribbed" lamps in his January 20, 1829, letter to Stutson. He claimed that customers preferred twisted ribs, but vertically ribbed fonts were also made well into the 1830's. The ribbed knops that made up the standard appear to be twisted. This may have been the result of twisting the assembly when the ringed wafer was applied to hold the bulb-shaped font. The ribs extend to the metal collar. *Courtesy of Richard A. Bourne Co., Inc.*

2044 BLOWN MOLDED CORNUCOPIA (PEACOCK TAIL) LAMPS WITH PRESSED LACY ACANTHUS LEAF BASE

McKearin GV–18

(a) Handled square base with ribbed socket 7½" H.
(b) Octagonal base with ribbed knops 7" H.
      1835–1840

Collectors of American glass usually call this blown molded pattern *Cornucopia* or *Horn of Plenty*. It bears a strong resemblance to a French pattern illustrated in an 1840 Launay Hautin & Compagnie catalog. The Paris firm referred to it as *Tail of Peacock*. The font is rarely encountered, but both bases are familiar when combined with other Sandwich upper units. The square base A has a primitively molded handle. The Acanthus Leaf pattern was pressed into each corner. The short ribbed standard was actually a shallow socket into which the separately made font was inserted. "Lamp sockets", as these may be called, were mentioned in a Jarves letter. The base is occasionally found with a lacy candle socket inserted into the "lamp socket" to make a chamber stick as shown in photo 4009. Lamp B is a combination more easily recognized, although it, too, is extremely scarce. Its standard is comprised of two ribbed knops. *Courtesy of Richard A. Bourne Co., Inc.*

2045 BLOWN MOLDED RIBBED LAMPS WITH PRESSED BASE

Similar to McKearin GI-15, GI-28

(a) Octagonal galleried base 7¾" H. x 3" Dia. font, 4½" Dia. base 1828–1835
(b) Square petaled base 8⅛" H. x 3" Dia. font, 3⅛" Sq. base 1835–1840

The study of glass is intriguing because of the mystery that surrounds certain pieces. Both conical fonts have a pattern of seventeen ribs and are exactly alike. The upper ends of the ribs are flattened and concentric rings surround the neck. Font A is on the galleried base shown previously, which was found in quantity at the Boston and Sandwich Glass Company. If base B was ever dug at the site, we're not aware of it, but descendants from several Sandwich families testified to Sandwich origin. The petals were easily broken, which may account for its rarity. Many may not have survived removal from the mold. The ribbed font in opaque lavender-blue was combined with the pressed Lion Head and Basket of Flowers base shown on the right of photo 2076, also dug in quantity at the site. *Courtesy, Sandwich Glass Museum, Sandwich Historical Society*

2046 FREE-BLOWN CONICAL LAMPS WITH PRESSED OCTAGONAL GALLERIED BASE

(a) Clear lamp with shaped wafers and hollow knopped center 11'' H. x 3'' Dia. font, 4'' Dia. base

(b) Opaque white fragment with knopped wafer 8'' H. x 3'' Dia. font, 4'' Dia. base 1828–1835

Lamp A was constructed in the same manner as the lamp with the bear paw base in photo 2017. Its octagonal base was pressed into stepped rows of beads, called *galleried* by collectors. A band of prisms is on the inside of the bottom step only, although it cannot be seen through the opaque glass of lamp B. The white lamp was taken in two pieces from a building at the factory site by William Casey in the 1920's. After his death, Mr. Casey's fragments were incorporated into the Barlow collection. The two pieces were glued back together and the glue appears as fiery opalescent in the photo. Melted fragments that overheated and burned in the annealing leer were also dug, proving that the lamp was manufactured in Sandwich. Blown fonts and standards have been found at the site, but once broken away from their pressed bases, they cannot be related to a specific base. This fact makes fragment B a very important piece of documentation. It is obvious that both lamps have identical fonts and bases, lamp A being taller because it has a hollow knop standard. It is not as obvious that the wafers of both lamps started out alike. The large knopped wafer on lamp B is usually associated with the Lion Head and Basket of Flowers base in photo 2076. This same wafer was reworked to form the shaped wafers on lamp A.

2047 FREE-BLOWN, CUT AND DECORATED BULB LAMP WITH OCTAGONAL BASE, WHALE OIL BURNER

1829–1835

Records show that as early as 1829, decorating of this quality was done at Sandwich as well as at the New England Glass Company in East Cambridge, Massachusetts. On July 29, 1829, William T. Mayo wrote a letter from the Boston office to William Stutson at the Sandwich factory. "We can sell 4 or 5 doz. roughed Cyl. Lamps 8 Sqrfoot whenever you send them. We paint them & make quite a pretty article. Make some of the tops small enough for a plated brass and pewter cap." Jarves, as agent of the Boston and Sandwich Glass Company, prepared a report for the Federal Government in 1832 in which he stated that five women were employed to paint on glass. To manufacture this lamp, the font was blown and fastened to the pressed base by a ringed wafer. The four-step base has a prism pattern pressed on the inside. After annealing, the lamp was sent to the cutting shop, where the upper part of the font was cut into a fan design and polished, and the lower part was roughed to appear frosted and give the paint something to "bite" into. Although a visitor to the factory in 1831 observed glass being stained, there is no way to determine whether the floral design of fleurs-de-lys and green leaves was painted in Sandwich or at the decorating facility in Boston. The collar was cemented to the neck and a burner was threaded onto the collar. Finally, the lamp was ready to be sold. *Reproduced by courtesy of The Magazine ANTIQUES*

2048 FREE-BLOWN LAMP WITH PRESSED BASE

5½'' H. x 2½'' Dia. font, 2⅜'' Sq. base 1830–1840

The pressed base on this lamp has been attributed to Eastern and Pittsburgh glass houses. Commercial mold makers manufactured the molds and sold them to any glass company that needed the service, so it is impossible to tell origin from the shape of the base alone. The base and the font were both dug at the Boston and Sandwich Glass Company site. Without a doubt, some were made in Sandwich. However, a buyer should be aware that, without documented attribution from descendants of a glassworker or an invoice preserved with the lamp at the time of purchase, positive proof of Sandwich manufacture cannot be obtained. This is true of several bases that date from this time period. Although we use the existence of a wafer as a tool to help us attribute a piece, be aware that other companies also used it as a method of joining the separate units. Regardless of the manufacturer, colored early lamps are very, very rare.

2049 FREE-BLOWN GLOBE FONT WITH PRESSED BASE, DROP TUBE WHALE OIL BURNER

4⅛'' H. x 2⅛'' Dia. font, 2⅛'' Sq. base 1828–1835

This delicate base with extended round corners has a prism pattern on the inside. There are three bands of prisms, stepped to conform to the stepped outer surface of the base. Therefore, only a small amount of hot glass was required to fill the mold and the lamp is light in weight. The date above denotes the manufacturing date of the lamp. The drop tube burner predates the founding of Jarves' Sandwich Glass Manufactory by many years and is the earliest type shown in this book that was used on American glass. Glass lamps blown to accept this burner had no necks; the tin disk rested loosely on the opening. Deming Jarves patented the cork improvement to the drop tube in 1822 to be used on font openings with short necks. The cork acted as a stopper. Jarves' cork tube burner and the threaded tube burner were in common use by the time he opened the Sandwich works, but this earlier drop tube burner would be supplied if requested by the customer.

2050 DROP TUBE WHALE OIL BURNER

1⅝'' H.

This is the earliest form of whale oil tube burner used on glass lamps with closed fonts (as opposed to primitive lighting devices in which the fuel reservoir was an open dish) made by the Boston and Sandwich Glass Company or glass factories that predate the Sandwich works. A metal disk with a tab rolled up to form a primitive handle set on top of the opening in the font. A ball of cotton was forced through the tube to act as a wick. When the font was full of whale oil, the wick burned brighter than when the last of the oil was concentrated in the bottom of the font. This problem was eliminated by making wicks of tightly braided cotton threads that allowed capillary action to carry a constant flow of whale oil to the flame.

2051 FREE-BLOWN GLOBE FONT WITH PRESSED BASE, THREADED WHALE OIL BURNER

4⅛" H. x 2⅛" Dia. font, 2⅛" Sq. base 1828–1835
Here is the same lamp fitted with a threaded collar and single tube whale oil burner. The principle of enclosing the fuel in a covered font and using a tube to support a wick vertically was patented in 1787 by John Miles of Birmingham, England. On glass lamps, it became necessary to cement a metal collar onto the neck of an enclosed font, to which the burner could be threaded. Lamps supplied with collars and burners were more expensive than when supplied with a drop tube burner or Jarves' cheaper cork tube invention. The light cast by most of these small lamps was not much of an improvement over candles, but lamps were cleaner, smoked less, and there was no wax to run onto the table. A burner screwed snugly into place prevented spillage in the event of an accident. Note the defect that was in the pattern on the plunger, breaking the precise lines of the prism bands. Bases with this defect were dug at the factory site. This characteristic helps to identify this lamp as Sandwich in the antiques marketplace.

2052 FREE-BLOWN BULB LAMPS WITH PRESSED BASE

8" H. x 2¼" Dia. font, 2⅝" Sq. base 1830–1835
Here again we see the extended rounded corners of a base commonly used at Sandwich. Keep in mind that several Eastern and Midwestern houses used this type of base, so its style cannot be used for identification. Inside the standard are razor sharp glass deposits left by the pontil rod. Extreme caution must be used when handling and washing the lamps. Pressed into the underside of the base at each corner is a fan pattern with a center dot that makes the fan resemble half of a daisy with five petals. Bases with this flower/fan motif were dug in quantity at the Boston and Sandwich factory site. Both collars are later replacements.

2053 FREE-BLOWN DECORATED BULB LAMPS WITH PRESSED BASE

9⅜" H. x 3" Dia. font, 3⅛" Sq. base 1830–1835
The condition of this perfect pair of decorated lamps is outstanding when you consider that they have been together for over 150 years. The pressed bases were made in the same mold. The free-blown fonts are as close to a matching pair as you will find. The metal ringed collar on lamp A is original. The collar on lamp B is old, but is a replacement that is one size too large. Close scrutiny reveals that the flowers were once a brilliant yellow and the leaves were emerald green. It has been written that early colors faded and wore off because the glass was not refired in a decorating kiln. In an article published in the December 1925 issue of *Antiques Magazine*, author Charles Messer Stow stated that he had a little notebook in Deming Jarves' writing that was dated 1828, in which Jarves recorded directions for making a kiln. The notebook was titled *Deming Jarves Glass Staining Receipts, Boston*, so the kiln appears to be one designed to set the stain. The kiln's inside dimensions were 3' long, 1'10" wide and 1'6" deep. A copy of Stow's article is preserved in The Rakow Library at The Corning Museum of Glass. Even the stain and paint applied to glass in the 1890's did not hold up well to repeated washing.

2054 FREE-BLOWN ENGRAVED CUT BULB LAMP WITH PRESSED BASE

9¼" H. x 2¾" Dia. font, 3¼" Sq. base 1830–1845

This base with extended round corners is a common one that was also used by other glass companies. Patrick F. Slane, who established the American Flint Glass Works in South Boston, illustrated it in a patent of March 26, 1845, for an improvement of glass lamps. Molds were purchased from moldmaking establishments, which was a separate business in itself. Fonts with this cut design have been dug from the factory site. Occasionally a cutter cut too deeply into the surface, so the piece was discarded to be used as fill to extend the factory yard into the swampy areas that surrounded it. Be aware that all of these lighting devices were made by joining separate units together. Any font could be combined with any base that was manufactured during the same time period.

2055 FREE-BLOWN GLOBE LAMP WITH PRESSED SCALLOPED CIRCULAR BASE

3¼" H. x 2¼" Dia. font, 2¼" Dia. base 1830–1835

There are eleven scallops in each of the three steps on the base, yet the base was pressed in a three-sectioned mold. This meant that two sections had four scallops each, while the third had only three scallops. The flattened knop was pressed as part of the base. Keep in mind that this lamp is only slightly over 3" in height. It was also made as a toy lamp with the smallest of handles applied to the upper half of the font and a tiny bulb-shaped lamp glass fastened to the burner coronet by a set screw. It is pictured in *Early Lighting A Pictorial Guide*, published by The Rushlight Club. Small lamps had many uses; they were placed in windows to guide a loved one home, used on hall tables to guide the elderly through darkened hallways, and used in sickrooms to leave a soft, comforting light in place of a harsh, larger flame. Some were used for heat to melt the wax that was used to seal letters before the advent of envelopes.

2056 FREE-BLOWN GLOBE PEG LAMPS

4¼" H. x 2¾" Dia. 1830–1850

A peg lamp is nothing more than a font with a peg beneath it that can be inserted into the socket of a candlestick, lantern or wall sconce, and into the metal fitting of a hanging lamp. The diggings at Sandwich show that hundreds of peg lamps were made, most so plain that no one can tell today which glass house made them. This photo shows pieces that had been in the hands of a Sandwich family. Unless these plain little pieces have family ties, they are impossible to authenticate as Sandwich glass.

2057 FREE-BLOWN BULB LAMP WITH PRESSED SCALLOPED SQUARE BASE

9¼'' H. x 3'' Dia. font, 3½'' Sq. base 1835-1845
This unusually flat base was also used on a candlestick with a blown socket. It has four steps that rise to a short, circular stem. Stubby pillars of glass surround the stem just above the uppermost scalloped step. A ringed wafer holds the font to the stem. Beneath the base in the center is a jagged ridge of glass that was left when the pontil rod was broken away. Use extreme caution when handling Nineteenth Century glass. This manufacturing ''defect'' does not deter from value, except in the mind of someone who has been injured because of it. This lamp is exceedingly attractive for one with such a primitively constructed base. At an antiques show in 1987, we saw its mate with a whale oil burner threaded to a ringed collar, still filled with thick, amber whale oil.

2058 FREE-BLOWN FONT WITH PRESSED QUATREFOIL BASE, WHALE OIL BURNER

6⅛'' H. x 3'' Dia. font, 2¾'' Sq. base 1830-1840
The black specks that can be seen inside the glass are called *gall*, which is a residue of impurities in the batch. It is unusual to see a piece with as many specks (more than fifty) as this one has. Records show that pieces with specks were sold by the lot at trade sales, which were wholesale auctions attended by a glass company's major buyers. There are several large chips beneath the base that were caused by the release of the spider pontil that held the lamp while it was being worked on. If the chip cannot be seen when the lamp is set in an upright position, the manufacturing characteristic should not deter from value.

2059 FREE-BLOWN BULB LAMPS WITH PRESSED QUATREFOIL BASE, WHALE OIL BURNER

11½'' H. 1830-1845
These pressed bases are very slender for their height. Each base is comprised of five steps made up of four rounded lobes, above which is a narrow standard molded in one piece with the lobed base. The hot glass was forced into shape by an extremely deep plunger that penetrated to within ⅛'' of the wafers. If you find double plunger marks on the base, or other defects caused by the plunger, they do not deter from their value. They are the result of manufacturing error when the pressing industry was in its infancy. The base is held to the bulb font by a thick three-knopped wafer that was not reworked. The ringed collars and threaded burners appear to be original to the lamps. Many metal lamp fittings were purchased from Boston manufacturer William Carleton, who originally bought Jarves' patent for the cork tube whale oil burner. *Courtesy of The Toledo Museum of Art (Acc. No. 67.98 A&B)*

2060 FREE-BLOWN BULB LAMPS WITH PRESSED QUATREFOIL BASE, FLUID BURNER

(a) 13¼" H.
(b) 13⁹⁄₁₆" H. 1830–1845

These lamps are taller than the previous ones. They hold more fuel and have fluid burners capable of providing more light. Lamp B is almost ½" taller than lamp A. The difference is in the blown fonts. They are otherwise a perfect pair. Both fonts were roughed in the cutting shop to approximately the same height so that they could be painted. Don't pass up old lamps that were painted. This work was done at Sandwich by 1831. The Toledo Museum of Art acquired a large collection of lamps and candlesticks in 1967. The authors were fortunate to have access to them for study. Museum glass not on display in the main gallery is preserved in a glass study room that the museum makes available for serious research. The room is arranged like the book stalls in a library; the cases are only the depth of book shelves so that each piece can easily be studied. An accession number identifies each piece of glass. All written information about each item is cataloged in the same room and can be located by referring to the accession number. It was our pleasure to be involved with a museum that was planned for use by the serious scholar. *Courtesy of The Toledo Museum of Art (Acc. No. 67.99 A&B)*

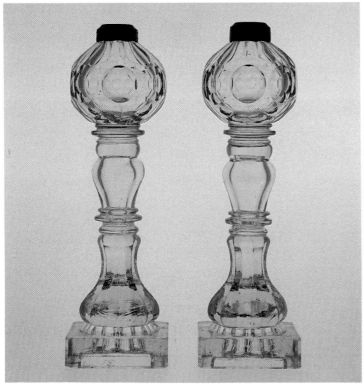

2061 FREE-BLOWN CUT PUNTY LAMPS WITH PRESSED OCTAGONAL STANDARD AND SQUARE BASE

11" H. x 3⅛" Dia. font, 3⅜" Sq. base 1835–1845

Some of the cutting done at Sandwich shows great quality. These fonts have punties cut around the center and flutes above that carry the design to the collar. Each font was attached with a wafer to a free-blown hollow center unit, which Jarves referred to as the bulb. Sometimes the glass blower inserted a coin into the hollow center. Below the bulb, another shaped wafer was used to fasten the octagonal standard. This standard was pressed in one piece with the square base. This base and standard can be found in a smaller size combined with vase units and candle sockets. Jarves' early letters and the earliest factory sloar book give us a good understanding of the company's product and construction methods. *Courtesy, Sandwich Glass Museum, Sandwich Historical Society*

2062 FREE-BLOWN CUT BULB LAMPS WITH PRESSED OCTAGONAL STANDARD AND SQUARE BASE, WHALE OIL BURNER AND LIVERPOOL LAMP GLASS

(a) Lamp 10⅜" H. x 2½" Sq. font, 3½" Sq. base
(b) Liverpool lamp glass 4¾" H. x 3⅛" Dia.
(c) Combined size 15½" H. 1830–1840

Here is an excellent example of assembling two units into a tall lamp without using a blown knop center. The base was held directly to the font with a wafer. The unusually long, drawn-out bulb font made it difficult for the wick to absorb the final inch of oil from the bottom. The fonts are square because four deep flutes were cut into the thick sidewalls of an originally 3" Dia. bulb font. The lamp glasses are secured to the coronet around the burners by a set screw and permanent hook. They had to be removed each time the lamps were lit, so many were broken. The technique employed in decorating the glasses was called *roughed and cut*. The records made no distinction between

Continuation follows glossary.

2063 FREE-BLOWN GLOBE LAMP WITH PRESSED BASE, FLUID BURNER

6'' H. x 3'' Dia. font, 3¼'' Sq. base 1828–1835

In the early 1830's, experiments were made to perfect man-made lighting fuels that burned cleaner and whiter than whale oil. They were extremely explosive, so burners were redesigned to help eliminate accidents. This fluid burner with caps is correct for the time of production, as is a two-tube whale oil burner. Note how the prism pattern beneath the base angles to the right, leaving an unpatterned area on the left. The plunger struck the base at an angle and the base was forever improperly patterned. When you find antique glass with a production defect, do not hesitate to buy it, because it is unique and may be the only piece of its kind with that particular defect. The dark areas in the base are a greenish-black gall that floated on the surface of the hot glass in the pot and was generally removed. This lamp was also made in a smaller size. *Courtesy, Sandwich Glass Museum, Sandwich Historical Society*

2064 FREE-BLOWN CUT BULB LAMPS WITH PRESSED BASE

10¼'' H. x 3'' Dia. font, 4'' Sq. base 1828–1835

These lamps descended down through the family of decorator Annie Nye, who worked for the Boston and Sandwich Glass Company in the 1880's. The stepped base was also used in candlesticks and can be seen in photo 4014 of Volume 4. Note the difference in the two ringed wafers. This minor production characteristic does not hurt the value of an otherwise perfectly matched pair. The cut grape design was a common one. There are generally three bunches of grapes and a vine that encircles the font. In addition to the documentation provided by Annie Nye's family, fragments with the grape design have been dug at the factory site. Electrical adapters were soldered to the original collars and are next to impossible to remove. If you wish to adapt oil lamps to electrical use, do not solder the new fittings. Value is greatly diminished.

2065 FREE-BLOWN CUT LAMPS WITH PRESSED BASE

8¾'' H. x 3¼'' Dia. font, 4¼'' Sq. base 1830–1840

This is a well-executed pair of fonts for free-blown work. The cut grape and vine designs are an exact match, indicating that these lamps have always been together. Both collars were replaced, probably in the 1870's, when this style of collar came into use. When buying lamps at high retail price, be sure that the collars are of the period and that the threads are in good condition. The stepped bases with rounded corners were originally well executed, although they show much damage now. Note that the plunger with its prism pattern went further into the base of the lamp on the right. This does not change the value of the pair. As can be seen in other photos, this base was also made with no pattern beneath the base. *Courtesy, Sandwich Glass Museum, Sandwich Historical Society*

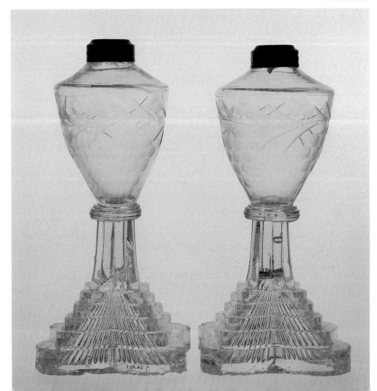

2066 FREE-BLOWN CUT LAMPS WITH PRESSED BASE, FLUID BURNER
13⅛" H. 1830–1840

This base was also used on candlesticks. The five steps are smooth on the outside and the prisms are on the inside. A blown knop center added height and was held to the other units by large, shaped wafers. Flutes were cut into the font after the glass was evenly cooled in the annealing leer. The ringed collar is the style usually attributed to the New England Glass Company, but metal-working machine shops sold collars, burners and fittings to any glass factory that ordered them. Patrick F. Slane used ringed collars at the American Flint Glass Works in South Boston, and illustrated one on a patent that was granted to him on March 26, 1845. The stepped bases of various configurations also are not exclusive to the Boston and Sandwich Glass Company, but were used by other factories in the greater Boston area. Molds were purchased by the factories and did not belong to individual glassworkers. *Courtesy of The Toledo Museum of Art (Acc. No. 67.96 A&B)*

2067 FREE-BLOWN CUT LAMP WITH PRESSED BASE
11½" H. x 3" Dia. font, 4¼" Sq. base 1830–1840

Here is the same type of lamp shown previously with a hollow knop between the upper and lower units to give it height. A design of cut swags and tassels surrounds the upper half of the font, with cut ovals around the lower half. A shaped wafer connects the font to the hollow blown knop in the center. A second shaped wafer was used to connect the knop to the base. Very rarely, a coin was placed in the center knop. This would greatly enhance its present-day value. The plunger that hollowed out the pressed base did not have the pattern of prisms on it. The Boston and Sandwich Glass Company made both types of bases, as did other glass factories. This lamp very likely had a lamp glass that was cut in the same swag and tassel design. The collar is original and the base is in pristine condition, so this lamp would bring top retail price on the antiques market. *Courtesy, Sandwich Glass Museum, Sandwich Historical Society*

2068 FREE-BLOWN GLOBE LAMPS WITH PRESSED QUATREFOIL BASE, WHALE OIL BURNER
10⅝" H. x 3" Dia. font, 4" Sq. base 1830–1845

One of the most difficult things to do when blowing glass was to make a matching pair. The bases were a simple matter because they were pressed in a mold, but the rest was assembled by free-blowing a center "bulb" unit and a font unit and then assembling the units by connecting them together with a series of shaped, or bladed, wafers. After the blown units were assembled, the pressed base was fastened to a pontil rod adapted with a four-armed spider attachment. The hot wafer was applied to the top of the standard and, while the wafer was still in a molten condition, the blown assembly was applied to the wafer. After a good bond was assured, the pressed base was broken away from the spider, leaving inner chips under the base at each place where the spider was attached. This chipping was a part of the assembly process and does not deter from value. The accompanying illustration shows how the four arms of the spider were used to hold the base.

Fig. 5 A pontil rod with a four-armed "spider" attachment was fastened to the bottom of the base. The base was held in this manner while the blown knop center unit was fastened to it with a bladed wafer. When the work was completed, the pontil rod was broken away, chipping the inside of the base. These inside chips are not always found on later pressed pieces. In 1857, Hiram Dillaway patented a glassware holder that supported the base on the outside (see patent following photo 2161).

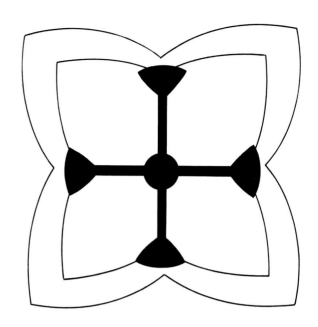

2069 FREE-BLOWN GLOBE LAMPS WITH PRESSED SQUARE BASE, FLUID BURNER

7½" H. x 3¼" Dia. font, 3½" Sq. base 1830–1840
Beginning in the early 1830's, the retail customer had his choice of fuels, so glass companies supplied their wholesale agencies with both types of burners mounted on the same style of lamp. When lamps that combined pressed bases with blown fonts were popular, wholesale orders to the factory were substantial. Utilizing but a single mold, one pressed base could be turned out every two minutes. At this rate, a shop of glassworkers had one minute to take a glob of molten glass out of the pot, carry it to the mold, shear it from the blowpipe and allow it to drop into the mold receiver, and insert the plunger to force the glass into shape. It took another minute for the glass to cool sufficiently in the mold to maintain its shape. This speedy rate of thirty pieces per hour was hard for a shop to sustain over an extended period of time. The answer was to order from the mold maker several molds of the same pattern. Because the molds were hand made, there were slight variations, especially on the plungers. On this pair of lamps, the plunger used on lamp A had a prism band with fine lines. The plunger was inserted deeper into the mold than the plunger used to make lamp B, which has a coarse prism band. Yet, every other detail indicates that the lamps have been together since they were produced, so the minor difference in the prism band does not affect value. Be aware that if each lamp was purchased separately by a collector or dealer, the inevitable difference in the color of the glass, resulting from the use of different batches, would make them less valuable.

2070 FREE-BLOWN GLOBE LAMPS WITH PRESSED EYE AND SCALE CYLINDRICAL BASE, WHALE OIL BURNER

11¾'' H. x 4⅛'' Dia. font, 4⅛'' Dia. base 1836–1840
This pair of lamps was given to the Sandwich Historical Society in 1913 by the daughter of Enoch Hinckley, for whom they were made. Hinckley was a master carpenter, ship-builder and the landlord of Swift's Tavern in West Sandwich, now Sagamore, Massachusetts. He also built the sloop *Sandwich* for the glass company in 1827. The lamps are very heavy. The bases were pressed after coal became the principle fuel for heating the glass. The Eye and Scale pattern is on the outside and distorts the pattern of prisms that is pressed on the inside of the base. *This prism pattern differentiates the Sandwich Eye and Scale base from that of other factories.* Look into the base of the lamp on the right. Note the thickness of the glass and the prisms *that can be felt* on the inside. The large hollow free-blown knop above the base was held in place by a wafer. The free-blown font was attached in a like manner. Two other glass companies made similar Eye and Scale bases. The most frequently found are light in weight and were crudely made, possibly by Thomas Cains. The cylindrical bases were blown molded, therefore are closed across the bottoms, which have rough pontil marks. We have seen these as lamp bases combined with blown molded paneled fonts and free-blown bulb and cylindrical fonts. In c. 1840, the French firm of Launay Hautin & Compagnie, selling agents for Cristalleries de Baccarat and Cristalleries de Saint-Louis, devoted one page in their catalog to illustrate a full line of tableware in this *draperie* pattern. A lamp font was not shown, but the cylindrical base was combined with a bowl to make a high foot nappie. *The French base has a rayed star that covers the closed bottom.* It is the opinion of the authors that if a French Eye and Scale lamp had been made, it would have medium weight and be closed across a star bottom. *Courtesy, Sandwich Glass Museum, Sandwich Historical Society*

2071 BASE OF ABOVE LAMPS

This close-up shows the erratic effect that resulted from combining the wrong two patterns. The Eye and Scale pattern was on the mold and the Prism pattern was on the plunger. The Eye and Scale pattern was selected by Deming Jarves for use in his first attempt to press a tumbler. Collectors have automatically associated all glass in this pattern with Sandwich, regardless of whether it was pressed or blown molded. The Sandwich lamp has an open bottom and prisms on the inside.

Page from original c. 1840 Launay Hautin & Compagnie catalog illustrating their *draperie* tableware. Note the rayed star in the bottom view of the French cylindrical base. The blown molded tumbler in the top row is often mistaken for Jarves' pressed tumbler. *The Corning Museum of Glass, Corning, New York*

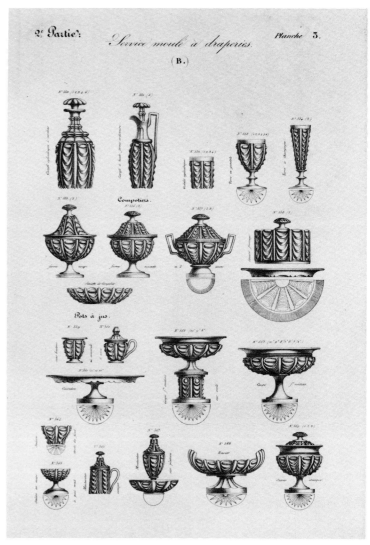

2072 BLOWN MOLDED EYE AND SCALE LAMP WITH PRESSED CIRCULAR BASE

9'' H. x 2⅝'' Dia. font, 4¼'' Dia. base 1835–1840

The wafer method of construction was used to combine units of lamps, candlesticks, vases, and tableware throughout the Boston and Sandwich Glass Company's entire sixty-three years of production. The existence of this lamp proves this point. Most Eye and Scale lamps that are found in the antiques market were constructed in a single mold and were not made in Sandwich. The lamp shown here was made in Sandwich and has a wafer just above the pressed base. The font was blown into a mold and has a delicate, unique quality. If the lamp had been made in one piece, the mold marks could be followed continuously from the base to above the pattern on the font. But you will never find a mold mark on a wafer, because the wafer was a separate disk of glass that was not put into a mold. This circular base can be seen on a candlestick in photo 4019 of Volume 4. The Eye and Scale font was also combined with a pressed hexagonal base that has a pattern of horizontal lines and fans, and the flaring hexagonal candlestick base shown in photo 4027.

2073 METAL COLLARS
1825–1909
Great quantities of brass and pewter collars were unearthed at the factory site. The pewter collars decayed from the hundred years they were in the ground and are of little use other than to the historian. The brass collars were in excellent condition, undamaged by time. They can easily be brought back to full polish.

2074 BRASS COLLARS AND FEEDER CAP
1825–1909
The eight collars shown here represent every size of brass collar dug from the Boston and Sandwich site. From left to right, their diameters are 2⅜'', 1⅞'', 1½'', 1⅜'', 1¼'', 1⅛'', 1³⁄₃₂'', and 1¹⁄₁₆''. The feeder cap shown in the lower right fits the two smallest collars. *Feeders* were separate openings in fonts through which kerosene was poured. They were most often used in suspension lamps that hung over tables and in wall brackets. A large number of pewter collars were also found, but they were so badly decayed that sizes could not be determined.

2075 METAL FLUID BURNERS (CAPS) AND COLLARS
1825–1860
Over four hundred collars and fully as many burners were dug at the Boston and Sandwich Glass Company site. All of the collars had cement in them and most had broken glass attached, showing that lamps were sold with collars already cemented on and burners threaded in place.

2076 FREE-BLOWN GLOBE LAMP WITH PRESSED LION HEAD AND BASKET OF FLOWERS BASE
7¼'' H. x 2¾'' Dia. font, 3⅛'' Sq. base 1830–1855
This lamp is often attributed to the New England Glass Company alone because some of them were signed as such, but heavy deposits of burnt fragments, shown in the foreground, indicate Sandwich manufacture also. However, the Sandwich lamps have button feet beneath the base and were not signed. The basket of flowers on each of the four sides and the lion head on each of the four upper corners of the base were molded in deep relief. The clear fragment on the left has a ringed wafer, while the opaque white fragment has a knopped wafer. The globe font is the one most frequently encountered. Variations include free-blown bulb and conical fonts and blown molded ribbed ones as shown in photo 2045. The lamp was made over a long period of time; the cork tube whale oil burner, the threaded tube whale oil burner and the tapered tube fluid burner are all original to this pattern. Occasional pastel opal shades attest to 1850's production.

2077 BLOWN MOLDED BANDED LEAF LAMP WITH PRESSED LION HEAD AND BASKET OF FLOWERS BASE, WHALE OIL BURNER AND BULB LAMP GLASS

(a) Lamp 7⅝″ H. x 2¾″ Dia. font, 3″ Sq. base
(b) Bulb lamp glass 5¼″ H. x 3¼″ Dia.
(c) Combined size 13″ H. 1830–1855

Up until this point in time, most fonts were unpatterned and decorative motifs were molded into the bases. This very rare silver-blue lamp has a band of leaves around the font and vertical ribs above and below the band. The font was held to the base with a large knop wafer. Note the button feet beneath the base, which could be machined to level the lamp. The threaded burner and the ring that holds the lamp glass were cast in one piece of brass. The bottom rim of the lamp glass, called the *fitter*, is flared to fit under a hook on one side of the ring and a set screw on the other side that can be tightened to hold the lamp glass in place. Because the flared fitters are easily chipped, care must be taken to remove and replace the lamp glass. Lamp or window glass that was roughed in the cutting shop to soften the light or provide privacy was sometimes called *obscured* in early advertisements. The term *bulb lamp glass* was used by Jarves in a letter to William Stutson dated November 23, 1825, in which Jarves described and illustrated a variety of lamp glasses. *Courtesy, Sandwich Glass Museum, Sandwich Historical Society*

2078 WHALE OIL BURNER AND LIVERPOOL LAMP GLASS

(a) Burner 2″ H. x 1⅛″ Dia.
(b) Liverpool lamp glass 3⅞″ H. x 3″ Dia. 1825–1845

Here is the whale oil burner most often encountered on the lamp with the pressed Lion Head and Basket of Flowers base. The burner predates the lamp, however. On November 23, 1825, Deming Jarves told Superintendent William Stutson that there was much demand for lamp glasses and advised Stutson to make several different kinds. Four out of Jarves' six illustrations show the flaring lower rim that fit under the set screw and metal holding tab of the burner. The flaring upper portion was called a *tulip neck*. Liverpool lamp glasses were ordered with "½ Tulip" and "¾ Tulip" necks. An 1829 letter from Albany, New York, glass dealer Gregory and Bain referred to a "painted lamp glass". Lamp glasses in perfect condition are seldom found today. Most were broken and the few that remain are likely to be chipped from carelessness in removing them from under the holding tabs and set screws.

2079 BLOWN MOLDED BANDED LEAF PEG LAMPS

4″ H. x 3″ Dia. 1830–1855

With the addition of a glass extension that could be inserted into a candle socket or metal lamp fitting, any font that was shaped with stability in mind could be marketed as a peg lamp. Although the addition of cork tube burners would complete a lamp to the satisfaction of a collector, it is more likely that, as peg lamps, the Banded Leaf fonts had threaded collars and burners to lessen the chance of a spill. Peg lamps were often sold with candlesticks in matching colors. The candlesticks then served a two-fold purpose; they held candles when desired and served as the base of a lighting device. A pair of clear Banded Leaf peg lamps are in the authors' collection. *Courtesy of Richard A. Bourne Co., Inc.*

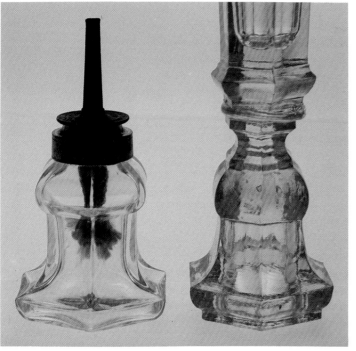

2080 BLOWN MOLDED HEXAGONAL LAMP, FLUID BURNER

(a) Lamp 2½'' H. x 2⅛'' Dia.

(b) Matching pressed candle socket 2⅝'' H. including extension; 2⅛'' Dia. 1840–1860

This unusual photo was taken to show how the same form could be adapted to multiple use. There is no question that two different molds were used. The candle socket was pressed, with the plunger making the hole for the candle. To make the night lamp, glass was blown into a similar mold from the neck. Little lamps were cataloged as night lamps, but were used for other purposes. According to family descendants, this particular one had been on a desk and had been used for many years to heat wax with which to seal letters. The wax had to be held at the proper distance from the flame in order to melt it. The flame burned at one steady rate with no way to control it.

2081 BLOWN MOLDED LAMP, FLUID BURNER AND BULB LAMP GLASS

(a) Lamp 2½'' H. x 2'' Dia.

(b) Lamp glass 2½'' H. x 1⅝'' Dia.

(c) Combined size 5¼'' H. 1830–1870

The lower unit appeared in McKee and Brothers catalogs as late as 1868, where it was sold as a night lamp. The burner should be equipped with a long length of wick that coils around the bottom of the font for maximum use of the burning fluid. When the wick shortened up, as shown here, very little fuel was available to the flame, necessitating constant refilling. This lamp has a free-blown lamp glass with a folded rim that was marketed as an accessory to control the heat. A metal fitting designed to slide up and down the burner tube was cemented to the opening in the bottom of the lamp glass. It is shown here in its lowest position. When the glass was pushed down to the bottom of the tube, the flame with its maximum heat was available above the glass for melting wax, or for use in an apothecary shop as a Bunsen-type burner.

2082 ABOVE LAMP WITH LAMP GLASS IN RAISED POSITION

If one wished to lower the heat, the lamp glass could be raised up the tube, as shown here. The flame would be farther away from the rim of the lamp glass, decreasing the heat. It has been suggested that in this position it may have been used to light cigars. It was often used in a sick room to heat a spoonful of butter and honey mixture given to control croup. The lower lamp unit is commonly found at antiques shows because it was made in quantity by many glass factories. Fragments of the upper lamp glass were dug in quantity at the Boston and Sandwich Glass Company site with the hole through the center of the bottom, but no metal fitting. No one had been able to tell us its purpose until the complete assembly was found at an antiques show.

2083 BLOWN MOLDED HAND LAMP, FLUID BURNER AND BLOWN FIERY OPALESCENT LAMP GLASS

(a) Lamp 1⅜'' H. x 2¼'' Dia.
(b) Lamp glass 2⅛'' H. x 1⅛'' Dia.
(c) Combined size 4¾'' H. 1838–1845

This lamp was blown into an unpatterned mold to give it form, after which the handle was applied. In the 1800's, the burner was called a *cap*; the worker whose job it was to cement the collar in place was a lamp *capper*. The opalescent lamp glass, called a *chimney* in later years when used to provide the draft for a kerosene burner, is held in place by a four-pronged fitting that slides up and down the fluid burner tube. In this manner, the heat could be adjusted for maximum efficiency. Most lamp glasses were clear glass. It is most unusual to find a burner with a fiery opalescent glass. It is possible that the lamp glass was made at another glass works to the specifications of the burner manufacturer. Fiery opalescent glass was first made in Sandwich in 1838, so this is still a realistic, probable date regardless of its origin. *Courtesy, Sandwich Glass Museum, Sandwich Historical Society*

2084 FREE-BLOWN CUT LAMP WITH PRESSED HEXAGONAL BASE, WHALE OIL BURNER AND LIVERPOOL LAMP GLASS

(a) Lamp 7¾'' H. x 2⅞'' Dia. font, 4¼'' Dia. base
(b) Liverpool lamp glass 3½'' H. x 2¾'' Dia.
(c) Combined size 11¾'' H. 1840–1855

The font on this lamp was blown, then hand-tooled into the desired form. After the lamp was annealed, it was sent to the cutting shop, where the floral design was cut and polished into the font. The pressed base was commonly used on candlesticks and can be seen combined with a pressed hexagonal socket in photo 4042 of Volume 4. However, the uniqueness of this lamp is its original lamp glass, identified as *Liverpool* in Deming Jarves' November 23, 1825, letter to William Stutson. He referred to the upper flared portion as a *tulip neck*; the one shown in this photo is "⅓ Tulip". Jarves also directed that some be made with "¾ Tulip". On December 8, 1827, Jarves stressed the importance of making the lower portion globe-shaped so that the flame had room and would not heat the neck. "The lamp sellers begin to find the shape they require not good to last—as the heat soon breaks them without a glass chimney." He illustrated the wrong and right way to make them.

2085 BLOWN MOLDED PANELED LAMPS WITH PRESSED HEXAGONAL BASE, WHALE OIL BURNER

(a) Amethyst 8½'' H. x 2¾'' Dia. font, 4¼'' Dia. base
(b) White 7½'' H. x 2½'' Dia. font, 3¾'' Dia. base
1840–1855

This flaring hexagonal base was commonly used on candlesticks. The font was blown into a mold with a pattern of six panels, after which it was held to the pressed base by a wafer that is hidden inside the knop beneath the font. The wafers on some experimental pieces can be very thin—sometimes no more than the thickness of a layer of mucilage if the units were to be pasted together. When investigating a lamp that you think has this type of construction, study the vertical marks made by the seams of the

Continuation follows glossary.

2086 BLOWN MOLDED PANELED LAMP WITH PRESSED HEXAGONAL BASE IN ORIGINAL BOX, WHALE OIL BURNER

(a) Lamp in box 7½" H. x 2½" Dia. font, 3¾" Dia. base 1840–1847

(b) Lamp beside box 8⅝" H. x 2⅞" Dia. font, 4¼" Dia. base 1840–1850

Early in Sandwich glass history, a general store in Portsmouth, New Hampshire, owned by John Sise, began to carry Sandwich glass along with other dry goods. A working relationship developed between Sise and the Boston and Sandwich Glass Company that resulted in his store becoming known as "the Sandwich store in Portsmouth" (see notebook dated 1888 pictured in Chapter 11 of Volume 4). In 1952, when Sise's home, then in the hands of his grandson, was disposed of, this box with its lamp was found in the attic along with twenty-seven other pieces of Sandwich glass. The lamp had never been used and was still packed in salt marsh hay. A Boston newspaper dated 1847 lined the deteriorating bottom of the box. The amethyst lamp on the right matches the lamp in the box but is one size larger.

2087 BLOWN MOLDED PANELED LAMP WITH PRESSED HEXAGONAL BASE

8⅛" H. x 2¾" Dia. font, 4¼" Dia. base 1840–1850

This font has twelve panels that continue to the neck. The hot glass was forced against the walls of the mold by air pressure. After removal from the paneled mold, the font was attached to the pressed base by the usual common disk wafer. An identical lamp in the authors' collection has two wafers. For some reason while construction was taking place, the first wafer placed on the standard cooled and did not adhere to the knop extension of the font, so a second hot wafer was applied. Both lamps have the same value. If you find a pair of lamps with one wafer on one lamp and two wafers on the other lamp, consider them to be a matching pair if this is the only difference. See photo 3019 to study a pair of green vases with this production variation. The metal collar here with its stamped, rounded rings is a later replacement.

2088 BLOWN MOLDED OCTAGONAL LAMP WITH PRESSED HEXAGONAL BASE, WHALE OIL BURNER

5" H. x 2" Dia. font, 2⅝" Dia. base 1840–1850

Large amounts of fragments of this lamp were dug at the Boston and Sandwich Glass Company site. An amber fragment is shown on the left and an opaque green fragment is on the right. Although this was a small lamp, the base was held to the font by a *wafer*, a small disk of glass about the size of a quarter. After the upper and lower units were removed from their respective molds, the hot wafer was placed atop the base and, while still in a molten condition, the font was pushed into the molten wafer, sealing the two units together forever. This original ringed collar is often used as a means of attribution solely to the New England Glass Company, but many broken lamps dug from the Sandwich site have this pewter collar. All glass companies purchased their metal fittings from many outside sources, making identification by collar design unreliable. The New England Glass Company and the Boston and Sandwich Glass Company both worked closely with William Carleton, owner of one of Boston's largest lamp assembly plants.

2089 BLOWN MOLDED OCTAGONAL PEG LAMP, WHALE OIL BURNER

4½" H. x 2½" Dia. 1838–1845

This lamp was a very important find when it was dug at the site of the Boston and Sandwich Glass Company factory. There were several peg lamps made from the same mold tightly clustered together, indicating that a box ready for shipment had been dropped. The box had rotted away, leaving the cluster of lamps that carried the ringed collar and burner many antiques dealers and auctioneers attribute to the New England Glass Company only. The dug lamps ready for market are proof positive that ringed collars were used at Sandwich. The lamp was blown into a two-piece mold that had four panels in each half. The underfilled peg in no way detracts from the value of the piece. The fact that it was part of a boxful shows that it passed inspection and was good enough to be packed. Factory managers expected that up to 10 percent of the glass would be sold as seconds at wholesale trade shows (auctions).

2090 BLOWN MOLDED PANELED PEG LAMPS

(a) Ten panels, whale oil burner 4⅛" H. x 2" Dia.
(b) Fourteen panels, fluid burner 4⅞" H. x 2⅛" Dia.
    1840–1860

The simplicity of paneled peg lamps makes it impossible to attribute a particular factory, but we know from the diggings that these types of peg lamps were produced in quantity at Sandwich. The diameter of the font and the length of the peg were critical to their intended use. Lamp A, with its narrow diameter and short peg, was inserted up through the bottom of hanging hall lights and in straight-sided lamp glasses. Lamp B fits nicely into a candlestick that has a pressed base and blown socket, as well as into several of the largest pressed candlesticks. The long extension stabilized the font when in use. Lamps dug at Sandwich had both types of peg extensions; the rounded end as in A and the flat end as in B.

2091 BLOWN MOLDED PANELED PEG LAMP, WHALE OIL BURNER

4⅞" H. x 2⅛" Dia. 1840–1860

This is the fourteen-paneled peg lamp shown previously, fitted with a whale oil burner and inserted into the free-blown socket of a Sandwich candlestick. Candlesticks manufactured by combining pressed bases with free-blown, wide-rimmed sockets were ideally suited to take peg lamps, as shown on the left. At the time of production, the blown upper unit of the candlestick was called the *nozzle*. The candlesticks were wholesaled by the glass company "with or without *sockets*", which was the term used for the metal inserts. Blown candle nozzles varied in diameter, so the metal sockets standardized the openings. When the metal socket was replaced by a peg lamp with a long peg extension, the result was a very useful lighting device. The bottom part of the lamp unit rested firmly on the wide rim of the candlestick and the long peg extension stabilized the device when in use. The combination of a candlestick and a peg lamp allowed for greater use of the candlestick.

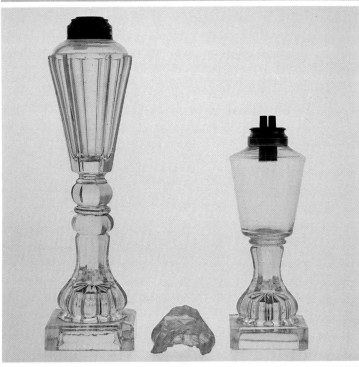

2092 PRESSED OCTAGONAL LAMPS WITH PRESSED OCTAGONAL STANDARD AND SQUARE BASE, FLUID BURNER

9½'' H. x 3⅛'' Dia. font, 3'' Sq. base 1840–1860

Here is a beautifully matched pair of lamps, properly weighted at the base to maintain stability. The base was pressed into shape by a lemon squeezer-type plunger; a prism pattern can be seen through the glass. Any excess glass from this base was forced out of the mold through the top of the standard. The pressure from the plunger forced air into the glass that can be seen as bubbles in the top of both standards. By this time in our study, the reader's eye should automatically center on the telltale wafer, easily seen in this photo. Note that unlike the previously shown paneled fonts, these fonts were pressed. The unpatterned glass above the panels was then closed in to form the domes. The fluid burners are correct for this time period. *Courtesy, Sandwich Glass Museum, Sandwich Historical Society*

2093 LAMPS WITH PRESSED OCTAGONAL STANDARD AND SQUARE BASE, WHALE OIL BURNER

(a) Pressed hexagonal font 12½'' H. x 3⅛'' Dia. font, 3⅜'' Sq. base
(b) Free-blown cylindrical font 8¼'' H. x 3'' Dia. font, 3'' Sq. base 1840–1860

Note how proportion alters the usability of a lamp. Lamp A is heavy and has a base that is 3⅜'' Sq., but it is unstable despite its weight because of its extreme height. By the time it was filled with fuel and fitted with a burner and lamp glass, it was topheavy. Now look at the proportions of lamp B. The base was pressed in the same style without the knop above the standard. The font is shorter and has no knop extension. The lamp is squatty and stable—a strictly utilitarian lighting device that cannot be called beautiful. Lamp A with its six panels separated by V-grooves has more appeal to a collector, but Lamp B had more appeal to a Nineteenth Century housewife. Keep in mind these words spoken by a member of the Board of Directors. "We are in the business of making money, not glass." Collectors and glass students often make the mistake of associating only one popular type of glass to a particular factory, and fail to realize that the factory that produced an exotic art glass also manufactured common items for everyday use. These money makers were the backbone of every flint glass company.

2094 PRESSED OCTAGONAL LAMP WITH PRESSED MONUMENT BASE

10¼'' H. x 3¼'' Dia. font, 3½'' Sq. base 1840–1860

The font has eight plain panels that continue below the bottom edge of the font onto a ½'' H. extension. It was made by pressing glass into an octagonal tapered mold that was open at the top. The plunger was circular; the eight panels cannot be felt on the inside surface. The excess glass above the pattern was drawn in to form the dome with a neck to receive the collar. Although simple in form, the weight of the base gives the lamp stability. Great quantities of these lamps were made in clear glass as well as an assortment of colors. The use of the wafer made it possible to attach this font to any number of bases and, generally speaking, the base and font are the same color. If you find a combination such as canary and clear, examine the lamp carefully to determine whether it is a "make-do". This severely limits the value and, although there are "make-do" collectors, the piece does not belong in a Sandwich glass collection.

2095 PRESSED FLUTE FOUNTAIN (CARDAN) LAMP WITH PRESSED DIAMOND THUMBPRINT (DIAMOND AND CONCAVE) CIRCULAR BASE, WHALE OIL BURNERS

11½'' H. x 6¾'' Dia. 1855–1860

When made with a cutting wheel, a dished out circle was called a *punty*. The same pattern when pressed into the surface was known as Concave. This pattern, now called Diamond Thumbprint, was illustrated in a McKee and Brother catalog listed as ''pressed D. and C. pattern''. The Diamond Thumbprint pattern was used on two types of lamps. It was pressed into a circular font similar in form to the Cable font in photo 2172, which was joined to a glass base with a wafer. It is a font that is seldom found in the antiques market. The second type was the unique Cardan lamp shown in this photo, called a *fountain lamp* at the time of production. Most Cardan devices were made of tin or pewter—very few glass examples exist. The whale oil was consistently fed to the two burners by the barometric principle that resulted from experiments in the mid-1550's by Italian philosopher, physician and mathematician Girolamo Cardan. The large Flute pattern font is marked ''PATENT APPLIED FOR''. A patent for a mold design by which the connecting burner cups could be pressed was granted to Henry Wright Adams of New York on August 19, 1856. A patent for the lamp itself was issued to Wright on June 30, 1857. The font shown here was joined to a Diamond Thumbprint base that was generally fastened to a large Diamond Thumbprint bowl. The small Flute patterned octagonal burner cups into which the fuel was fed each have a threadless rim over which was placed a metal cap with a double tube whale oil burner. On the one Cardan cap dug by author Barlow from the Boston and Sandwich Glass Company site, inside threads accepted a common threaded burner. The barometric feed principle was used on several Sandwich articles, such as a blown bird fountain made very early in the company's history and a pressed mucilage stand patented by Elisha Morgan in 1867. *The Corning Museum of Glass, Corning, New York*

2096 WHALE OIL BURNER FROM FOUNTAIN LAMP

1850–1855

This cast metal cap with its two-tube whale oil burner was dug from the site of the Boston and Sandwich Glass Company. It appears to be an earlier version of the caps shown on the Diamond Thumbprint fountain lamp. The cap is nothing more than a cover with a center hole that has coarse threads to accept the common whale oil burner shown on the right. This coarsely threaded burner fits the coarse threads of a ringed collar, such as is shown in photo 2089. When the burner needed to be replaced, a burner with the same thread gauge had to be purchased. Otherwise, cross-threading damaged the fittings. This dug burner is additional proof that glass fountain lamps were made at Sandwich, but not all fountain lamps are Sandwich.

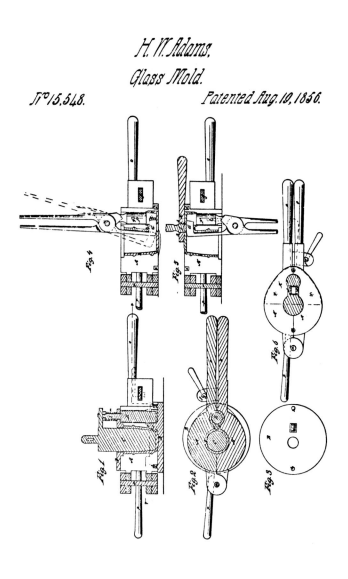

H. W. Adams,
Glass Mold.
Nº 15,548.
Patented Aug. 19, 1856.

Henry Wright Adams of New York, New York, perfected a mold for pressing glass fountain lamps and patented it on August 19, 1856. The patent was designated No. 15,548. ''The manufacture of such a lamp of glass has been considered by glass manufacturers to be, if not impossible, an operation of very great difficulty. This mold renders the operation of making such lamps perfectly simple and easy.'' Adams' mold was a complicated arrangement whereby the font, a single burner cup, and the top and sides of the connecting arm were pressed simultaneously. Upon completion of this operation, a specially designed tool resembling tongs was inserted into the large font, as shown in Figure 4. This implement removed glass from the sidewall of the font, opening the font to the connecting arm. Subsequent steps pressed glass into the bottom of the connecting arm and closed the upper part of the font. It is obvious that a fountain lamp with two burner wells required an even more intricate mold.

H. W. ADAMS.

Lamp.

No. 17,658.

Patented June 30, 1857.

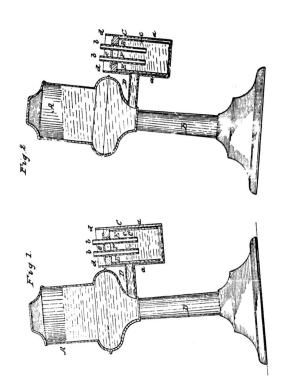

In an effort to prevent oil spillage when a glass Cardan lamp was carried, Henry Wright Adams of New York patented an improvement on June 30, 1857. The lamp was called a ''fountain lamp'' in his patent No. 17,658. Adams deepened the cup beneath the burner so that its bottom was some distance below the burner tubes and the glass extension arm that connected it to the font. He lined the sides of the cup with a metal cylinder so that air in the cup could not escape back into the font when the lamp was tilted, thereby allowing excess fuel to enter the cup and overflow. Fuel entered the cup by passing from the font into the extension arm, then downward between the glass wall of the cup and its bottomless metal liner. The lamp had to be filled by removing the metal cap with its burner and holding the lamp almost horizontally with the burner cup above the font. The spout of the lamp filler or oil can was inserted into the cup, from which the oil flowed to the outside of the metal liner and through the extension arm into the font. The complicated mold in which the glass was pressed, the nonsensical manner in which the lamp was filled, the overflow problem, and the difficulty of keeping the font clean attest to the reason why so few exist today.

2097 LAMPS WITH PRESSED OCTAGONAL STANDARD AND SQUARE BASE

(a) Pressed Thumbprint and Arch 9⅜'' H. x 2¾'' Dia. font, 3'' Sq. base
(b) Pressed Bigler 10'' H. x 2¾'' Dia. font, 3'' Sq. base 1840–1860

To a Bigler pattern collector, both fonts would be acceptable as variants of that pattern, but George and Helen McKearin differentiated between the two forms shown here in their book *American Glass*. Lamp A, Thumbprint and Arch, is almost cylindrical with straight sides and a horizontal ring both above and below the pattern. As noted on page 61 of Volume 3, we would prefer to call this pattern *Two-Printie* because of its similarity to the patterns known as *Three-Printie* and *Four-Printie*. Lamp B is known as *Bigler*. It has a smaller diameter at the bottom of the font; the sides taper. There are no rings above and below the pattern, but the horizontal bar of glass that separates the upper ''printie'' from the lower ''printie'' appears to be more prominent. Both fonts have a vertical V-groove that separates each of the six panels of ''printies''. The standard of lamp B with its eight concave panels is very easily damaged. Note the cutout just above the square base, thinning the glass to a sharp edge. A much more serviceable base can be seen on lamp A, though it is not as aesthetic. *Courtesy, Sandwich Glass Museum, Sandwich Historical Society*

2098 PRESSED THUMBPRINT AND ARCH LAMP WITH PRESSED MONUMENT BASE

11⅝'' H. x 3⅛'' Dia. font, 3½'' Sq. base 1840–1860

As stated previously, this pressed pattern is often accepted as a variant of Bigler. The six-sided knop below the font is part of what is known as the *font extension*, which is molded in one piece with the font. The hand-formed wafer that attaches the font extension to the base can be seen below the pressed knop. This combination of a Thumbprint and Arch upper unit and Monument lower unit was also made into a vase, which can be seen in photo 3032. As you study this series of books, you will note that there are many tones of yellow glass. They were all called *canary*. Yellow glass with a green tone was called *green canary*.

2099 MONUMENT BASE FRAGMENT

1840–1860

One of the finest collections of fragments dug from the site of the Boston and Sandwich Glass Company's factory is preserved at The Bennington Museum in Bennington, Vermont. This fragment is one of many Monument bases dug in Sandwich, but keep in mind that the base was also manufactured by the New England Glass Company, located in East Cambridge, Massachusetts, using a duplicate or similar mold. *When an item or pattern is documented as having been produced by one particular factory, this does not infer that it was made by that factory exclusively.* Commercial mold makers in Boston and New York supplied every glass factory in their area with their molds. When a particular mold became popular, it was duplicated and sent out to all interested parties. Note the circular standard extension above the Monument base. All dug fragments of this base and all Monument base lamps and vases documented as Sandwich have this circular standard. The authors believe that a similar base with an octagonal standard was not used by the Boston and Sandwich Glass Company. *The Bennington Museum, Bennington, Vermont*

2100 BLOWN MOLDED THREE-PRINTIE BLOCK LAMP WITH PRESSED OCTAGONAL STANDARD AND SQUARE BASE

9⅛'' H. x 3'' Dia. font, 3⅛'' Sq. base 1835–1840

This pattern takes its name from the three horizontal rows of blocks, each block having a circular *printie*, or *punty*, in it. This particular lamp is a transitional piece; the pattern was designed when all fonts were free-blown or blown molded, but was continued as a pattern that adapted itself to pressing, as shown in subsequent photos. If a pattern was blown into a mold, as was this font, the glass on the inside follows the contour of the mold. There are soft mold marks on the outside where the hot glass was forced against the seams of the mold by lung power. If the same pattern was pressed into a mold, the inside surface is relatively smooth. There is a wafer between the font and the pressed base. Other factories made this pattern, both blown molded and pressed. A visitor to the factory in 1838 reported that lamp fonts were blown and were then attached to pressed bases.

2101 PRESSED THREE-PRINTIE BLOCK LAMPS WITH PRESSED OCTAGONAL STANDARD AND SQUARE BASE

10'' H. x 3'' Dia. font, 3⅛'' Sq. base 1840–1860

This pair of lamps combines simple lines, excellent color, strength, balance and beauty. The fonts were *pressed*, and after the plunger was removed the unpatterned glass was drawn in to form the dome. On the inside of the font, the glass feels smooth; it does not follow the contours of the mold. The marks left by the plunger forcing hot glass into the seams of the mold are sharply delineated. This pattern is attributed by some scholars to the Boston and Sandwich Glass Company alone, but in the summer of 1952, while excavating under railroad yards in East Cambridge at the former site of the New England Glass Company, quantities of fragments with this pattern were unearthed. The fragments had a different base that was pressed in one piece with the Three-Printie Block font, helping to strengthen the authors' belief that the East Cambridge factory used superior construction methods to the Sandwich and Mount Washington works. Fragments dug at the Sandwich site have a wafer between the font and the standard.

2102 PRESSED THREE-PRINTIE BLOCK

(a) Lamp with pressed octagonal standard and square base, whale oil burner 9¾'' H. x 3'' Dia. font, 3⅛'' Sq. base 1840–1860
(b) Vase with expanded rim, pressed octagonal standard and square base 10'' H. x 5'' Dia. 1845–1860

The same mold was used to press the upper unit of the vase and the font of the lamp. The unpatterned glass above the blocks that was flared out to make the rim of the vase was closed in to make the dome and neck of the lamp font. When the glassworker flared the vase, he pulled the pattern upward, drawing the round printies into ovals. The knop beneath the pattern is an extension of the upper unit. The wafer is under the knop. The square base gave the lamp stability, but was too small for a vase with such a wide rim if it was filled with flowers. If the vase had been meant to be ornamental or to hold potpourri, it would survive.

2103 PRESSED THREE-PRINTIE BLOCK LAMP WITH PRESSED OCTAGONAL STANDARD AND SQUARE BASE

10'' H. x 3'' Dia. font, 3⅛'' Sq. base 1840–1860

Do not let color be your guide. Although this pattern is a duplicate of the previous ones, we show this pale blue one to emphasize this. It is not a poor photo, but is an excellent likeness of a color often mistaken for Depression Era glass made in the 1900's. At an antiques show, we glanced at this piece from across the aisle and dismissed it as a reproduction. Only after it was purchased by a colleague who took the time to examine it closely did we realize its value. We subsequently bought it from the new owner. We do not believe that it is possible to attribute a lamp to a particular factory by its metal collar. Deming Jarves' letters ordered a certain lamp to be manufactured with perhaps three choices of collars and burners. Diggings at the site prove that all collars produced in the Boston and New York area were used by the Boston and Sandwich Glass Company. Keep in mind that most lamps on today's market do not have their original collars. Extended use wore the threads, so collars were replaced.

2104 PRESSED FOUR-PRINTIE BLOCK LAMP WITH PRESSED HEXAGONAL BASE

(a) Lamp 11⅛'' H. x 3¼'' Dia. font, 5⅜'' Dia. base 1840–1850
(b) Candlestick with pressed hexagonal base 7½'' H. 1840–1860

This lamp has one of the tallest pressed fonts made at Sandwich during this time period. The font held a generous supply of whale oil. It was lengthened by the addition of a fourth row of blocks, beneath which is a large knop extension that was pressed as part of the font unit. The base was pressed separately and was joined to the font with a wafer. The same base was used to make candlestick B. Its pressed socket, attached to the base with a wafer, appears to be out of proportion, but the combination resulted in a very stable unit that could be used with little fear of knocking it over. The mold used to make the font of lamp A was also used to make the upper unit of a vase. One can be seen in photo 3037 in Volume 3, combined with this same hexagonal base.

2105 PRESSED FOUR-PRINTIE BLOCK LAMP WITH PRESSED MONUMENT BASE

12'' H. x 3¼'' Dia. font, 3½'' Sq. base 1840–1850

This is a beautifully proportioned, usable, tall lamp. The knop that gave the lamp stature and grace was molded in one piece with the font. Jarves' method of forming separate units that were then combined allowed the company to market lamps in a large variety of styles, but resulted in a flaw that annoys a present-day collector of pristine pairs. In assembling the units, no time was given to line up the pattern so that it faced forward when the base was placed parallel to the edge of a shelf or mantle. The vertical groove between the blocks is not centered, nor is a vertical row of four blocks. Its matching mate would also have been misaligned, but in a different way. The heavy Monument base is unusually thick, so the use of a deeply penetrating plunger is easily seen. Note the dark horizontal area below the wafer. This is the point where the plunger completed its penetration. The pressure from the plunger forced the hot glass to fill all voids in the mold, assuring high quality of the finished product. *Courtesy, Sandwich Glass Museum, Sandwich Historical Society*

2106 BLOWN MOLDED ELONGATED LOOP LAMP WITH PRESSED BASE

6'' H. x 2¼'' Dia. font, 2⅝'' Sq. base 1840–1860

Here again is the diminutive base with extended round corners that was used by Eastern and Midwestern glass houses. Keep in mind that when we discuss Eastern factories, the term includes glass works all along the coast— the greater New York City, Philadelphia. But there is no doubt that many were made in Sandwich in a variety of colors. The font, blown into a mold that had eight ovals, was held to the base with a common disk wafer, even though the lamp is only 6'' H. including the ringed collar. The style of collar was used since the factory began. According to Jarves' 1832 report to the Federal Government, all metal fittings used on glass were purchased, so do not attempt to document origin by hardware.

2107 BLOWN MOLDED ELONGATED LOOP HAND LAMP, WHALE OIL BURNER

3½'' H. x 2½'' Dia. 1840–1860

This lamp has six loops and is an excellent example of a very small one adapted to adult use. If it had a tiny handle small enough for only a child's fingers to grasp, it would be classified as a child's lamp, but this handle is expanded to take at least two fingers of an adult's hand. The fingers could protrude through to the second joint and the lamp could be carried comfortably, even with the wick ignited. Note the ringed collar, which was used by the Boston and Sandwich Glass Company, the New England Glass Company, the Mount Washington Glass Company, the American Flint Glass Company, and assuredly many more. Dealers and auctioneers often attribute a lamp to a certain glass house based on the collar that holds the burner in place, and they usually associate this collar with the New England Glass Company. Many ringed collars were dug from the site of the Boston and Sandwich works. One can be seen on a peg lamp in photo 2089 that was dug from the factory yard.

2108 PRESSED LOOP SAFETY LAMP WITH PRESSED HEXAGONAL BASE

(a) Lamp 9⅞'' H. x 3¼'' Dia. font, 4¼'' Dia. base

(b) Safety tube 1840–1860

Here is the simplest of the Loop patterns. Only four loops surround the font that are so large they square off the bulb-shaped font. Lamps equipped with patented safety tubes are sought after by collectors. The purpose of the tubes was to act as a safety device against explosion by supposedly separating the air, and therefore the flame, from the fuel. Most tube safety devices were based on the invention of Sir Humphrey Davy in 1816. Isaiah Jennings adapted Davy's principle to burning fluid in the early 1830's, and several other improvements were patented over the next two decades. The solid tube shown here is permanently attached beneath the cemented collar and cannot be removed from the lamp. It is likely that a second tube, smaller in diameter, was permanently attached to the burner. This solid tube lamp was difficult to fill with fuel because air was trapped in the top of the font outside the tube.

2109 PRESSED LOOP (LEAF) LAMPS WITH PRESSED OCTAGONAL STANDARD AND SQUARE BASE

(a) Clear 8⅜'' H. x 2½'' Dia. font, 2⅜'' Sq. base
(b) Canary 9¾'' H. x 3'' Dia. font, 3⅛'' Sq. base
   1840–1865

The aesthetic lines of Sandwich glass lamps often take on a beauty that in itself elevates the lamp to a high degree of excellence. The pattern, called *Leaf* when it was made, can be found on many pieces of tableware, but the slender silhouette of a lamp lends itself to this elongated motif. Lamp B is a common size with a font extension that was made in many colors. Lamp A is a rare size that is difficult to find. It has a very small collar that is difficult to fit to a burner, so, if you find lamp A with a burner, the burner significantly adds to the value. Canary was a popular color. The Boston and Sandwich Glass Company erected a furnace specifically for the making of it. They called it "the canary furnace".

2110 PRESSED LOOP (LEAF) LAMPS WITH CIRCULAR BASE

8¾'' H. x 3'' Dia. font, 4¼'' Dia. base 1840–1860

The ability to manufacture identical lamps so that matching pairs could be sold became perfected when glass factories were able to press both the fonts and the bases. Note carefully the exactness of this pair. There is a slight extension beneath the font that is exactly the same on both lamps. There is a slight extension above the standard that is identical on both lamps. The gaffer took particular care to make identical the wafers that connect the fonts to the bases. The result was a perfect pair of lamps that would realize a high price on today's antiques market. This pattern that we call *Loop* today was known as *Leaf* during the time of production. The pattern was made by many companies in the East and the Midwest. *Courtesy, Sandwich Glass Museum, Sandwich Historical Society*

2111 PRESSED WAISTED LOOP LAMPS WITH PRESSED MONUMENT BASE

(a,b) 11⅜'' H. x 4½'' Dia. font, 3½'' Sq. base
(c) 11¼'' H. x 4½'' Dia. font, 3½'' Sq. base
   1840–1860

The Waisted Loop lamp came with an assortment of other bases as well as the Monument base shown here. For some reason, the glassmakers showed complete disregard for lining up any of the six panels of Loop pattern with the sides of the Monument base during the final stage of manufacture, when the font was attached to the base with a wafer. Note how the bases are misplaced when the fonts are lined up so that the Loop patterns all face in the same direction. This would not be true of New England Glass Company or Mount Washington Glass Works products assembled with wafers. Panels would be lined up so that a pair placed on a mantle or table would appear to be identical. Note the plain standard on these Sandwich lamps. Other glass companies made the Waisted Loop lamp with a paneled standard. The New England Glass Company also made this font molded in one piece with a hexagonal base, so if you find a Waisted Loop lamp without a wafer, buy it knowing that it is not Sandwich.

2112 WOODEN PATTERN FOR PRESSED GAINES (SANDWICH LOOP) HAND LAMP

For lamp 3⅜'' H. x 2⅝'' Dia. 1850–1870

Glass company catalogs list the original name of this pattern as *Gaines*, and the authors believe that this name should be retained. Collectors know it as *Sandwich Loop*, but it was also made by several Midwest factories. A Cape Cod Glass Company list of glassware, which is comprised of four order sheets listing that company's entire line, shows that a wide variety of Gaines tableware could be ordered in opal or flint. (Editor's note: In the language of the day, *flint* meant clear, colorless glass.) A Gaines hand lamp is listed on the fourth page of the Cape Cod order list. The wooden pattern shown here was one of a group sold by James E. Johnston of Sandwich to Colonel A. H. Heisey, founder of A. H. Heisey and Company of Newark, Ohio. Twelve elongated loops surround the pattern.

2113 PRESSED CIRCLE AND ELLIPSE (LEAF AND CONCAVE) LAMPS

(a) Pressed Monument base 10⅛'' H. x 3'' Dia. font, 3½'' Sq. base
(b) Pressed octagonal standard and square base 10¾'' H. x 3⅛'' Dia. font, 3⅜'' Sq. base 1840–1860

The fonts of both lamps were identical when they were removed from the mold, but the hand work necessary to close in the domes resulted in a difference in shape and color. The same amount of glass made thinner to form the rounded shoulder of font B makes the lamp look two-toned in the photo. The intermingling of upper and lower units was a practice that continued throughout the whale oil and burning fluid period, so learning the patterns and shapes of the separate units will help you identify Sandwich glass, even if you locate a combination that the authors have not been able to show you. If each unit is a documented Sandwich pattern, and they are joined by any of the documented wafer shapes shown in this chapter or in Chapter 2 of Volume 3 (Vases and Flower Containers), the lamp can be accepted as a Sandwich product. Lamp A has a 1920 replacement collar to adapt it to electricity. *Courtesy, Sandwich Glass Museum, Sandwich Historical Society*

2114 PRESSED CIRCLE AND ELLIPSE (LEAF AND CONCAVE) LAMPS WITH PRESSED HEXAGONAL BASE

9⅛'' H. x 3'' Dia. font, 5¼'' Dia. base 1840–1860

This font is illustrated in a McKee and Brother catalog believed to have been printed in 1859–1860. The Pittsburgh, Pennsylvania, firm identified it as ''Pressed L. and C.'' and noted it could be purchased with either a whale oil burner for $4 a dozen wholesale or a fluid burner at $4.66 per dozen. When one considers that these lamps burned with an open flame, were hazardous if knocked over and were constantly in areas where children played, it would seem reasonable by today's standards to maximize the stability of the base. We consider this pair to be beautifully proportioned. The fonts are the same as shown in photo 2113, but the safety factor in the design of these bases is apparent. Note the beautifully executed wafers that fasten the fonts to the bases. For once, care was taken to line up the panels of the fonts with the panels of the bases.

2115 PRESSED CIRCLE AND ELLIPSE (LEAF AND CONCAVE) LAMPS WITH PRESSED OCTAGONAL STANDARD AND SQUARE BASE

(a) 11⅛'' H. x 3'' Dia. font, 3⅜'' Sq. base
(b) 11⅜'' H. x 3'' Dia. font, 3⅜'' Sq. base 1840–1850
This lamp was originally designed to be shorter, with the font setting directly on the standard, separated by a wafer. As the need for additional height became apparent, extensions were added in the form of the hexagonal knop above the standard. By this means of stretching, the lamp could be manufactured in several heights. A taller lamp extended the light farther out into the room with less shadow cast by the table. The wafer can plainly be seen between the extensions. This pair of lamps is extremely scarce in any color, so the slight difference in height does not detract from value. The fonts were pressed into a mold, so the height is uniform up to the top row of circles. The domes were closed in by hand, and the worker did a better job on lamp B. Henry F. Spurr, last manager of the Boston and Sandwich Glass Company, included a formula for ''Green or Peacock Blue'' with his ''Glass Receipts''. When the color leans toward green, collectors call it ''peacock green''.

2116 PRESSED RING AND OVAL LAMP WITH PRESSED HEXAGONAL BASE, FLUID BURNER

8'' H. x 3'' Dia. font, 4⅛'' Dia. base 1850–1865
This lamp is beautifully proportioned; the diminutive font complements the candlestick base on which it stands. It must have been a popular combination because many can be found in clear glass and, although scarce in color, several different colors were photographed in preparation for this book. However, we choose to show this green one because green Sandwich glass is very scarce today and commands highest prices in the antiques market. Without documentation in the form of original factory drawings or catalogs, there is no way of knowing the original name of this Ring and Oval pattern. To differentiate between this pattern and the Circle and Ellipse pattern previously shown, relate the name *Ring and Oval* to the horizontal ring that surrounds the font between the upper ''circles'' and the lower ''ovals'' that are called *ellipses* in the previous pattern. This Ring and Oval font mold was used to make a beautiful blue vase that is pictured in Richard Carter Barret's *A Collectors Handbook of Blown and Pressed American Glass*. On the lamp shown here, the wafer that holds the upper unit to the base was expertly placed so that it appears to be a continuation of the horizontal ring motif below the ovals. *Courtesy, Sandwich Glass Museum, Sandwich Historical Society*

2117 PRESSED RING AND OVAL LAMP WITH PRESSED HEXAGONAL BASE, ARGAND KEROSENE BURNER AND GLOBE

(a) Lamp 7⅞'' H. x 3'' Dia. font, 4¼'' Dia. base 1850–1865
(b) Globe 4½'' H. x 4½'' Dia. 1875–1887
(c) Combined size 13¾'' H. to top of globe

By 1850, production of long, narrow fonts had been discontinued in favor of shorter fonts that kept the bottom ends of the wicks of fluid burners closer to the flame. After the discovery of kerosene, called *coal oil* during the 1850's and 1860's, lamps originally designed for explosive fuels were gradually converted to take advantage of the new illuminant that was safer and brighter. This Plume and Atwood Victor Argand burner was commonly used as a "conversion kit". As a flat kerosene wick was fed through the burner, it wrapped itself around a tube and emerged as a round wick. The tube provided a center draft. The use of different burners sometimes meant changing the gauge of the threads of the collar, so it is possible today to find a matching pair of lamps with two different sizes of threaded collars from different time periods. Another method of changing thread gauge was to screw in a metal adapter. The single lamp glass used on whale oil and fluid burners was replaced by two pieces, a chimney to control draft and a globe or shade to soften the glare. The wreath on this globe was acid etched.

2118 PRESSED STAR AND PUNTY LAMP WITH PRESSED HEXAGONAL BASE

9¾'' H. x 3¼'' Dia. font, 4'' Dia. base 1840–1865

As you study the next four lamps, note how a slight change in size of either the upper or lower unit determined its usefulness. Here is a slender version of the Star and Punty lamp. The font is small in diameter. The base, too, although similar in form, is small in diameter. There is a plain knop extension beneath the font that was molded as part of the upper unit; a vertical mold mark can easily be seen in the photo. This plain knop is an important identifying feature. The accompanying illustration shows the difference between the Sandwich lamp with its plain knop and the Mount Washington Glass Works with its detailed hexagonal font extension ending in a circle of down-tipped petals similar to those found on Mount Washington Petal candle sockets, shown in Figures 1 and 3 of Volume 4. The down-tipped petals was Mount Washington's method of making the wafer less obvious. *Courtesy, Sandwich Glass Museum, Sandwich Historical Society*

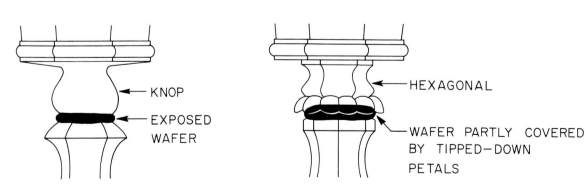

B. & S.

MT. W.

Fig. 6 The extension beneath the Sandwich Star and Punty font is an unpatterned knop. The Mount Washington font has a hexagonal extension that terminates in petals, or beads. This beaded extension was hollowed out to hide a common disk wafer.

2119 PRESSED STAR AND PUNTY

(a) Lamp with pressed hexagonal base 9¾'' H. x 3⅛''
    Dia. font, 4⅜'' Dia. base
(b) Spoon holder 4¾'' H. x 3½'' Dia. 1840–1865

Here is the same pattern on a more serviceable lamp. As
in the previous example, the sides of the font are almost
vertical so that, when filled, it was not topheavy. Unlike
the following example, the extension beneath the font is
solid glass and could be pressed firmly into the hot wafer.
The upper portion of the standard is solid glass and the
base is larger, giving the lamp strength to withstand an accident without breaking. The opaque blue spoon holder
matches in pattern. It is more commonly found without
a foot and sat flatly on the table. In colored glass, it was
made as part of a set that included kitchen lamps. In clear
glass, it matched Star and Punty tableware as well as clear
glass lamps. See *Barlow-Kaiser Sandwich Glass Price Guide* for
clear glass value.

2120 PRESSED STAR AND PUNTY LAMP WITH PRESSED COLUMNAR STANDARD AND SQUARE BASE

11'' H. x 4'' Dia. font, 4⅜'' Sq. base 1840–1865

Here is a combination that is not often found in good condition. The Columnar standard was held to the font,
which has no extension, by a large wafer. This lamp is
sometimes found in the antiques marketplace with the upper and lower units joined by a metal connector. The lamp
was not manufactured that way. In the late 1800's, a
repair kit was sold to salvage damaged lamps. Even if you
find a pair of lamps with the metal connectors beneath the
fonts, do not make the mistake of thinking they are in
original condition. This combination was prone to accident
because the heavy fuel-filled tapered font snapped off from
the hollow, slender standard. Understand that the lamps
that may be considered the most beautiful to a collector
may have been unmanageable in an 1860's home.

2121 PRESSED STAR AND PUNTY LAMPS WITH PRESSED HEXAGONAL BASE, FLUID BURNER

(a) 9½'' H. x 3½'' Dia. font, 4½'' Dia. base
(b) 9¾'' H. x 3½'' Dia. font, 4½'' Dia. base
    1840–1865

The Star and Punty pattern was frequently used by Sandwich glassmakers. It was used on colognes as shown in
photos 3101 and 3102. This sturdy pair of lamps are
beginning to show signs of deterioration. The surface of
the glass that is exposed to the atmosphere is breaking
away. It is sometimes caused by expansion and contrac-
tion of minute particles of fire clay that were present in the
sand and did not wash away during the cleansing process.
Too much alkali in the glass and moisture in the air drawing out the soda are also contributing factors. If given
enough time, it is the opinion of the authors that the piece
will be destroyed. Complete destruction may take hundreds of years, so this ''sand finish'' does not devalue the
piece. When purchased by the authors, lamp A was
equipped with this adjustable burner that was designed to
regulate the light.

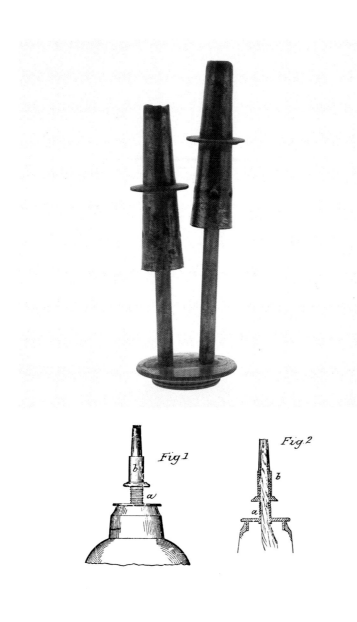

2122 FLUID BURNER FROM ABOVE LAMP

This is a close-up of the adjustable fluid burner shown previously. The wick tubes are straight-sided and are considerably longer than the tubes of a common fluid burner. A tapered tube with a finger grip is fitted to each wick tube. The wicks were drawn through the inner tubes until they protruded ½'' or more. The outer tapered tubes were slid up the inner wick tubes until the correct lengths of wick were exposed. When the wick burned down and the amount of light decreased, the outer tube was slid down to expose more wick. The concept of adjusting the light by means of a sliding tube had merit, but straight-sided wick tubes were dangerous when man-made fluids were used. Unless the tubes were tapered to fit snugly around the wicks, the fluid oozed over the top and ran down the outside of the lamp. This danger was alleviated when Isaiah Jennings patented straight tubes with tapered tops that were threaded, as shown in the patent illustration.

Isaiah Jennings of New York, New York, was granted patent No. 7492 for an improvement to the adjustable fluid burner on July 9, 1850. Jennings tapered the upper portions of both the inner wick tube and the outer movable tube. He threaded the straight-sided portions so that the length could be adjusted by screwing the outer tube onto the inner one. When searching for adjustable fluid burners, remember that they can be found without threads as shown in photo 2122 and with threads as shown here.

2123 PRESSED STAR AND PUNTY THREE-LIGHT GIRANDOLE WITH PRESSED CLIMBING IVY STANDARD AND SQUARE BASE, WHALE OIL BURNERS

18½'' H., 5¼'' Sq. base, 5¼'' H. x 3¼'' Dia. each font 1842

Large lighting devices that stood on mantles were common in the early Victorian Era. The patterns on the glass fonts varied. This girandole was purchased as part of a three-piece set. The set was bought by Mrs. Beebe Booth in 1842, from the Boston store of the Boston and Sandwich Glass Company. Mrs. Booth was the maternal grandmother of Pulitzer Prize novelist Booth Tarkington. This lamp and the two candlesticks that made up the set came to the Tarkington home in Kennebunk, Maine, about 1920. They were placed on the mantle over the fireplace, where they remained for many years. Unfortunately, the candlesticks were given away in the 1950's. According to family records, a tag that hung on the lamp had this name and address on it; ''H. N. Hooper Casting and Assembly Company, Boston, Massachusetts''. In the Boston City Directory, Henry N. Hooper and Company was listed under *Lamp Makers, Brass Foundries* and *Bell Founders*. Glass company records show a long business relationship with Hooper. His company cast the factory bell that was hung in 1833 as part of an improvement program. The pressed Star and Rosette prisms have been dug at the Boston and Sandwich Glass Company site by the hundreds. The dug prisms were badly discolored by the hundred or more years they lay in the soil. A few minutes with a buffing wheel return them to their original brilliance. At the time the girandole was purchased for the Barlow collection, three of the prisms were broken and two were missing. With the large inventory of dug prisms available to the authors, it was an easy matter to restore the girandole to its original state.

2124 ABOVE GIRANDOLE WITH CORONETS AND PRISMS REMOVED

The intricately designed metal coronets and the glass prisms were removed so that the assembly could be studied. Note that the metal sockets were not meant for candles. They were filled with cement, and the pressed fonts with pegs attached were permanently adhered. There has been speculation about the approximate time when *pressed* fonts were first made. Documentation shows that all Sandwich fonts were blown or blown molded until 1838. On January 11, 1839, the New England Glass Company's Henry Whitney and Thomas Leighton patented an "improvement in the manufacture of glass socket lamps". It was a method of making blown fonts with attached pegs. Pressed fonts were not mentioned nor illustrated. The documented purchase date of this girandole proves Sandwich marketing of pressed fonts with pegs by 1842, so the generally given date of 1840 appears to be correct. Spun brass fittings with alternating bright and satin finish bands were occasionally used as connectors on kerosene lamps as shown in photo 2292. After the fonts were assembled and the cement had set, the metal work was attached to the glass standard by the use of a brass ring also filled with cement. The standard then became a permanent part of the lamp structure.

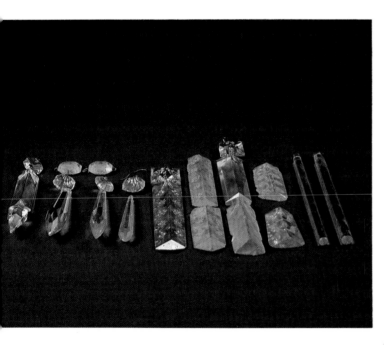

2126 PRESSED GIANT SAWTOOTH

(a) Lamp with pressed hexagonal base 11⅛'' H. x 3⅝'' Dia. font, 4⅝'' Dia. base

(b) Spoon holder 6¼'' H. x 3⅝'' Dia. 1840–1860

These matching pieces are excellent examples of how certain forms were combined with other elements to produce different items. To make lamp A, the Giant Sawtooth font was pressed and was attached to its base by a wafer that can be seen beneath the large knop. The unpatterned glass was drawn in to form the dome and neck of the font. A different mold was used to press the footed spoon holder B. Its base was part of the same mold. The glass above the pattern was sheared off and reheated to make a smooth rim. This was called *fire polishing*. These large, heavy lamps were advertised as kitchen lamps and the spoon holder was made to match. No glass company invoices have been found that refer to an item called a *spill holder* during this time period. The Giant Sawtooth spoon holder was also made in brilliant blue.

2125 PRISMS DUG FROM FACTORY SITES
1850–1890

Prisms were not manufactured in Sandwich, although all of the prisms shown here were dug from the sites of the Boston and Sandwich Glass Company and the Cape Cod Glass Company. A Mount Washington Glass Company catalog has been found that includes drawings of prisms accompanied by writing in German text, so we believe that, like marbles that were used in metal stoppers (see page 160 in Volume 3), prisms were imported from Germany. Many types and sizes were used. To give you an idea of sizes, the pressed Star and Rosette prism in the center is 5'' H. and the slender rods on the right are 5½'' H. All of the dug prisms had polished units that were completely assembled with wires intact. We did not find any that were discarded because they were damaged during production. None had pressed designs that were off center, none had shattered before polishing was completed, none were misshapen from overheating. The prisms found on all lamps made in the New England area are interchangeable, so it is evident that every glass company and lamp assembly company purchased them from outside sources.

2127 PRESSED FLATTENED SAWTOOTH HEXAGONAL LAMP WITH PRESSED HEX-AGONAL BASE

(a) Lamp 10¾" H. x 3⅝" Dia. font, 5" Dia. base
(b) Spoon holder 5⅜" H. x 3⅝" Dia. 1840–1855

During the pressing era great quantities of pattern glass lamps were produced. These lamps are identified by the name of the pattern that is on the font. The wafer can easily be seen between the upper and lower units. We cannot stress this too strongly because, while other factories also used this method of construction, if you find lamps of any pattern that were molded all in one piece, Sandwich can be eliminated as the place of manufacture. The spoon holder that accompanies the lamp was placed on the kitchen table to match the kitchen lamp. The term *spoon holder* was generally used in the New England area. The Pittsburgh, Pennsylvania, firm of McKee and Brothers used that term into the late 1860's, but their 1871 catalog illustrates *spooners*, so, to the collector, either term is correct.

2128 PRESSED FLATTENED SAWTOOTH CYLINDRICAL LAMP WITH PRESSED DOLPHIN STANDARD AND HEXAGONAL BASE, WHALE OIL BURNER

11¾" H. x 3⅜" Dia. font, 4½" Dia. base 1840–1860

The dolphin has become the most famous fish depicted in glass. The patterned font is attached to the Dolphin standard with a wafer. The Dolphin was molded in one piece with the base. Note the concentric rings beneath the base. Matching dug fragments of this base also have circles. Only rarely is a candle socket encountered on this base, but the authors have seen a pair of canary ones. A similar lamp in the family of the *Acorn's* master, Roland Gibbs, is a beautiful blue. Although Dolphin lamps, candlesticks, epergnes and high footed nappies (compotes) are synonymous with Sandwich, Jarves' Mount Washington Glass Manufactory and several Pittsburgh and European houses made their own variations. A comparison of some Dolphin candlestick bases may be found in Chapter 3 of Volume 4. See photos 4333-4336 in Volume 4 for information about Dolphin epergnes.

2129 PRESSED DIAMOND POINT (MITRE DIAMOND) LAMP WITH PRESSED HEXAGONAL BASE

9¾" H. without neck x 3" Dia. font, 4" Dia. base 1840–1870

Although nearly complete, this lamp is a fragment from the former Casey collection. William Casey collected broken glass that was taken out of the abandoned Boston and Sandwich Glass Company buildings from 1915 to 1927. The largest fragments in existence today are the result of Mr. Casey's effort. Note the facetted knop beneath the font, pressed into the upper unit at the time the font was made. A large wafer is clearly visible between the knop and the standard. An original New England Glass Company catalog illustrates many tableware pieces in the *Mitre Diamond* pattern. This lamp clearly had production problems. Even if the neck had not broken when the lamp capper cemented on the collar, it may have been marketed as a second. The unpatterned band above the diamonds meanders around the font, distorting the piece.

2130 PRESSED INVERTED DIAMOND AND THUMBPRINT SAFETY LAMP WITH PRESSED HEXAGONAL BASE AND REMOVABLE FONT, FLUID BURNER

9¾'' H. x 3⅛'' Dia. font, 4⅛'' Dia. base 1855–1870
This is one of the most unusual lamps in the authors' collection. That portion of the piece that normally forms the dome of the font is a separate unit of glass that was cemented to the glass font after a metal fuel reservoir was inserted. Patent No. 12,550 for the metal reservoir was issued to Elbridge Harris of Boston on March 20, 1855. Its purpose was the prevention of injury resulting from fracture of the glass. If the glass shattered, the can confined the fluid and fire was averted. Harris suggested that fluid burners be adapted with ''protectors'' on the order of the safety tube patented by John Newell in 1853. The patterned glass font is connected to the hexagonal base with the usual wafer.

2131 UNITS OF ABOVE LAMP

(a) Lamp stand 8⅜'' H. x 3⅛ Dia. font, 4⅛'' Dia. base
(b) Removable metal font with glass dome, fluid burner 4¾'' H. x 2⅞'' Dia.

Here is the lamp shown previously with its metal fuel reservoir removed. You often see lamp stand A sold as a ''spoon holder on a high standard''. This was not its intended use when it was manufactured. Note the plain rim above the upper patterned band that supports the glass dome, pressed as part of the open glass font. Unscrupulous antiques dealers sometimes take a lamp that has broken around the collar and have it ground down so that it can be sold as a ''spoon holder on a high standard''. But the aforementioned plain rim will be missing and close inspection of the upper surface of the patterned band will reveal that is was ground and polished. At best, it is a lamp part; one unit of a two-unit assembly. Your chances of completing the assembly by finding the metal container with its glass dome intact is unlikely.

2132 PRESSED PANELED WAFFLE SAFETY LAMPS WITH PRESSED HEXAGONAL BASE AND REMOVABLE FONT, WHALE OIL BURNER

(a) Complete lamp 9¼'' H. x 3⅛'' Dia. font, 4'' Dia. base
(b) Lamp stand 8½'' H. x 3'' Dia. font, 4'' Dia. base
(c) Removable metal font with metal dome, whale oil burner 3⅜'' H. x 3⅛'' Dia. 1855–1870

One of the most unusual pairs of lamps ever to be found was this pair with removable fonts. They were tucked away in a North Andover, Massachusetts, attic and had never been used. The reservoir and its flat dome are both metal, with the collar soldered into place and threaded to take the burner. This method of manufacture was also suggested in Elbridge Harris' 1855 patent. Lamp A is complete as it would appear with whale oil in it. Note that a wafer holds the upper and lower glass units together, as with any other Sandwich lamp. Keep in mind that, when examining lamp stand B, there must be an inner rim that extends about ¼'' above the upper band to hold the can securely in place. The group of stand lamps with Harris' patent metal fuel containers all have the same base.

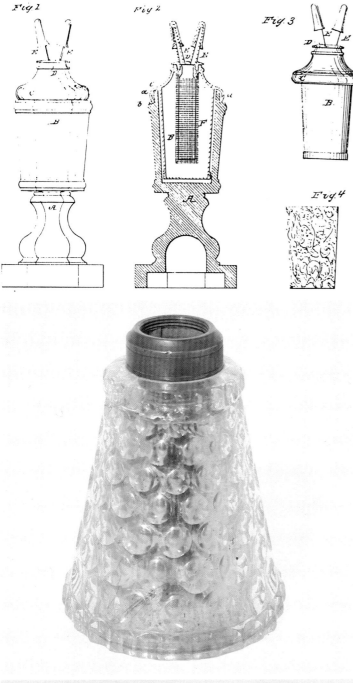

Elbridge Harris of Boston patented the metal fuel receptacle for a glass lamp on March 20, 1855. As stated in his patent No. 12,550, its purpose was to prevent "injury to clothing, furniture, and the danger to persons arising from the fracture of glass lamps." The metal reservoir could be used for heavier whale and lard oils, but "my improvements have special claims in relation to security from accidents in the consumption of highly inflammable mixtures of alcohol and hydrocarbons." To that end, Harris suggested the use of the safety tube, as shown in Figure 2. His patent specifications included a reference to the common form of hand lamp in which the bottom was left open to receive the metal reservoir (see photo 2133). If an unpatterned glass lamp was to be used, the metal could be covered with ornamental paper as seen in Figure 4.

2133 PRESSED BABY THUMBPRINT HAND SAFETY LAMP
4⅝" H. x 3¾" Dia. 1855–1870

This unusual hand lamp was discovered with its handle intact in one of the outbuildings at the Boston and Sandwich Glass Company site in the late 1890's. It was stored in an attic in Sandwich with several other large fragments that became part of the Barlow fragment collection. Other fragments of this lamp were unearthed in quantity in an area where unusable articles were discarded in the 1850's. There is no glass across the bottom of the lamp. It was left open to insert the metal fuel can that follows the configuration of the glass and secures to the collar. According to patent No. 12,550 issued to Elbridge Harris on March 20, 1855, the glass part of the lamp was to be blown or pressed as usual. "The body of the lamp is left open at the top, or bottom, like a drinking glass." Harris' metal container prevented accidents caused by the explosive nature of burning fluids. When fitted with a fluid burner, Harris used a safety tube that extended downward into the can, as shown in his patent. However, the tube was not a part of Harris' patent. When fitted with a burner for heavier whale oil or lard, Harris claimed that the metal conducted heat to liquify the fuel while the glass protected the metal from radiation.

2134 WAFFLE AND THUMBPRINT (PALACE)
(a) Pressed lamp with pressed hexagonal base, three "printies" in panel, fluid burner 9¾" H. x 3½" Dia. font, 4⅛" Dia. base
(b) Blown molded hand lamp, three "printies" in panel, whale oil burner 4⅛" H. x 3½" Dia.
(c) Pressed lamp with pressed hexagonal base, two "printies" in panel, whale oil burner 10½" H. x 3⅝" Dia. font, 4⅝" Dia. base 1840–1870

Here is a good example of slight variations that take place when a factory went from one mold to another. The font of lamp A has a vertical row of three circular indentations in each panel. The horizontal band above the pattern is smooth and the band around the bottom of the font is serrated. The larger lamp C has only two circular indentations in each vertical row and both the upper and lower bands are serrated. *These slight variations in moldmaking do not denote origin.* Another variation of lamp C has an open font to receive a glass-domed metal fuel container such as can be seen in photo 2130. It has no bands above or below

Continuation follows glossary.

2135 WOODEN PICKWICKS

(a) Dark wood 4⅜'' H. x 1⅜'' Dia. 1825–1870
(b) Light wood 3⅜'' H. x ⅝'' Dia. 1840–1870

The simplest style of pickwick that was inserted into the slot of a whale oil tube to raise the wick was a steel pin. One end had a sharp point and the other end was looped so that it could be hung from a chain that was fastened around the lamp. Obviously, a sewing needle would suffice. Pickwick A was an expensive, finely-turned piece that was used in better homes. When not in use, the sharp point was protected by inserting it into the hole that was drilled through the slender shaft of the wide-based holder. Pickwick B served the same purpose, but cost less and was commonly used in working class households. At the other end of the price scale were ivory pickwicks with ivory pins. When one realizes how many whale oil lamps were used in the home and workplace, the question arises, ''What happened to all of the pickwicks?'' Many were discarded, so pickwicks now sold by experienced antiques dealers command a high price. But, with perseverance, the dedicated collector may still find one. They have been assimilated into other categories, exhibited as ''individual toothpicks that one carried in one's pocket''. Search through boxes that contain household odds and ends such as sewing items.

2136 VEGETABLE IVORY PICKWICKS

(a) Amber 2¾'' H. x ½'' Dia.
(b) Dark red 2⅝'' H. x ⅝'' Dia.
(c) Black 3⅛'' H. x ⅝'' Dia. 1840–1870

Vegetable ivory came from the ivory-nut, the nut from a species of palm, that was often the size of a hen's egg. It could be machined into any shape, dyed into a number of colors and then cured by heat. Umbrella handles were made from this substance. Pickwicks A and B have real ivory picks, as shown in the foreground. Pickwick C has a steel pin for a pick. Its turned finial was threaded to screw into the lower unit. Pickwicks could only be used with whale oil burners because they had slots in the tubes to expose the sides of the wicks.

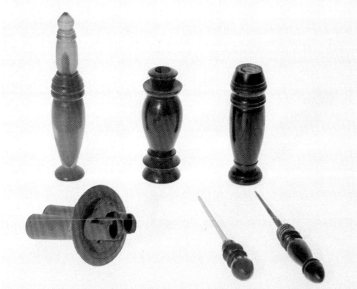

2137 PRESSED SMOCKING LAMP WITH PRESSED CIRCULAR BASE, WHALE OIL BURNER

9¼'' H. x 3½'' Dia. font, 4⅜'' Dia. base 1840–1855

This lamp has an interesting circular base that was usually used on candlesticks. We identify the base as a candlestick base because the bulk of the fragments that were dug at the factory site were attached to candle sockets. The pattern called *Smocking* by collectors can be found on many different tableware items, but it made a poorly designed lamp. Note that the pattern starts out small above the wafer that connects the font to the base, and expands until it culminates in thick, sharp mitres. These sawtooth tips are easily chipped when the lamp comes in contact with another item, so most Smocking lamps have major damage in this area. Refer to the *Barlow-Kaiser Sandwich Glass Price Guide* for information on pricing damaged pieces.

2138 PRESSED SANDWICH STAR LAMPS WITH PRESSED HEXAGONAL BASE, WHALE OIL BURNER

(a) Small 9⅞'' H. x 3'' Dia. font, 4'' Dia. base
(b) Medium 10½'' H. x 3½'' Dia. font, 5'' Dia. base
    1840–1860

It is believed that this pattern was unique to Sandwich, so collectors have given it the name *Sandwich Star*. It dates from the early 1840's on the whale oil lamps shown here, to the late 1850's, as shown by a larger 11¼'' H. lamp and by a large Sandwich Star bowl that was combined with the Three-Dolphin standard shown on the lighting device in photo 2144. Both lamps shown here were made from clear glass, yet there is a marked difference in the color of each. The smaller lamp A takes on a black glass appearance and the larger lamp B has a brilliant transparency. This was caused by the use of different glass sand. According to the Massachusetts State Assayer who analyzed sand samples from Cheshire, there are impurities in sand, "the impurities being such oxides as color glass". Sand from Western Massachusetts was exceptionally pure, resulting in brilliant colorless glass.

2139 PRESSED ARMORIAL LAMPS WITH PRESSED HEXAGONAL BASE

(a) Small 9'' H. x 3⅛'' Dia. font, 4'' Dia. base
(b) Large 9¾'' H. x 3½'' Dia. font, 4½'' Dia. base
    1845–1855

This pattern has an interesting story. A like example of lamp A is the only piece of Sandwich glass that author Ray Barlow has seen bearing an original Boston and Sandwich Glass Company paper label. In May 1965, at an auction held at the Town Hall in Carver, Massachusetts, it went under the hammer for hundreds of dollars more than the author was able to bid. The paper label was in the form of a semicircle with the words "BOSTON & SANDWICH GLASS COMPANY" around the top and "ARMORIAL PAT." across the bottom. A picture of a glass blower was in the center.

Fig. 7 Boston and Sandwich Glass Company paper label, drawn from memory.

2140 PRESSED ARMORIAL LAMP WITH PRESSED HEXAGONAL BASE, KEROSENE ARGAND BURNER CONVERTED TO ELECTRICITY AND SHADE

(a) Lamp 9¾'' H. x 3½'' Dia. font, 4½'' Dia. base
(b) Shade 6¼'' H. x 5½'' Dia.
(c) Combined size 17'' H. 1845–1855

A lamp that was converted to electricity has lost its original antiquity and is devalued by the cost of converting it back to its original state. In some cases, the cost could be considerable. The original shade ring was retained, but it was soldered to the electrical fitting. To return the lamp to its original condition, it would be necessary to remove the original shade and prisms and replace the burner, chimney and shade ring, which cannot be salvaged once it has been soldered to an electrical fitting. These three pieces are difficult to find in their original configurations. The authors suggest that if you have an antique lamp with original fittings, and you wish to use the lamp for electric lighting, remove the antique parts and store them carefully away.

2141 PRESSED ARMORIAL SPOON HOLDER

5'' H. x 3¾'' Dia. 1845–1855

In an effort to differentiate between spill holders and spoon holders, the authors have examined advertisements, catalogs, invoices and order sheets from many glass companies. To date, we have yet to find a listing for a spill holder *during this time period* and into the 1870's. A *spill* was a small roll of paper or a slip of wood used to light lamps. The term came into use after 1847 and before 1859. It is often stated that the form of glass shown in this photo was used to hold spills, hence, the name. The mold that was used to make the lamp font was easily adapted to make the spoon holder shown here. We have had conversations with elderly people who remember that on their grandparents' kitchen table were ''kitchen lamps'' with a spoon holder to match, not to hold spills for the lamps, but to hold extra spoons. The reason for the confusion may be that *spills* are listed in the 1887 sloar book. However, without an illustrated catalog, we do not know their form. As far as is known, Armorial pattern was unique to Cape Cod. Glass historians have also attributed it to the short-lived factory in Falmouth.

2142 PRESSED LYRE (HARP) LAMP WITH PRESSED HEXAGONAL BASE, WHALE OIL BURNER

(a) Lamp, straight sides 9½'' H. x 3⅛'' Dia. font, 4⅛'' Dia. base
(b) Fragment, tapered sides 1840–1870

Lamp A has a base that was commonly used on kitchen lamps, held to the font extension by a wafer. Fragment B was one of many dug from the Boston and Sandwich Glass Company site. You can see where the knop extension broke away from the lower unit. In either configuration, straight-sided or tapered, they were usually purchased in pairs by the retail customer. The matching footed piece that lamp collectors refer to as a ''spill holder'' was sold as a Harp spoon holder by McKee and Brother in their 1859–1860 catalog. Its use to hold spills may have been secondary. A Lyre cologne can be seen in photo 3103.

2143 BLOWN MOLDED LYRE (HARP) HAND LAMP, FLUID BURNER

3¾'' H. x 3⅜'' Dia. 1840–1870

The Lyre pattern hand lamp mold was designed by a very clever mold designer of their time. It has six panels, five of which have lyres. The sixth was left blank to accept the ridged handle that was applied after the lamp was removed from the mold. The lamp is considerably larger in diameter at the bottom than at the top. This gave it stability if it got bumped when it was filled with burning fluid. It would slide along the table rather than tip over. A Harp handled lamp was illustrated in the 1859–1860 McKee and Brother catalog, who supplied either a whale oil or a fluid burner with it. This lamp is often seen with a single tube fluid burner.

2144 PRESSED THREE-DOLPHIN STANDARDS WITH CIRCULAR BASE AND LAMP GLASS

(a) Standard 5½" H. to top of knop; 5¼" Dia.
(b) Lamp glass 10" H. x 7" Dia.
(c) Combined size 17" H.
(d) Peg lamps 5" H. x 2" Dia. 1850–1860

In 1887, Princess Liliuokalani of the Sandwich Islands, now Hawaii, came to the United States to visit relatives of her husband, John Owen Dominis, who were living in Brookline, Massachusetts. This pair of lighting devices was presented to her by her relatives and was taken back to the Sandwich Islands. The Princess succeeded to the throne in 1891 and reigned as Queen Liliuokalani until 1893. After her death in 1917, they became the possession of a close friend, whose descendants presented them to the Sandwich Glass Museum. This standard with a circular base was also used on a kerosene lamp as shown in photo

Continuation follows glossary.

2145 PRESSED THREE-DOLPHIN STANDARD WITH HEXAGONAL BASE, LAMP GLASS AND PEG LAMP, FLUID BURNER

(a) Standard 6¾" H. to top of ball; 6" Dia.
(b) Lamp glass 9½" H. x 6" Dia.
(c) Combined size 17½" H.
(d) Peg lamp 5" H. x 2" Dia. 1850–1860

The Three-Dolphin standard on which this assembly was mounted is the most sought after in the Sandwich lighting series. The standard has been found in two sizes: the larger with hexagonal base shown here and the smaller with circular base shown previously. The tails of the dolphins come together and are joined by a ball-shaped knop, above which is a brass unit with a socket into which the peg lamp is inserted. The socket is so constructed that it can be equipped with either a lamp or a candle, as discussed in photo 4050. The lamp glass is cemented into a brass collar embossed with a grape motif that was also used on the hanging lamp in photo 2398. Providing that a small enough diameter peg lamp is inserted in the socket, a 1/3 turn of the lamp glass quickly removes it, as shown in the following photo. The arrangement was particularly useful in warm climates where a light was needed near an open window. The lamp glass prevented a curtain blowing in the breeze from coming into contact with an open flame.

2146 UNITS OF ABOVE LAMP

The lamp glass was removed to show how the peg lamp is held to the metal fitting that is cemented to the glass standard. A second peg lamp inserted through the metal collar of the lamp glass illustrates how the lamp glass slips over it if the proper peg lamp is used. If the peg lamp is too large to pass through the brass collar and must be inserted into the socket after the lamp glass is in place, the burner is difficult to light without a wand. A Dietz and Company catalog that dates from the mid-1860's illustrates a special torch, or lamp lighter, "for lighting lamps without removing chimney". It was a metal wand with the name "GLEASON" on it that appears to be about 14" L. After lighting a match and inserting it into a prong at one end of the wand, it was passed down to the burner from the top of the chimney or lamp glass.

2147 PRESSED TULIP LAMPS WITH COLUMNAR STANDARD AND SQUARE BASE

(a) 12⅜'' H. x 4½'' Dia. font, 4⅜'' Sq. base
(b) 12⅜'' H. x 4¾'' Dia. font, 4⅜'' Sq. base
    1845–1870

The construction of this lamp is discussed at length because reproductions have found their way into the collections of major museums and knowledgeable glass experts. The lamps shown in this photo with their original plated collars were made by the Boston and Sandwich Glass Company. But a pair of reproductions, with Twentieth Century collars, appears on plate 194 of George and Helen McKearin's *American Glass*. Ruth Webb Lee devoted a paragraph and a full-page photo to the "repro" in her book *Antique Fakes & Reproductions*, where she stated that it was first made in clear glass, then in two-color combinations such as a garish green font with a yellowish white base. Original Tulip lamps are difficult to find because the petals around the font were easily damaged, so when you find a perfect lamp in the antiques market with a Columnar standard, assume that it is a "repro" unless you can prove otherwise based on the differences shown in the illustration. Among other things, there were no distinct mold marks on the font extension of the green combined with blue reproduction lamps examined by the authors. The font was made from a well-fitted Twentieth Century mold that opened and closed electrically. *The "repro" does have a wafer.* We have seen the reproduction lamp with a replaced Nineteenth Century period collar, emphasizing once again that one cannot rely on a collar to prove age or origin. The deliberate manufacture and marketing of reproductions touches a particularly sensitive nerve of the authors. Even when sold new in gift shops, they eventually find their way into antiques shops managed by honest but unwary dealers. Unscrupulous antiques dealers buy new reproductions, sometimes at their place of manufacture, to increase their inventory as originals become difficult to obtain at a price that allows for a fair markup. They "forget" to mention the age, or they "don't know, but got it out of an old home".

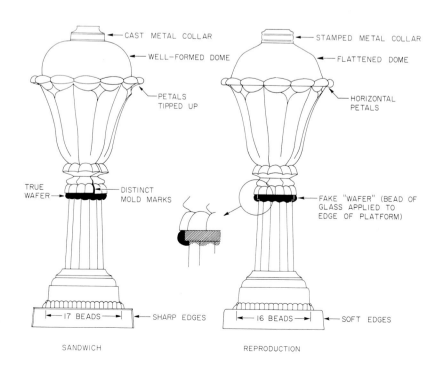

Fig. 8   The reproduction Tulip lamp was manufactured to deliberately deceive the Sandwich glass collector. It was made in a Twentieth Century mold that opened and closed electrically, so the mold marks are indistinct. After the reproduction lamp was removed from the mold, a fake "wafer" was made by wrapping a strip of glass around the edge of a platform molded on top of the standard. Look under the fake "wafer" in places where it does not hug the flutes of the standard. The platform is visible. Other obvious differences are the shape of the dome, the tilt of the petals around the font, and the number of beads pressed into each side of the square base.

2148 PRESSED TULIP LAMPS, FLUID BURNER
(a) Acanthus Leaf standard and square base 11⅜'' H. x 3¾'' Dia. font, 4⅛'' Sq. base
(b) Columnar standard and square base 11⅛'' H. x 3½'' Dia. font, 3⅛'' Sq. base 1845–1860

As the pressed glass era progressed, most lamps were manufactured with shortened fonts in which burning fluid or whale oil worked equally well. Lamp A has a larger font with an extension comprised of a knop, and below the knop a circle of beads. The beads combine nicely with the beaded upper surface of the Acanthus Leaf standard, making the wafer less prominent. The font extension on the slender lamp B has a completely different configuration. There were several variations of the original Tulip fonts. Note the well-formed domes as compared with the reproduction fonts discussed previously. Neither of these standards have been accurately reproduced to date. The base of lamp B does not have beads. *Courtesy, Sandwich Glass Museum, Sandwich Historical Society*

2149 WOODEN PATTERN FOR COLUMNAR STANDARD AND SQUARE BASE
5½'' H. x 4¼'' Dia. 1845–1860

Each glass base that was made at Sandwich began with a wooden pattern. This enabled the glass company to present to the commercial mold maker an exact sample of the required finished product. At the mold maker's establishment, the wooden patterns were soaked in oil, accounting for the dark patina that is on them today. Through a series of construction steps, the shape of the final mold was formed that would be filled with hot glass to make the article, in this case, a columnar standard with a square base.

2150 PRESSED ACANTHUS LEAF LAMPS WITH PRESSED ACANTHUS LEAF BASE
(a) 12½'' H. x 4¼'' Dia. font, 4⅜'' Sq. base
(b) 11⅜'' H. x 3¾'' Dia. font, 4⅛'' Sq. base 1840–1860

The Acanthus Leaf lamp was produced in many colors—most notably, blue and white. It is unusual to see it in clear glass. Note the wafer that holds font A to its base. It was much too large and fell over the standard, obliterating the beads beneath it. These manufacturing characteristics enhance value and give pieces individuality. The color of lamp B is known as *clambroth*, but was known as *alabaster* at the time of production. Alabaster appears to be soft and must be handled with extreme care. If you plan to make a purchase, be sure you examine for cracks and bruises. The surface may be shedding. If so, the overall appearance is dull. If the shedding is in the advanced stages, value can be diminished.

2151 PRESSED ACANTHUS LEAF

(a) Lamp with pressed Acanthus Leaf base 11⅜'' H. x 3¾'' Dia. font, 4'' Sq. base

(b) Pressed Scroll and Lily candle socket with pressed Acanthus Leaf lamp base 7⅞'' H. x 4'' Sq. base 1850–1860

There is no question that the designer of lamp A intended this font and base to go together. It is one of the few examples of a well thought out, planned combination. The pattern of six leaves around the font is repeated in a pattern of four leaves around the standard of the lower unit. The top of the standard has twelve beads around the outside edge and is hollowed out to accept the wafer, which can be the color of either unit. Twelve beads around the bottom of the font extension match the beads on the standard. Finding this lamp base combined with any other font would be unusual, yet, several candlesticks have been located with this base, as shown on the right. The pressed socket with its Scroll and Lily pattern was usually combined with a taller pressed hexagonal Acanthus Leaf lower unit, which was made in three sizes as pictured in photo 4041. That hexagonal lower unit carries a pattern of three vertical leaves alternating with the Scroll and Lily motif that is on the socket. The pattern surrounds the lower unit in three places: at the top of the standard, on the bulbous lower part of the standard and on the upper surface of the hexagonal base. On the square bases in this photo, the alabaster base on the left has nineteen beads on each of the four sides, not counting the corner beads. The clear square base on the right has eighteen beads on each side, not counting the corner beads. Each base is an old one.

Courtesy, Sandwich Glass Museum, Sandwich Historical Society

Fig. 9 The Boston and Sandwich Glass Company font extension has petals, or beads, that face upward and outward. Compare this illustration to the Mount Washington beaded extension shown in Fig. 6 on page 92 that was hollowed out to hide the wafer. On the Sandwich Acanthus Leaf lamp, the *standard* was hollowed out to accept a large wafer.

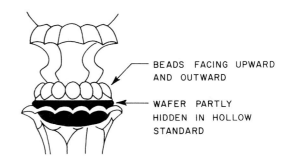

BEADS FACING UPWARD AND OUTWARD

WAFER PARTLY HIDDEN IN HOLLOW STANDARD

2152 FLUID BURNERS

(a) Two tubes

(b) Three tubes

(c) Four tubes 1830–1870

Burners with tubes that extend above the threaded disk were for burning man-made fluids. The tubes do not extend downward into the font as they do on whale oil burners. A single-tube burner may not be tapered, but burners with two or more tubes are tapered and angled out from each other. The burner is usually made of brass. The disk to which the tubes are attached is threaded to screw into the threaded brass collar that is cemented to the lamp. There are no slots in the sides of the tubes to allow the use of a pickwick, so they were difficult to thread. Also, slots in the side of a fluid tube were impossible to use because they would drastically change the air flow and, as the tube heated up, the wick would have ignited in the slot. To simplify threading the wick, a wick awl or fine crochet hook was inserted through the tube from the top. A wick previously soaked in burning fluid was hooked with the needle, drawn through the tube, and trimmed. The single-tube burner used on small lamps and the double-tube burner A are the most common. Three-tube burners can

Continuation follows glossary.

2154 FOUR-TUBE FLUID BURNERS

(a) With coronet for lamp glass
(b) For open flame 1830–1860

Generally speaking, fluid burners were meant to burn with an open flame. Very few can be found with a coronet, which was cast in one piece with the threaded disk. We believe that the lamp glass for this large coronet was cylindrical, open at both ends to allow the air to pass up through the openings between the cast arms that held the coronet. The rim of the coronet held the glass in place. There is no set screw to be tightened against a flared fitter. The lamp glass would have been extremely hot when all four wicks were ignited. It would also have been very difficult to extinguish the flames with the little caps. It appears to the authors that this type of burner may have been an attempt to manufacture an inexpensive lamp styled after elegant devices that had Argand burners and elaborately cut shades, designed to cast a glow over a large area.

2155 FLUID BURNER WITH CONVERTER ATTACHMENT

1¾'' H. 1863

Here is the common two-tube fluid burner. Slipped down over each tube are devices that supposedly improve the draft to the flame so that an ordinary burning fluid lamp could be converted to kerosene without the aid of a chimney and new burner. The wings of each attachment are marked ''T&N PAT MAR 24, 1863''. This late date for an improvement to a fluid burner suggests that it may have been an effort on the part of fluid burner and lamp manufacturers who were overstocked to prolong the use of their products into the kerosene era. A tiny hole near the edge of the burner cap indicates that the burner originally had a chain with brass caps, which was removed when this ''improvement'' was attached. A search of Patent Office records showed that the patent, No. 37,987, was granted to Abner G. Tisdel and William Nash of Watertown, New York.

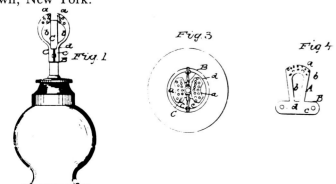

2153 TWO-TUBE FLUID BURNER WITH CORONET

1½'' H. x 2¾'' Dia. 1830–1860

This burner was on an Acanthus Leaf lamp when it was purchased. The piece was cast in one piece with the exception of the wick tubes, chain and set screw. Unusual lamp fittings should be important to any serious lamp collector. The monetary value of scarce burners can be substantial. If this one had three tubes, it would double in price. The burner bought separately to be mounted on a valuable colored lamp will increase the value of the lamp by more than the price of the burner. If you find a lamp glass with the proper size fitter, you again increase the value of the lamp by more than the price of the lamp glass. The authors have never seen a lamp glass or chimney on a fluid burner. An 1859–1860 McKee and Brother catalog pictured a camphene chimney. It was similar to a bulb-shaped kerosene chimney with a plain rim, but it had a tapered fitter. The fitters ranged in diameter from 2'' to 3½''.

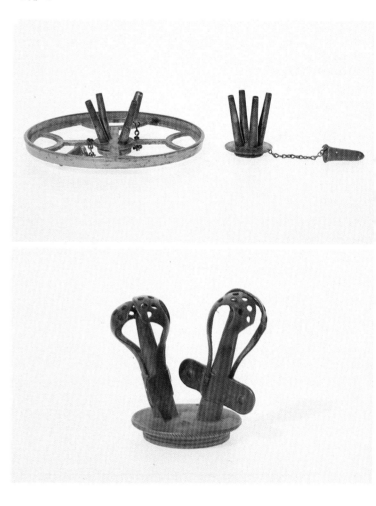

On March 24, 1863, Abner G. Tisdel and William Nash of Watertown, New York, were issued patent No. 37,987 for an ''improved attachment for converting other fluid (lamps) into coal-oil lamps''. Each attachment had two curved prongs that were perforated at their upper ends, forked at their lower ends, and attached to a clamp. The winged spring-clamp arrangement allowed the attachment to fit snugly around the tapered wick tube after it was adjusted so that the ''upper perforated parts of the prongs may be placed in a proper relative position with the top of the wick-tube as may be required to insure perfect combustion.'' It is not likely that the converter was widely accepted by the public. If so, more snugly-fitting converters would be found today in the antiques market.

2156 WICK HOOK (WICK AWL)

4¼'' L. 1840–1870

The awl-shaped tool with the added chain is a spring-loaded device that pulled the wick through the tubes of fluid burners. The hook was inserted into the opening until the smaller diameter metal piece nearest the hook was positioned firmly against the upper end of the tube. Continued pressure caused the larger metal sleeve to slide down over the smaller piece, compressing the spring and sending the hook well below the flat cap of the burner. When the wick was hooked and the wooden handle released, the wick was drawn into the tube and pulled out of the opening. The wick was trimmed, and the burner was screwed onto the lamp, ready to be ignited. Awls with fine wick hooks are likely to be mixed in with leather working tools at antiques shows and flea markets.

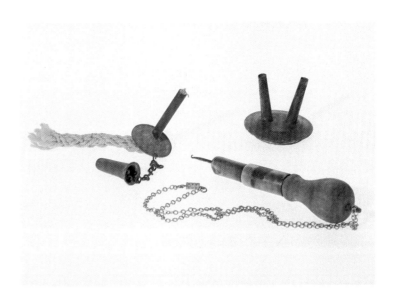

2157 PRESSED ACANTHUS LEAF LAMP WITH REEDED BRASS STANDARD AND MARBLE BASE, WHALE OIL BURNER

11'' H. x 3⅜'' Dia. font, 4'' Sq. base 1850–1860

This Acanthus Leaf font had a peg molded beneath the font extension so that it could be inserted into a brass standard. A variation of this font was reproduced in many colors, many of which can be found in flea markets mounted on old brass standards with marble bases. The reproduction font has no extension. The fuel reservoir sits directly on the brass standard. The brass standard pictured here is an early one that mimics the glass Columnar standard. During this period, lamps could be purchased with a choice of either a whale oil or a fluid burner.

2158 BRASS STANDARDS

(a) Stenciled with marble base 6⅝'' H. x 4½'' Sq. base
(b) Reeded 3¼'' H. x 1¾'' Dia. 1840–1870

A number of the fonts commonly attached to glass bases were also made with a peg extension. The extension had notches or slots, so the font could be permanently cemented to metal standards. The standards did not have vertical rods that passed completely through them. A short rod fastened to the standard at the lower end was bolted to the marble base. Standard A is a hollow brass column that was stenciled and blued. It was an inexpensive method of livening up an otherwise ordinary lighting device. Both Egyptian gray and Italian yellow-brown marble were used in the assembly of Sandwich lamps, so don't let the color of the marble influence your buying decision. Standard B is brass that was stamped into the reeded columnar pattern. If you were to disassemble a lamp that had not been previously tampered with, you will find the standards stuffed with newspaper. Careful removal of the newspaper may reveal the approximate date of assembly. However, the newspaper cannot determine the origin of the glass font, because a Boston glass company may have shipped a quantity of fonts to a lamp assembly company in another state. The assembly company may have been a small one with local trade or even a large one with a world-wide market.

2159 PRESSED ACANTHUS LEAF GIRANDOLES WITH MATCHING CANDELABRA

(a) Lamps 15¼" H. x 3⅝" Dia. font, 4⅝" L. x 3⅛" W. base

(b) Candelabra 16" H.; 6" L. x 4" W. base
    1850–1860

Here is the same Acanthus Leaf font permanently mounted in a metal socket above a cast metal standard depicting a maiden. A larger version of the same standard holds the branched candlestick. The combination on the fireplace mantle gave both types of lighting. We have also seen a three-piece set consisting of a pair of green Acanthus Leaf lamps flanking an Acanthus Leaf three-light girandole similar in configuration to the girandole in photo 2123. The set was complete with five fluid burners with coronets as shown in photo 2153. Because of the weight of the font when filled with fuel, the metal standard does not stand straight. Any attempt to straighten it would snap the metal, so, when it needed straightening, the center screw beneath the marble base was loosened. A wooden shim was slid under the feet of the figure and the screw was retightened. Candelabra B was given to Sandwich historian Francis (Bill) Wynn by a Sandwich resident. It came out of the home without its prisms. All of the prisms now in place were dug from the factory site by Mr. Wynn, who polished and hung them. At the time the Wynn collection was purchased by the authors, it contained more than six hundred prisms in usable condition. Although they were dug from the site, they were not made in Sandwich. An article in the *Sandwich Observer* on December 25, 1847, noted that Egyptian and Italian marble was used by the glass company. The serious collector should take advantage of any opportunity to acquire fittings for lighting devices. In no other category of collecting will your "spare parts department" be so necessary.

2160 PRESSED HEART LAMPS WITH PRESSED HEXAGONAL BASE, VAPOR BURNER

10" H. x 4" Dia. font, 4½" Dia. base 1845–1860

By the mid 1800's, a greater percentage of lamps were designed for stability than were used in the days of whale oil. A whale oil lamp if knocked over did not explode. As other fuels were developed, manufacturers as well as consumers became safety-conscious. No amount of caution eliminated the hazards presented by the gasoline burners shown here. "Gas oil" was equal to 95 octane gasoline today. To light this lamp, it was necessary to have another source of heat that could be directed to the elbows of each of the four tubes. Tiny holes the diameter of a human hair vented the fumes and allowed ignition. The heat from the flames kept the burner tubes at a high enough temperature to vaporize the gas drawn up the wick, maintaining the flame. The rarity of vapor burners attests to their limited appeal. The newspapers related many instances of people "burnt to a crisp" by exploding lighting devices. On two-color pieces, the wafer could match either the upper or the lower unit, but both wafers should be the same color on a perfectly matched pair. The Heart lamp has been reproduced several times during the 1900's. In 1988, the authors purchased a pair of blue "repro" Heart lamps from an "antiques dealer" who had recently bought them new, by the dozen. The dealer had already replaced the 1988 collars with old ones.

2161 PRESSED HEART LAMP WITH PRESSED HEXAGONAL BASE

10¼" H. x 3⅞" Dia. font, 4¾" Dia. base 1845–1860

The Heart pattern was an extremely versatile one that was adaptable to many items. It was used on vases, as shown in photos 3039 and 3040 in Volume 3, and colognes, as shown in photo 3104. An occasional rare color surfaces, such as fiery opalescent, at one time owned by the authors. This strange combination of a clear upper unit held by a clear wafer to a colored base adds significantly to value. The base has a refinement of line not seen on many hexagonal ones. The Heart font in clear glass combined with a clear glass base of the design shown in the preceding photo is common. It was made in nine sizes that ranged from 6½" to 11" high with fonts that held less than one pint to as much as one quart. *The Bennington Museum, Bennington, Vermont*

During the first half of the Nineteenth Century, a glass article that required handwork after it was removed from the mold was hand-held by attaching a pontil rod to the center of the bottom or inside the hollow of a pressed standard. Upon completion of the handwork, the rod was snapped off. This left chips in the article or sharp pieces of excess glass that could cut if the article was not handled carefully when it was being washed. By the 1850's, stands were devised to hold the article. The surface remained untouched by the pontil rod, and the device saved the labor cost of an extra glassworker who held the pontil rod while someone else completed the handwork. On August 11, 1857, Sandwich's Hiram Dillaway patented an improved holder that had interchangeable "yokes" to fit many different forms of glass. While lamps were not illustrated, they were mentioned in the specifications as one of the articles that could be held "during the manipulations that are necessary in their manufacture". The authors, with knowledgeable dealers and collectors, have examined several lamps, particularly in the Heart series, *Continuation follows glossary.*

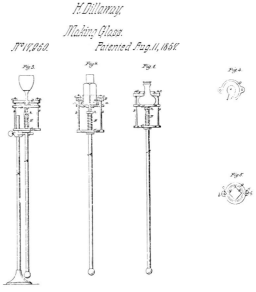

2162 PRESSED ASHBURTON

(a) Lamp made from egg cup mold, whale oil burner
    3⅞" H. x 2¼" Dia.
(b) Egg cup 3¾" H. x 2¾" Dia. 1840–1870

This lamp does not have a wafer. It was made by first pressing an egg cup. Instead of flaring an egg cup rim, the glass above the pattern was closed in to form the dome of the font and drawn upward to form a neck on which to cement a collar. The single tube whale oil burner is correct. The font holds slightly more than two ounces of fuel, so the lamp was only for short-term use. To the uninitiated beginning collector, the value placed on this Ashburton night lamp would be staggering. "It's only a little lamp," he might think. But this piece has three things going for it: small lamps in patterns normally used on full-size fonts are always in demand because they are rare and do not take up much space; the pattern itself is collectable in a great variety of tableware pieces; and, last, any pressed or blown molded piece that was made by adapting a mold designed for another purpose is unique. The term *egg glass lamp* was used in the sloar book as early as October 29, 1826. Egg cup B is a standard form that was produced by the Boston and Sandwich Glass Company as well as other factories in the East and Midwest. *Courtesy, Sandwich Glass Museum, Sandwich Historical Society*

2163 BLOWN MOLDED PILLAR

(a) Lamp with pressed circular base 6'' H. x 2¼'' Dia. font, 3½'' Dia. base

(b) Wooden pattern 5¼'' H. x 2½'' Dia. 1835–1845

The name of this pattern is *Pillar*. Do not associate the word with the type of construction known as *pillar molding*. There are eight convex panels around the font, with a vertical row of concave "printies" in each row. The eight panels continue onto the font extension, where each is the same width as each of the eight panels on the standard just below the wafer. Although an inexpensive item at the time of production, care was taken to line up the eight panels on the example in the photo. Wooden pattern B was used to make a mold for a font one size larger. It is upside down, standing on its neck. The uppermost part of the wooden pattern is the font extension to which the wafer was attached. The wooden patterns for both sizes of fonts were together until sold separately by a New Jersey antiques dealer in the early 1960's. This Pillar pattern in tableware was made over a long period of time by the Boston and Sandwich Glass Company and into the 1870's by Bakewell, Pears and Company.

2164 BLOWN MOLDED FONT WITH PRESSED CIRCULAR BASE

6'' H. x 2¼'' Dia. font, 3'' Dia. base 1840–1850

This lamp is in a private collection in Sandwich and has been traced back to 1840 through a glassworker's family. Even though the lamp is quite small, a wafer was used to assemble it. Study the unusual base, one which is seldom seen. The pattern of two rows of printies on the font was molded in low relief. The oversized collar is a later replacement. Be aware that companies making glassware merchandised their products to every economic level. Collectors are inclined to associate a well documented glass works with the type of glass for which it is known best *at the present time*, i.e., Sandwich Lacy, Mount Washington Burmese, Wheeling Peach Blow, New England Glass Company Amberina. We sometimes neglect to recognize that each company also made tavern glass, laboratory glass, nipple shells, urinals, and unimportant lamps such as this one and the one shown previously.

2165 PRESSED PRISM AND CRESCENT LAMP WITH PRESSED HEXAGONAL BASE, WHALE OIL BURNER

9½'' H. x 2⅞'' Dia. font, 4'' Sq. base 1845–1860

This pattern is a variation of a pattern that was produced in a limited number of tableware pieces. The lamp font, however, has an added horizontal band of printies around the upper part. These stand lamps were also called *kitchen lamps*, as listed in a McKee and Brother catalog for 1859–1860. Even at this late date, lamps were supplied with either whale oil or fluid burners, the whale oil burners being less expensive. When looking for tableware to match pattern glass lamps, keep in mind that tableware pieces were not made in sets because they were designed to be used with complete porcelain and pottery sets. For example, a factory glass catalog for a certain year may only show lamps, sauce dishes and sugar bowls. Another catalog from another factory may list nappies, bowls and celeries. And tumblers appear on the same page as non-matching spittoons and bird fountains. *Reproduced by courtesy of The Magazine ANTIQUES*

2166 BLOWN MOLDED OVAL HOBNAIL LAMP FRAGMENT

4¼" H. x 3⅜" Dia. 1850–1870

This pattern of convex ovals was used by several factories. The authors examined several complete lamps with fonts that were joined to their pressed glass bases both without wafers as well as with them. This Oval Hobnail font was dug at the site of the Boston and Sandwich Glass Company, where it had been discarded because it broke above the wafer after the collar was cemented in place. Many fragments of this pattern have been dug including a complete finial and pieces that match colognes and vases as shown in Volume 3. One of the lamps studied was fitted with a fluid burner which appeared to be original.

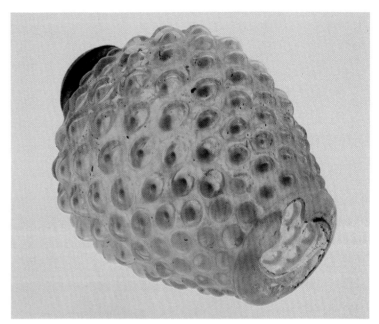

2167 PRESSED EARLY MOON AND STAR (STAR AND PUNTY, STAR AND CONCAVE)

(a) Lamp with pressed hexagonal base 9¼" H. x 3½" Dia. font, 3⅞" Dia. base
(b) Hand lamp 3⅞" H. x 3" Dia. 1850–1870

The use of heavenly bodies as motifs was common on early glass. Sunburst and Comet were patterns used as often as the pattern of moons and stars shown here. This pattern was identified as *Star and Punty* in the list of glassware manufactured by the Cape Cod Glass Company, where many fragments were dug in canary and blue as well as in clear. Some Pittsburgh houses called it *Star and Concave*. Collectors and writers who preceded the authors named it *Early Moon and Star* to distinguish it from a late Pittsburgh pattern they referred to as *Moon and Star*. The font of lamp A is attached to a familiar Sandwich base. Lamp B was also pressed and has a handle that was molded in one piece with the font. A newspaper report noted that lamps were being pressed with their handles at the Cape Cod Glass Company works. Quantities of clear and colored fragments were also dug at the Boston and Sandwich Glass Company site and the New England Glass Company site in East Cambridge, Massachusetts. *Courtesy, Sandwich Glass Museum, Sandwich Historical Society*

2168 BLOWN MOLDED BULL'S EYE AND ROSETTE LAMPS WITH HEXAGONAL BASE, FLUID BURNERS

9½" H. x 3" Dia. font, 4¼" Dia. base 1840–1860

Here is a very busy pattern. The Bull's Eye circles alternate with the encircled Rosettes around the font, below which are Gothic arches. Small stars can be seen above center between each circle. There is a serrated band above and below the pattern on the font as well as on a matching spoon holder. Fragments dug at the factory site include a variant on which each Bull's Eye has three concentric circles inside it. Note particularly where the fonts were joined to the bases with wafers. At the time of manufacture, the flat disk wafers were made in exact size to conform to the diameter of the font extension, and it is difficult to tell that wafers were used. Tumblers and other pieces were made in this pattern, but a usable number of forms would be difficult to locate.

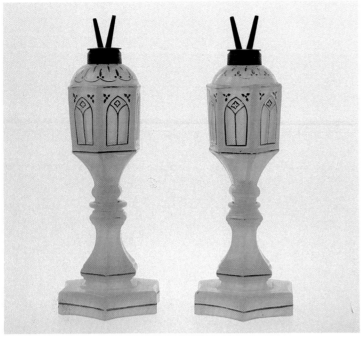

2169 PRESSED GOTHIC ARCH LAMPS WITH PRESSED HEXAGONAL BASE, FLUID BURNER

11'' H. x 4¼'' Dia. 1840–1850

When shopping for burners to complete your lamps, remember that fonts were shortened as the burning fluid era began. Fluid burners were not safe on lamps with tall fonts. The large knops beneath the fonts were molded as part of the upper units. Note the wafers beneath the knops. Wafer A is considerably larger than wafer B, yet in all other respects—the blue tinge, the gilding, the collars and burners—the lamps are a perfect pair. This minor difference in wafer size does not affect value. Gilding was extremely attractive, so it was used in abundance to increase sales. It is difficult, however, to obtain glass with gilding intact because repeated washing caused it to wear. Although we know that the New England Glass Company sold gilded pieces as early as 1832, the authors have not been able to prove that this method of decoration was used at Sandwich before the coming of William Smith in the 1840's. *Courtesy of The Toledo Museum of Art (Acc. No. 68.17 A&B)*

2170 PRESSED HORN OF PLENTY (COMET) LAMPS

(a) Pressed Monument base 10½'' H. x 3¼'' Dia. font, 3½'' Sq. base
(b) Pressed hexagonal base 10⅜'' H. x 3'' Dia. font, 4⅛'' Dia. base 1845–1870

This pattern was called *Comet* by the Pittsburgh, Pennsylvania, firm of McKee and Brothers. Many forms of tableware were made in clear glass. Oval dishes are occasionally found in opaque white, and several pieces are known to exist in canary and blue. A popular pattern was often continued over a long period of time with variations that add to the excitement of collecting. Although these lamps are approximately the same size, their height was obtained by different methods. Lamp A has an extremely tall standard molded in one piece with the Monument base. One can see in the photo how far the plunger was inserted. The opening beneath the base extends half way up into the standard. A wafer connects the standard to a flat-bottomed font. The hexagonal standard of lamp B is

Continuation follows glossary.

2171 PRESSED HORN OF PLENTY (COMET) LAMP WITH PRESSED HEXAGONAL BASE, KEROSENE BURNER AND SHADE

(a) Lamp 10¼'' H. x 3'' Dia. font, 4'' Dia. base 1845–1870
(b) Shade 5¼'' H. x 4⅝'' Dia. 1855–1870
(c) Combined size 16'' H.

If you were to go into a retail store during the Victorian Era to purchase an inexpensive ornate lamp, this is what you might walk out with. It is a Horn of Plenty kitchen lamp fitted for parlor use. A highly elaborate prism ring was placed over the shoulder of the font, with hanging pressed Star and Rosette prisms. A coronet, called a *shade ring* as we entered the period of coal oil, held a shade to diffuse the harsh glare. All of this paraphernalia made the lamp difficult to fill, so ornate fixtures were placed where only occasional light was necessary. The single lamp glass used with whale oil and fluid burners generally gave way to a chimney combined with a shade or globe. However, this Hutchenson's patent burner was designed to provide a draft without a chimney.

2172 PRESSED CABLE LAMP WITH PRESSED HEXAGONAL BASE

8½'' H. x 3'' Dia. font, 3⅞'' Dia. base 1845–1865
The word *cable* had been in the vocabulary long before the laying of the first Atlantic Telegraph Cable that collectors like to associate with this pattern. Sandwich historian Francis (Bill) Wynn, who spent years excavating fragments from the site of the Boston and Sandwich Glass Company, insisted that *cable* meant *rope*. We are inclined to agree. Mr. Wynn's research and ours indicate that Sandwich manufacture of the Cable pattern predated the forming of Cyrus W. Field's company in New York which, after several unsuccessful attempts in the mid–1850's, completed the last mid-ocean splice at 1:00 PM on July 29, 1858. Webster's 1847 dictionary defines *cable* as ''a large strong rope or chain, used to retain a vessel at anchor. A cable is composed of three strands, each strand of three ropes, and each rope of three twists.'' It is logical that a Cable pattern would have meaning in a community that depended so heavily on the sea. Six vertical lengths of Cable pattern alternate with six fans below the horizontal cable band.

2173 PRESSED CABLE WITH RING LAMP WITH PRESSED HEXAGONAL BASE

9¾'' H. x 4½'' Dia. font, 4⅝'' Dia. base 1855–1865
The Cable and Ring pattern was popular for many years, spanning the time from whale oil to fluid and kerosene. The enormous size of this font attests to this fact. Kerosene burned faster than earlier fuels, so kitchen lamps were made to hold larger amounts for longer light. If Cable pattern variants were designed to commemorate the Atlantic Cable, what was the purpose of the rings? A cable used on a ship was run through an anchor ring and was braided back upon itself. Rope cables and chain cables were advertised for sale in Cape Cod newspapers dating back to the 1830's. This lamp has six vertical lengths of cable pattern with a ring around each. A six-pointed star was pressed between each length, below the upper horizontal cable band. After the font was pressed, the unpatterned glass above the pattern was closed in to form the dome. Reheating to complete the dome blurred the cable band.

2174 PRESSED CABLE WITH RING LAMP WITH PRESSED HEXAGONAL BASE, KEROSENE BURNER

This Cable and Ring lamp described previously was perfect to use when fuel was needed for heating. It was sturdy and its base was wide enough in diameter and heavy enough to offset the weight of any accessory that might be placed atop the burner. Special burners and chimneys were manufactured to hold hair curling irons, teapots, vaporizers and the like. This burner was patented by Michael Collins of Chelsea, Massachusetts, on September 19, 1865. The patent date is embossed on the thumbwheel of the burner. According to Catherine M. V. Thuro in her book *Oil Lamps The Kerosene Era in North America*, it was manufactured by Holmes, Booth and Haydens of Waterbury, Connecticut.

2175 PRESSED CABLE WITH RING LAMP WITH PRESSED HEXAGONAL BASE, TEAPOT

To illustrate how lamps were used for heat, the authors placed a teapot on the Collins patent burner. A tin chimney extends through the center of the teapot; the bottom rim fits on the scalloped, perforated flange of the burner and is held stable by firm pressure of the flexible metal tabs against the inside. The top of the metal chimney inside the pot is fluted, as shown. The chimney forms the inner wall of a chamber that holds water. The cylinder that forms the outer wall is 2'' in diameter larger than the chimney, and, when filled with water and placed on the lighted burner, the water would boil in eight minutes.

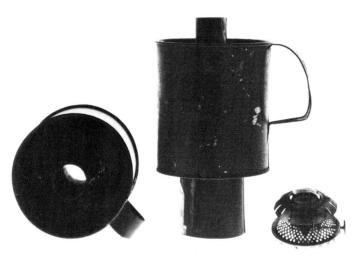

2176 "SICK ROOM COMPANION"

(a) Upper unit for food
(b) Lower unit for water
(c) Collins kerosene burner

The use of this two-piece tin accessory is fully described on the lower unit. "SICK ROOM COMPANION... FURNISHES LIGHT AND SHADE...COOKS OR WARMS FOOD FOR INVALIDS OR INFANTS BY STEAM...KEEPS THE ATMOSPHERE OF THE ROOM MOIST...NO BAD ODORS OR BURNED FOOD." The upper unit was removable so that warm soup could be served while water in the lower unit continued to vaporize. The inner tube of the upper unit A fits snugly around the inner tube "chimney" of lower unit B. Below the water chamber of unit B is an opening covered by a thin sheet of mica, or isinglass. The opening allowed some light from the flame to penetrate the darkness.

2177 BLOWN MOLDED CABLE WITH RING HAND LAMP, FLUID BURNER

2¾'' H. x 2⅛'' Dia. 1845-1865

The Cable with Ring lamp series was extensive. Several sizes of the kitchen, or stand, lamps were made and several sizes of handled lamps as well. A Boston and Sandwich Glass Company invoice to Portsmouth, New Hampshire, retailer John Sise dated October 5, 1861, listed two dozen Cable hand lamps with brass fluid caps. Company records did not differentiate among Cable patterns, so we cannot tell if the lamps sent to Sise were plain Cable or the variant shown here. This one is the smallest we have found. Sometimes decanter stopper molds were used upside down to make small lamps, but not in this case because the cable runs through the ring in such a manner that the upper part of the ring is behind the cable and the lower part of the ring can be seen. If you were to turn this lamp upside down and imagine it to be a stopper on a decanter, the pattern would be upside down in relation to the pattern on the decanter. There are six lengths of cable around the font. The handle was applied between two panels, so the pattern did not interfere with the gaffer's work. Many times, especially on little lamps or creams, the tail of the handle is damaged. This hurts the value of the piece considerably. If the body of a piece is cracked where the handle was applied, do not let an unscrupulous dealer convince you that it "happened in the making". The piece did not leave the factory in that condition.

CHAPTER 3

LAMP SHADES AND GLOBES

1825-1908

The production of lamp shades and globes to satisfy the needs of the lighting industry was important to the stability and success of most flint glass houses. *Lamp glasses*, as they were called when Sandwich's glass industry was in its infancy, were required for proper draft of the cylindrical-wicked Argand burner that was invented in the late 1700's. The lamp glass most resembled a small globe with a chimney-like opening above. Wide diameter shades were made to rest on the fonts of sinumbra lamps that employed burners based on Argand's principle. In the 1840's, large globes were manufactured that were fitted to lard-burning lamps. All of the aforementioned lighting devices were constructed from metal, but the metal lamp manufacturers depended on the glass manufacturers to furnish the globes and shades.

Fortunately for an in-depth study of Sandwich lighting accessories, a number of business letters written by Deming Jarves in the 1820's have survived. The letters included orders for lamp glassware and Jarves' simple illustrations on how to form it. These documented shapes are shown on glass lamps in Chapter 2 and in several photos that follow. However, beyond Jarves' correspondence and the few early metal lamps that have *documented* Sandwich shades and globes, information is scarce. Lighting devices examined by the authors that were part of the households of factory glassworkers were simple glass, tin and pewter hand and table lamps. The larger lighting devices with expensive fuel-feeding mechanisms that would have been used in the homes of management are not as easily accessible. Without strong documentation, a collector should not purchase an early metal lamp and assume that the glass shade or globe is Sandwich, because all of the struggling American glass factories made the same types of lamp glasses, shades and globes.

Documentation in the form of catalog pages printed in the 1870's makes collecting shades and globes from the kerosene and gas era much easier. We can be comfortable with the knowledge gleaned from the eight pages of the 1874 Boston and Sandwich Glass Company catalog that follow, together with etching plates and decals that are housed in the Sandwich Glass Museum. Glassworkers' family collections have many examples that were taken home from the factories. Fragments of shades and globes that were dug at the Sandwich factory sites show the printed, engraved and etched designs that were used.

As shown on the 1874 catalog pages that follow, Sandwich lamp shades can be divided into four forms. *Cone shades with ring necks*, as shown in the Barlow-Kaiser photo 2185, are the most common. Less often seen are cone shades with a flared upper rim that was known as a *Tucker* or *Tucker top shade*, as shown in photo 2189. The *Peerless shade*, shown in the center of the third row on page 68 of the 1874 catalog, is the most difficult to find. To the right of the Peerless shades are two *Vienna shades*, another of which can be seen in photo 2193. The Vienna shade is shaped like the Tucker, but the bottom rim, or *fitter*, is smaller than the diameter of the shade.

Opal cone shades with ring necks are the most exciting to collect. Over one hundred different ring-necked cone shades were photographed for inclusion in the 1874 catalog, showing an unbelievably large assortment of designs and their variants. We can assume that catalogs issued in preceding and subsequent years pictured additional designs. So, when you find a cone shade with a design that is not depicted in the 1874 catalog, look in the catalog for a shade that has one part of the design painted or transferred onto it and another shade that has the rest of the design on it.

If you find a shade at an antiques show with a design that is not shown in the 1874 catalog or in this study of Sandwich lighting devices, proving it to be Sandwich will be difficult. Other glass houses made shades with similar designs.

Opal globes that were manufactured at the time the 1874 catalog was released can be divided into two categories, those used on kerosene lamps and those used on gas lighting devices. Kerosene globes had a larger diameter fitter that rested on a metal ring that surrounded the kerosene burner. Gas globes had a small diameter fitter so that they could be used to control the draft of the gas burners in use at that time (see Chapter 8). The gas globes were also highly decorated, as shown on page 69 of the catalog. By the late 1870's, the fitters on gas globes were increased in diameter for use on greatly improved gas burners. This new size was adaptable for use on kerosene burners.

In some cases, highly decorated opal gas globes interfered with the light. As gas burners were perfected that imparted a more even flame with an incandescent glow, globes were made from clear glass that was acid-etched into floral designs that completely covered the surface. The form of the upper rim was changed from a closed-in rim to an outwardly flaring configuration that directed the light upward and outward.

The manufacture of shades for candle-burning fairy lamps is documented in the 1887 Boston and Sandwich Glass Company sloar book. During the week of May 31, 1887, the shop of Nicholas Lutz made seventy-four blue shades, seventy red shades and seventy-three "fairy lamp shades to pattern". Forty-seven opal shades and twenty ruby shades were made during the week of June 6. Judging from the sloar book entries, all shades appear to have been made in solid colors. The authors do not have enough corroborating evidence to determine the types and patterns that could be reliably attributed to Sandwich.

Some of the striped (latticinio) shades that are occasionally found at antiques shops and shows could very well have been made by the shop of Nicholas Lutz. Many of the striped fragments dug from the factory site are small, so there is no way to tell whether they were from kerosene lamp fonts or fairy lamp shades. To date, we have not encountered a fairy lamp in the private collections of descendants of Sandwich glassworkers.

THESE SIMPLE HINTS WILL HELP YOU IDENTIFY SANDWICH LAMP SHADES AND GLOBES

In addition to the eight pages of lamp glassware reprinted in this chapter, study the cut, engraved, etched and decorated designs on tableware and vases pictured in the 1874 Boston and Sandwich Glass Company catalog. The reprint of the catalog has probably been the most valuable original document available to the glass collector and antiques dealer.

On decorated opal glass, look for depth and for perspective in hand-painted landscapes, leaves in shadow, flowers bending toward and away from the viewer.

Lamp shades with blown-out "puffy" patterns were not made in Sandwich.

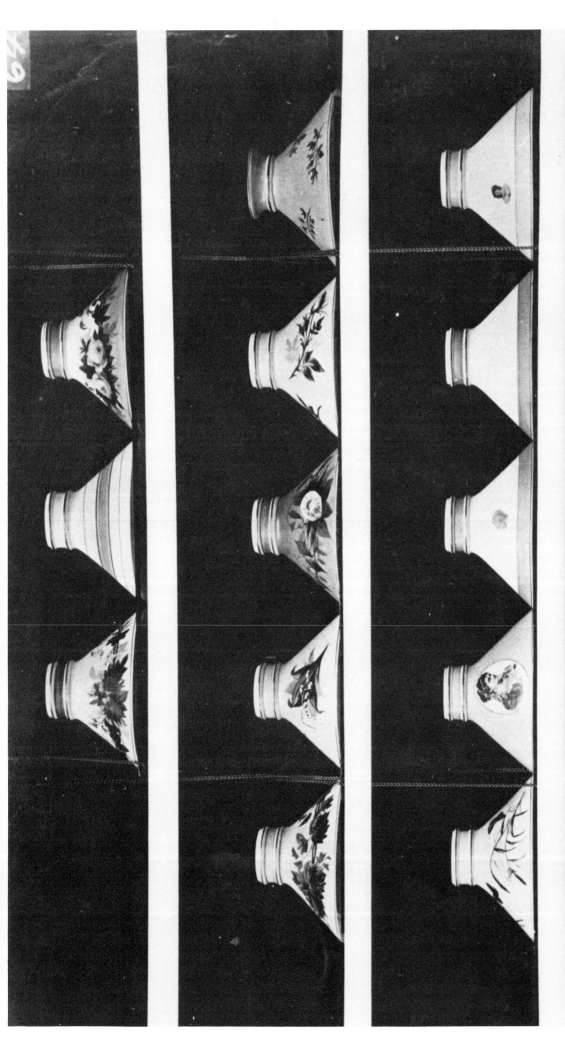

Page 64 of the 1874 Boston and Sandwich Glass Company catalog. The 10'' decorated opal cone shades all have ring tops except the Tucker top shade on the right of Row 2. Wholesale prices ranged from $13 per dozen for Row 1 No. 2 with the floated band to $40 per dozen for the heavily decorated shade in Row 2 No. 1. *Courtesy, Sandwich Glass Museum, Sandwich Historical Society*

Page 65 of the 1874 Boston and Sandwich Glass Company catalog. The 10'' decorated opal cone shades all have ring tops except the Tucker top shade in the center of Row 5. Some were completely hand painted and some were decorated by a combination of hand painting and transferred decals, called *decalcomania* or *decalcomanie* at the time of production. *Courtesy, Sandwich Glass Museum, Sandwich Historical Society*

Page 66 of the 1874 Boston and Sandwich Glass Company catalog. The 10" decorated opal cone shades all have ring tops. Identical designs were used on dome shades, which were not yet in style when this catalog was printed. It is satisfying to match a shade that you have purchased to a shade pictured in this catalog, but be aware that the elements of each design were combined in different ways. For example, the great blue heron in Row 4 No. 4 may be combined with the delicate painted band that surrounds the center of the shade in Row 4 No. 5. *Courtesy, Sandwich Glass Museum, Sandwich Historical Society*

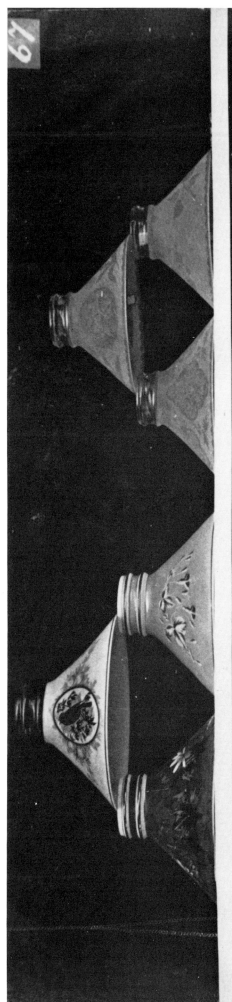
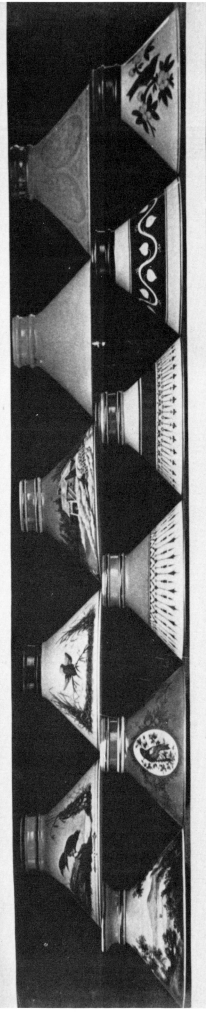

Page 67 of the 1874 Boston and Sandwich Glass Company catalog. All of the opal cone shades have ring tops except for the Tucker top shade with the landscape in Row 4 No. 1. This landscape and the snowscape in Row 3 No. 3 were the most expensive opal shades on this page, wholesaling for $36 per dozen. The four "decorated flint cone shades" pictured on the upper right were designs that were acid-etched onto clear glass. *Courtesy, Sandwich Glass Museum, Sandwich Historical Society*

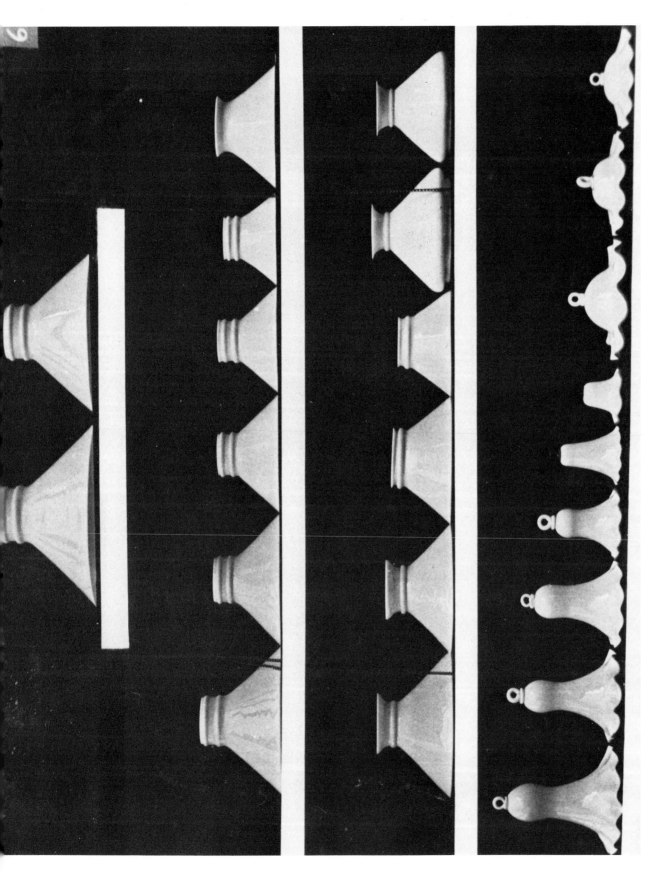

Page 68 of the 1874 Boston and Sandwich Glass Company catalog. Beginning with the top row, a 12″ opal cone shade with ring top is pictured, followed by 11″, 10″, 9″, 8″, 7″, 6″. Row 2 ends with an 8″ opal cone shade with Tucker top. Whether ringed or not, the flared top was identified as *Tucker*. Row 3: 12″ and 10″ opal Tucker top, two opal Peerless shades, two opal Vienna shades. Row 4: 8″ opal smoke bell with glass ring followed by 7″, 6″, 5″, 4″ opal smoke bell with metal ring followed by 3″; 8″ opal smoke shade with glass ring followed by 7″, 6″. *Courtesy, Sandwich Glass Museum, Sandwich Historical Society*

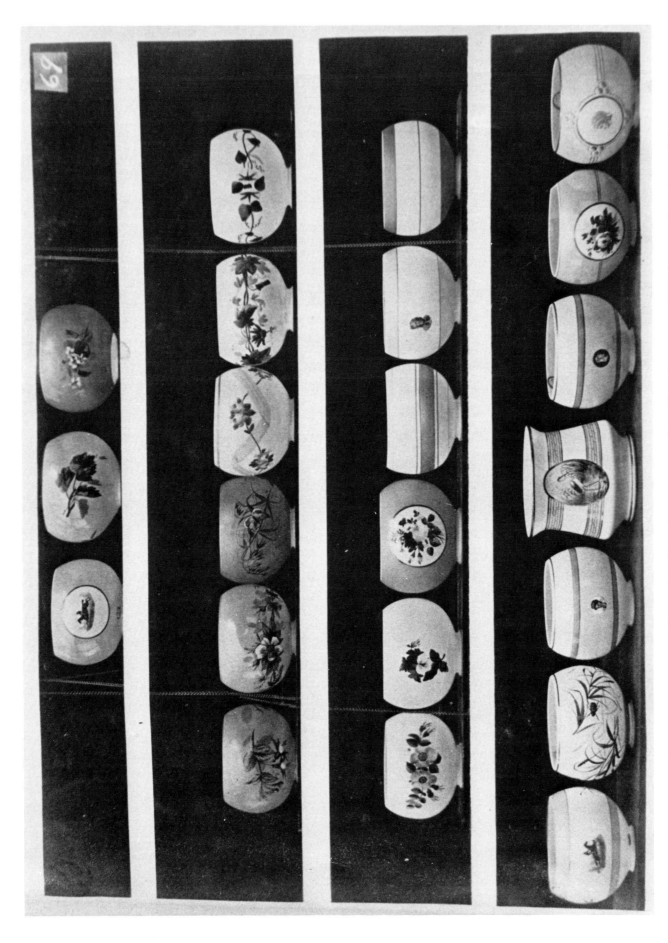

Page 69 of the 1874 Boston and Sandwich Glass Company catalog. Here is a page of 7″ decorated opal gas globes, except for the opal flower pot in the center of the bottom row. However, the flower pot is important to our study because the Key motif inside the horizontal bands was used as a border surrounding the medallion on a smoke bell. Most of the gas globes have small flared fitters. The transition to a larger diameter fitter was made by 1878. The larger fitter allowed the gas globe to be mounted on the globe ring of a kerosene lamp. *Courtesy, Sandwich Glass Museum, Sandwich Historical Society*

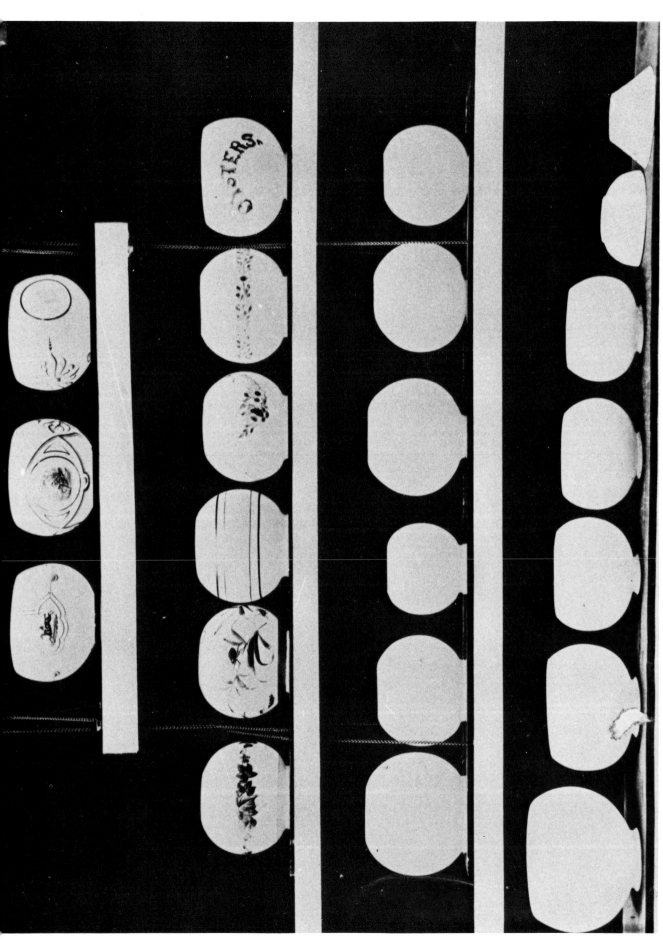

Page 70 of the 1874 Boston and Sandwich Glass Company catalog. Here is a variety of opal globes used for gas or kerosene. Row 1: 7" decorated gas globes. Row 2: decorated kerosene globes except for the lettered gas globe marked "OYSTERS". Row 3: 5" kerosene globe followed by 4", 3½"; 7½" Argand gas globe followed by 7", 6½". Row 4: five gas globes followed by a "globe shaped disc" and a "cone shaped disc". *Courtesy, Sandwich Glass Museum, Sandwich Historical Society*

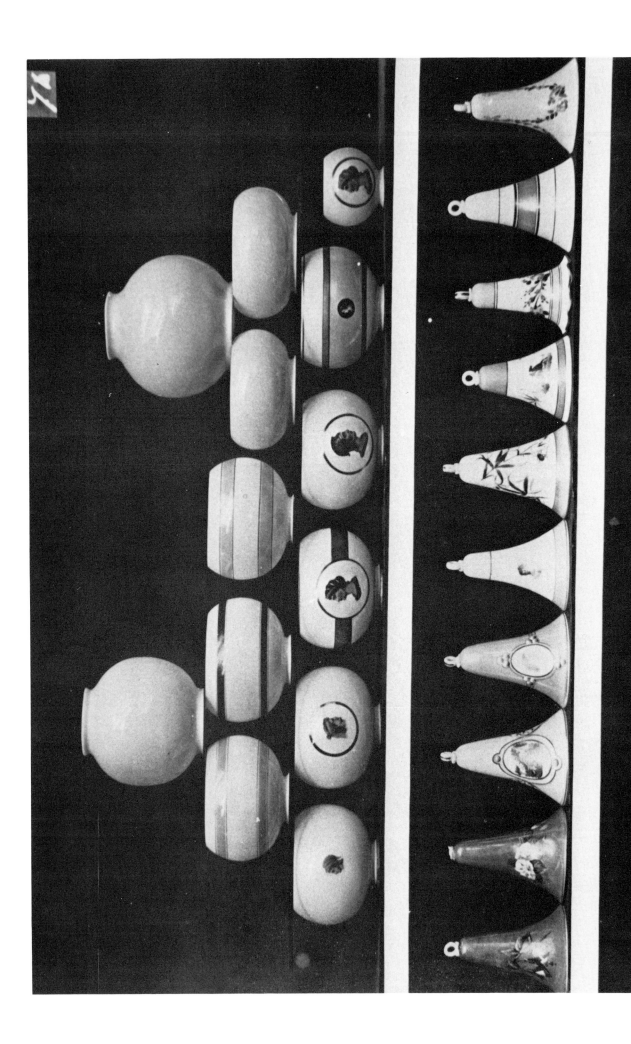

Page 71 of the 1874 Boston and Sandwich Glass Company catalog. Row 1: two opal hall globes, which had fitters at the top and bottom that secured into metal rings on the lighting fixture. Row 2: two decorated gas globes with small fitters, followed by two opal "flat shape" gas globes with the new large fitter. Row 3: five common size gas globes followed by a decorated toilet gas globe. Row 4: 6" and 7" decorated opal smoke bells with glass ring. The price list that originally accompanied the catalog referred to some designs by number and some by name, such as the "decorated Festoon" smoke bell at the extreme right. *Courtesy, Sandwich Glass Museum, Sandwich Historical Society*

2178 CUT ARGAND LAMP GLASS, LIVERPOOL SHAPE

1832–1840

When production of glass began at the Sandwich Glass Manufactory in 1825, Deming Jarves wrote detailed letters from Boston to his brother-in-law William Stutson, whom Jarves had put in charge of the glass works in Sandwich. As superintendent, it was Stutson's job to convey Jarves' instructions to the glass blowers so that the free-blown glass conformed to customers' specific needs. Jarves' letter dated November 23, 1825, contained drawings and measurements for several styles of lamp glasses. A Liverpool lamp glass is shown here. The fitter could be made straight-sided or flared, depending on the style of the burner. The upper portion was called the *tulip*, illustrated by Jarves with a plain rim. If a customer were to order this lamp glass, he would have asked for a "Liverpool lamp glass with ¾ tulip and turn-down rim". On December 8, 1827, Jarves advised Stutson to make the lower portion globe-shaped and the neck portion wider. "...being obliged to make them so narrow—cutting in with tools destroys the temper of the glass." The design was cut into the shade after it was annealed and roughed. A large flower above the fitter resembles a bellflower. An undulating band of punties and rosettes surrounds the tulip, and a chain of punties was cut on the upper surface of the rim. *Classical America, Alexandria, Virginia*

2179 ABOVE LAMP GLASS ON ARGAND MANTLE ARM LAMPS

Here is an original set of four roughed and cut Liverpool lamp glasses mounted on a magnificent set of bronze lamps with Argand burners. Note the slight variation in each of the free-blown lamp glasses. The tulip of the glass on the far left angles sharply where it meets the upper portion of the globe. Now study the third lamp glass that is on the right burner of the center lamp. The tulip flares out from the globe as a gentle curve. Lamps such as these were advertised as "mantle arm lamps". This set is labeled "J.&I. Wilcox New York" and is from the estate of Admiral Richard Byrd, who lived in Boston until his death in 1957. The circular wick lamps were invented by Swiss chemist Francois Aime Argand in the early 1780's. *Classical America, Alexandria, Virginia*

Deming Jarves was the sole owner of the Sandwich Glass Manufactory when he wrote this November 23, 1825, letter to William Stutson. Stutson was his brother-in-law and was in charge of operations at the Sandwich works. Jarves illustrated the styles of lamp glasses that were to be made. In the order in which they appeared in the letter, Jarves' drawings were referred to as *Liverpool lamp glass* (with tulip neck), *Mallory, globe lamp glasses, globe* (no neck), and another Liverpool lamp glass with tulip neck. *Courtesy, Sandwich Glass Museum, Sandwich Historical Society*

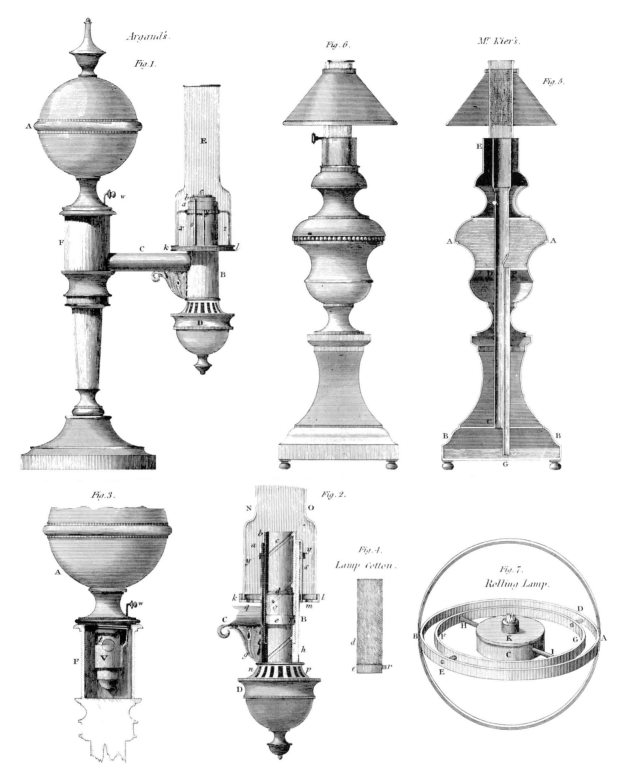

Argand's.

Fig. 1.

Fig. 6.

Mr. Kier's.

Fig. 5.

Fig. 3.

Fig. 2.

Fig. 4.
Lamp Cotton.

Fig. 7.
Rolling Lamp.

This is Plate 1 from the lamp section of *Ree's Cyclopedia of Sciences and Literature*, which was published in Philadelphia, Pennsylvania. The work took five years to complete. This plate, the authors have been advised, dates from c. 1815. Swiss chemist Francois Aime Argand was in Montpellier, France, when he perfected a lamp that gave a light equal to six or eight candles. In 1784, he patented it in England, describing it as, "A lamp so constructed as to produce neither smoak nor smell and to give considerably more light than any lamp hitherto known, by converting the smoak into flame, by causing a current of air to pass through the inside of the flame and by producing another current of air on the outside of the wick by means of a chimney." Figure 1 shows a complete Argand lamp. Font A held the heavy whale oil or colza oil. A mechanism that shut off the fuel when the lamp was not in use can be seen in Figure 3. The fuel was fed through the tubular arm C to the burner, in which concentric metal tubes held a cylindrical wick, as shown in Figure 2. Figure 4 shows Argand's cylindrical wick, or "lamp cotton". Although other people also designed concentric tube burners, the name *Argand* was used as a generic term into the 1900's.

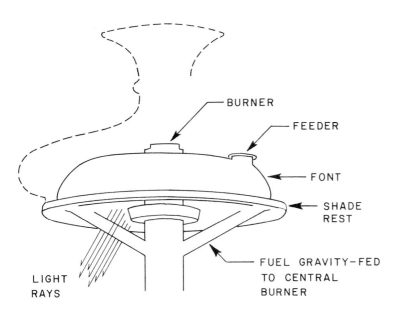

BURNER

FEEDER

FONT

SHADE REST

FUEL GRAVITY-FED TO CENTRAL BURNER

LIGHT RAYS

Fig. 10   The sinumbra lamp was designed to provide a downward light without casting a shadow. The burner was set on the standard below a hollow metal ring that acted both as a font for the fuel and as a rest for the shade. The shade had to be removed to fill the hollow ring font, which had a capped feeder. The font was supported in turn by two hollow tubes through which fuel was gravity fed to the burner in the center. The burner design was based on the principle perfected by Francois Aime Argand in the 1780's. The earliest fuels used in Argand burners were sperm oil and colza oil, made from the seeds of colza, a variety of cabbage. Even though highly refined, they were very heavy and worked best when draining downward toward the wick. Sinumbra shades have very narrow necks compared to kerosene shades.

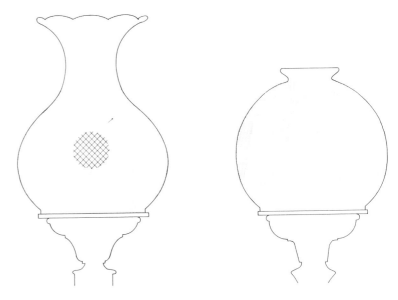

Fig. 11   Here are two styles of roughed and cut glass globes that were used on metal solar lamps in the 1840's and 1850's. Designs cut during this time period were bold. The fitter of the globe secured to a metal ring that rested on or surrounded the font.

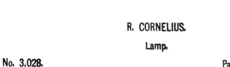

R. CORNELIUS.

Lamp.

No. 3,028.   Patented April 6, 1843.

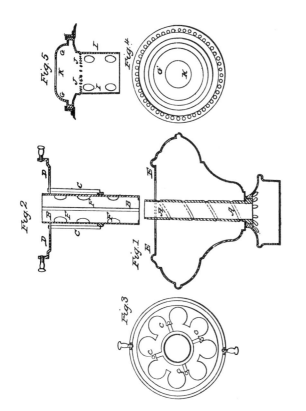

Popular in the 1840's, solar lamps had fonts in which the fuel surrounded the burner mechanism. This patent No. 3028 for a solar lamp that burned lard was taken out on April 6, 1843, by Robert Cornelius of Philadelphia, Pennsylvania. Fig. 1 shows the shape of the metal font that was in style at that time. The Argand burner shown in Fig. 5 took a slim, straight-sided chimney. A glass solar globe was secured by means of the set screws shown in Fig. 2.

2180 CUT ARGAND LAMP GLASSES

7½'' H. x 5½'' Dia. 1832–1840

This matching pair of cut shades is an excellent example of the type of ''lamp glasses'' that were used on lighting devices such as mantle arm lamps with Argand's burner. Some of the finest shades were cut during the first half of the Nineteenth Century. In this example, a combination of designs was lightly cut into the ground surface. Vesicas enclose a Strawberry Diamond design around the shoulder, with chains of punties above. Punties adorn the turned rim. A grape motif covers the lower portion. McKee and Brother showed a ''turn-over globe'' (i.e., referring to the turn-over of the rim) in the 1859–1860 catalog, but none are listed in later catalogs put out by McKee, Dietz, Russell and Irwin or any of the other catalogs available for study. It appears that the single style shown in the McKee catalog was a carryover for customers who had not yet converted to kerosene. Lamp glasses with turn-over rims are very, very scarce, so do not pass one by.

2181 CUT OVERLAY SINUMBRA (ASTRAL) SHADE ON SINUMBRA LAMP PRESENTED TO DEMING JARVES

(a) Shade 11'' H. x 14'' Dia.
(b) Lamp 21¾'' H. x 5⅞'' Sq. base
(c) Combined size 31⅜'' H. 1850–1860

Squatty, wide, boldly cut shades were produced to fit sinumbra lamps. The shadowless sinumbra lamp was first devised by George Phillips in 1820, five years before Jarves began making glass in Sandwich. Flint glass companies on the Eastern Seaboard and in the Pittsburgh area advertised their availability. One such announcement by Bakewell, Page and Bakewell in November 1828 listed ''an Assortment of ASTRAL, OR SINUMBRAL LAMPS On Pedestals and for Suspension''. The Boston and Sandwich Glass Company produced the shades in several sizes, as shown by a May 1826 invoice that referred to a 10'' astral shade. This ruby Overlay masterpiece would have been called a ''tulip Astral shade''. It was cut in a design of six-petaled flowers placed along continuous ribbons surrounding the shade. The prisms, which were not made in Sandwich, vary in size and have obviously been replaced over the years. The name ''DEMING JARVES'' was cut into the marble base. The Corning Museum of Glass has a solar lamp with a similar double-step marble base marked ''Thomas Leighton'', who became superintendent of the New England Glass Company in 1826 and died in 1849. Might both lamps have been assembled by lamp manufacturer William Carleton? *Courtesy, Sandwich Glass Museum, Sandwich Historical Society*

Jones, McDuffee and Stratton and its predecessor, Otis Norcross and Company, were Boston wholesale houses that handled glass made by the Boston and Sandwich Glass Company from the earliest days. This is page 42 from their catalog that appears to date from 1880 to 1890, showing six imported Faience lamps, five of which are fitted with a Sandwich shade or globe. The Boston and Sandwich Glass Company shipped separate fonts, pedestals, bases, shades, globes and chimneys to lamp assembly companies in Boston and elsewhere. The separate units were combined with units from other sources, both here and abroad. This catalog page documents that it is possible to find Sandwich shades and globes combined with foreign-made lamps and that lamp assembly companies were capable of "mixing and matching" unusual combinations. In 1889, Jones, McDuffee and Stratton bought all of the inventory and molds from the defunct Boston and Sandwich Glass Company works.

2182 TRANSFER PRINTS OF LADIES
1870–1887

The onset of non-lead opal shades and globes for kerosene lamps and gas brought about a demand for prints that could be transferred to the glass. *Decalcomania* or *decalcomanie* was "the art or process of transferring pictures and designs to china, glass, marble, etc., and permanently fixing them thereto". The term was shortened to *decal* in the Twentieth Century. This is a sheet of decals as purchased by the Boston and Sandwich Glass Company. All of the ladies' heads look to the left or right. This was more appealing on the rounded surface of a globe than a head facing forward. Generally, two or more were transferred onto each shade. A medallion in color, often black, was applied by brush after the print was in place. Horizontal bands were painted by a decorator (called a "liner"), and a background color was floated on. The shade was sent to the decorating kiln, where the piece was fired to set the color. *Courtesy, Sandwich Glass Museum, Sandwich Historical Society*

2183 TRANSFER PRINTS OF GREEKS AND ROMANS

1870–1887

These transfer prints were also found in Sandwich. They show Greek warriors, Roman gladiators and an assortment of men's heads from mythology. Each print has a red background, but the same designs have been found on glass without the background. Look closely at the faces and the headgear. If you find glass with these faces, you will have one more way to help attribute the piece to Sandwich. However, be aware that the prints were in demand by many glass companies and decorating houses that purchased them from the same sources, so the presence of a matching decal on a piece of glass does not guarantee Sandwich manufacture. *Courtesy, Sandwich Glass Museum, Sandwich Historical Society*

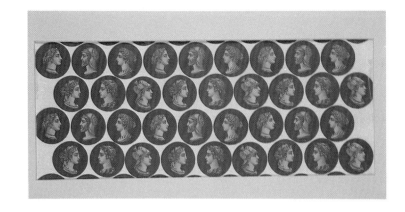

2184 TRANSFER PRINTS OF CHERUBS

1870–1887

This assortment has full-figure cherubs against a background of trees and bushes. The authors have not seen the cherubs transferred to glass without the other elements. When the decal was slid from the sheet onto the glass, the entire design was transferred. Prints were transferred onto other Sandwich items, many of which can be seen in the reprint of the 1874 Boston and Sandwich Glass Company catalog. *Courtesy, Sandwich Glass Museum, Sandwich Historical Society*

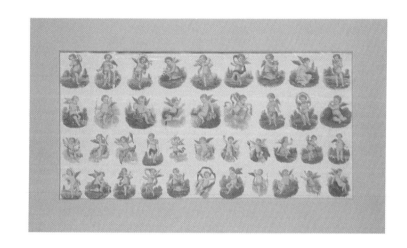

2185 BLOWN MOLDED OPAL CONE SHADE WITH RING TOP

5¾" H. x 9¾" Dia. 1870–1896

This was the most popular form of shade in the 1870's. In clear glass, it was frosted and etched with designs similar to those shown on globes in this chapter. Four examples were pictured on page 67 of the Boston and Sandwich Glass Company catalog. The authors have yet to purchase a clear etched example, but its production in opal glass was prolific. As shown on page 68 of the Boston and Sandwich catalog, it was made in seven sizes ranging from 6" to 12" Dia. The size in our photo was the most common 10" Dia., with the slight change in dimensions resulting from warping in the annealing leer or from the amount of excess glass that was machined from the rims. Undecorated, they were sold to be put on reading lamps. They were shipped as blanks to commercial decorators and lamp assembly houses that painted them to their own specifications. Records show that the Sandwich Co-operative Glass Company supplied blanks to all three Swann brothers: Edward J., who operated a decorating shop in Sandwich; Frederick, a partner in the New Jersey lamp decorating firm of Swann and Whitehead; and Ebenezer W. (See Chapter 16 in Volume 4 for this documentation.) Painting on china and glass at home using designs of their own choosing was the pastime of ladies in the late Victorian years. Shades that were painted too heavily or with busy designs cut down on the amount of light that the lamp put out. These amateur renderings can usually be distinguished from professional commercial ones.

2186 BLOWN MOLDED OPAL CONE SHADE WITH RING TOP DECORATED WITH DAISIES

5⅜" H. x 10" Dia. 1870–1887

Cone shades this size, with ring tops or "ring necks" as described in Union records, were the most common form of shade made. The beautiful work of Sandwich artists somehow set their shades apart from those executed in many other glass houses. The daisy chain completely surrounding the shade looks as though it had been fashioned in the field from daisies that had just been picked. Some are in full bloom, some are in bud, some lean toward the viewer, some bend away. The natural beauty captured forever on the shade is typical of the work done by the "females". (Editor's note: On June 29, 1858, Francis Kern was put in charge of "the room occupied by females". Decorating by women dates back to 1832.) See page 65 of the catalog for a similar shade. A vase decorated with daisies is shown in photo 3075. *Courtesy, Sandwich Glass Museum, Sandwich Historical Society*

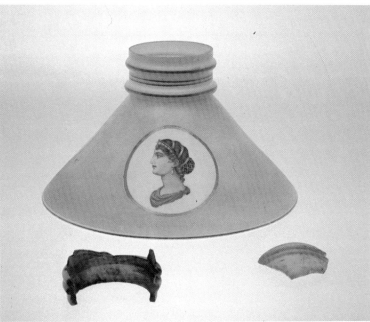

2187 BLOWN MOLDED OPAL CONE SHADE WITH RING TOP, GILDED AND DECORATED WITH LADY TRANSFER PRINTS

5⅜" H. x 10" Dia. 1870–1887

The mold that was used to make this decorated opal shade was the same style as the mold used to make the undecorated green student shade. The woman's head was a printed decal that was transferred from a sheet that was purchased from an outside source. The blue background was floated on by hand. The gilded lines were applied with a brush by spinning the shade on a decorator's wheel. In addition to the usual trim, this piece had two lines gilded between the rings of the neck. After the decorating was completed, the shade was sent to the decorating kiln, where heat caused the transfer prints and the applied pigments to become a permanent part of the shade. This decal is pictured on page 71 of the Boston and Sandwich Glass Company catalog.

2188 DETAIL OF ABOVE SHADE

Here is a close-up of the transfer print that appears on the opposite side of the previously shown ring top cone shade. The gilded medallion that frames the decal was hand applied. Note its unevenness, a good indication that the shade was decorated during this time period. This is the kind of detail to look for when you examine Sandwich shades. If the shade were a reproduction, the gold ring would be perfectly even. This transfer print can be seen on the gas globe illustrated on Plate 295 of the Mitchell, Vance and Company catalog. Other illustrations in the catalog show ring top cone shades inserted into the center extension units of gas chandeliers.

2189 BLOWN MOLDED OPAL CONE SHADE WITH TUCKER TOP, GILDED AND DECORATED WITH WARRIOR TRANSFER PRINTS

5" H. x 10½" Dia. 1870–1887

The simple lines on this shade and the ease with which it could be decorated are the reasons why the Boston and Sandwich Glass Company manufactured so many shades. Decorator Mary Gregory described in her diary a certain day on which she completely hand painted shades at the rate of fifteen minutes per shade. These shades have handwork that gave them appeal, yet were decorated in minimal time. The two warrior heads were transferred and the ground color was applied. The only detailed handwork required was the application of the gilded ovals that frame the prints and the narrow bands of gilding around the top and bottom of the shade. The dug fragment in the foreground matches the top of the shade.

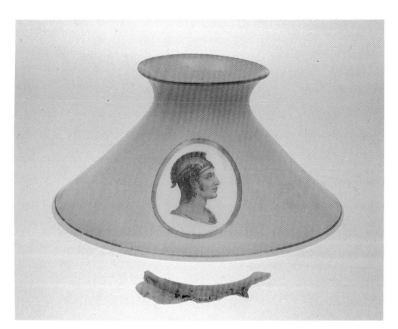

Michael Grady headed one of the shops responsible for making glassware for lamps during the closing years of the Boston and Sandwich Glass Company. The 1887 sloar book included "Tucker cones" in the assortment as well as library shades and crimped smoke shades. *Courtesy, Sandwich Glass Museum, Sandwich Historical Society*

2190 DETAIL OF ABOVE SHADE

Note the detail of the print that was transferred to the opposite side of the above shade. The eye is in shadow, the cheek has color. Some transfers can easily be mistaken for hand decorating. The white color that surrounds the head is the color of the glass before the ground color was applied, evidenced further by the white color inside these decorated shades. The gilt is badly worn at the bottom because people handled the shade when it was placed on and taken off the lighting device.

2191 BLOWN MOLDED OPAL GAS GLOBE, FLAT SHAPE, DECORATED WITH MYTHOLOGICAL TRANSFERS

5" H. x 8" Dia. 1870–1887

One of the most difficult items to preserve over a long period of time is a glass globe that is open on both the top and the bottom. They tend to crack when exposed to rapid temperature changes. Gas globes in particular are scarce. On one hand, when electricity became available, kerosene shades and globes remained on their lamps to be used when power failed. In contrast, because gas was piped from an outside source and gas fixtures were removed from walls and ceilings, there was no need or reason to take care of fittings because they had no future. Here is a fine example of a Sandwich gas globe in perfect condition. The design was listed as "Decorated Band and Medallion" at the time of production, as shown on page 71 of the catalog. The decorated gas globes on page 71 have a smaller fitter. The blank for the globe in our photo is the undecorated one that is farthest to the right on that page.

2192 SECOND VIEW OF ABOVE GLOBE

In the catalog, opal globes with straight fitters were identified as kerosene globes. All globes with flared fitters were identified as gas globes. However, a gas globe with a wide opening, such as is shown here, was sometimes adapted to kerosene lamps, especially on fonts that were suspended in chandeliers or brackets that fastened to a wall. Globe rings could be purchased that were placed on kerosene burners. They had three set screws to secure the flared fitter.

2193 BLOWN MOLDED OPAL VIENNA SHADE WITH TUCKER TOP FITTED TO PRESSED SHADE HOLDER

(a) Shade 5¼'' H. x 8'' Dia. 1870–1908
(b) Illuminator shade holder 3⅜'' H. x 7⅝'' Dia. 1888–1896

The Vienna shade has a fitter that is smaller in diameter than the body of the shade. Its strength lay in its form, which allowed the portion under the roll to rest on the flange of a metal shade ring or glass shade holder while the fitter secured it against horizontal movement. Because they chipped less easily, they were extremely successful into the 1900's and are still used today on electric student lamps. Two smaller sizes of opal Vienna shades were pictured on page 68 of the 1874 Boston and Sandwich Glass Company catalog. Production was continued at the Sandwich Co-operative Glass Company, where the Illuminator kerosene shade holder was also made. Both units were manufactured at Albert Vaughn Johnston's Boston and Sandwich Glass Company II, where small production runs took place in 1895 and 1896. This assembly can be seen on a lamp in photo 2307.

2194 UNITS OF ABOVE ASSEMBLY

Late in the kerosene era, Carl Votti invented the glass shade holder to take the place of the glass center chimney and metal shade ring or tripod. Votti's original patent was No. 182,973, which was issued on October 3, 1876. According to Patent Office records, the patent was reissued with more detail as No. 7511 on February 3, 1877. At this time, Votti assigned it to Bennett B. Schneider of New York. The patent was issued again as No. 10,087 on April 11, 1882, again assigned to Schneider. Fragments found at the Sandwich Co-operative Glass Company site were marked ''B B SCHNEIDER'S ILLUMINATOR PAT OCT 3, 1876 REIS APRIL 11, 1882''. When used with the proper burner that had apertures for the admission of air, ''the shade and shade holder together constituted the draft-inducing device for the burner''. The lamp burned cleanly and steadily, providing excellent light through the clear holder and a soft glow through the opal shade to light the room. The Illuminator shade holder can be found with and without the patent dates. It provides an excellent example of a private mold sent to the glass company that quoted the lowest price.

This patent was originally issued to Carl Votti of Newark, New Jersey, as No. 182,973 on October 3, 1876. It was reissued twice when Votti assigned it to Bennett B. Schneider of New York as No. 7511 on February 13, 1877, and again as No. 10,087 on April 11, 1882. Fragments of the glass shade holder bearing the 1876 and 1882 dates were found at the Co-op site. Votti suggested that the shade and glass holder had several advantages over the common chimney arrangement: the burner was readily accessible for cleaning and wick trimming; and the annoyance of a broken chimney was avoided.

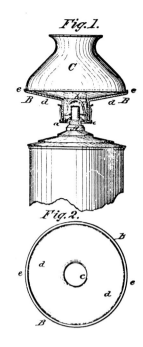

2195 BLOWN MOLDED OPAL VIENNA SHADE WITH TUCKER TOP DECORATED WITH FLOWER

5¼'' H. x 8'' Dia. 1870–1887

There were two styles of Tucker tops, one with a simple flare and the other with the ringed flare shown here. The decorated shades that we show both on lamps and alone represent all we have been able to find without damage in over thirty-five years of searching. This Vienna example is in the collection of descendants of gaffer John Murray. The design is delicate, but fills the surface nicely. On some shades, the design was repeated on the opposite side. The number of hand painted designs on Sandwich lamp shades is endless. The authors suggest that you refer to the shades, vases and flower pots shown in the 1874 catalog reprint. When shopping for shades to purchase, study their detail as if you were considering a painting on canvas. Look for perspective created by curled leaves, twisted stems, grayed shadows. Note here the foolish sapling germinating from a seed that did not know it was still part of a pistil. This whimsical touch may have been inspired by the acid-etched design in photo 2235.

2196 BLOWN MOLDED OPAL VIENNA SHADE WITH TUCKER TOP, DECORATED WITH MORNING GLORIES

4⅜'' H. to machined rim; 7¾'' Dia. 1872–1893

Our descriptions of various forms of shades were taken from Boston and Sandwich Glass Company records. A Vienna shade was shown on page 68 of their catalog. This term referred to the form of the lower portion, rolled under with a smaller diameter fitter. The shade pictured here should have a flared rim which must have been damaged. It was cut back to the decorated line on the ring, making its value significantly less. Vienna shades were used on the student lamps that became popular in the 1870's and on the clear glass Illuminator shade holder patented by Carl Votti of Philadelphia in 1876. The Morning Glory design was pictured on cone shades on pages 64 and 67 of the Boston and Sandwich catalog. There is no doubt that they were painted by a decorator trained by Edward J. Swann, who began working in Sandwich late in 1872. The design has all of his characteristics, but not his masterful touch. For more information about Swann, see Chapter 12 in Volume 4. Study also the decorated vases in Chapter 2 of Volume 3. *Courtesy, Sandwich Glass Museum, Sandwich Historical Society*

2197 BLOWN MOLDED OPAL CONE SHADE, GILDED AND DECORATED
5" H. x 9" Dia. 1875–1887

This shade is a family heirloom preserved by descendants of Hiram Dillaway and James D. Lloyd. The cone form with the top expanded into a lip was not pictured in the 1874 catalog, although similar gilded and decorated designs do appear. The lip was used to hang the shade from a metal ring on a suspension lamp. When searching for Boston and Sandwich Glass Company shades, watch for delicate, hand-painted, open designs that are intricate and well proportioned. Look for a combination of handwork, lined detail and floated color. The molds in which opal shades were blown were purchased by the Boston and Sandwich Glass Company and were not designed exclusively for its use. This particular form was also used by decorator Alfred E. Smith of New Bedford, Massachusetts, and can be seen in a Gillinder and Sons catalog. An undecorated one hangs in the center unit of an electric chandelier in the Florida home of Thomas Alva Edison.

2198 BLOWN MOLDED OPAL WIDE TOP CONE SHADE DECORATED WITH AUTUMN LEAVES
6" H. x 14" Dia. 1875–1896

Two clues help us to date this shade. First, the largest shade shown in the 1874 Boston and Sandwich Glass Company catalog was 12" Dia. and, second, this form was not shown at all. However, autumn leaves were painted onto Sandwich shades more often than many other motifs, so the 1874 catalog is the best original source when checking shades to see if they were painted in Sandwich. Autumn leaves were painted on a ring top shade on page 65 of the catalog. A design with similar wisps of dried grass is shown on page 69. The arrangement of a chain of wispy leaves and wildflowers is a simple one. Even though the flat leaves were quickly executed, there is a subdued shadow, as if the sun was shining onto the design. The authors have seen this shade on a suspension lamp meant to be hung from the ceiling.

2199 BLOWN MOLDED OPAL CONE SHADE DECORATED WITH WINTER SCENE
5" H. x 14" Dia. 1880–1887

This large shade was in a lamp that hung over the dining room table of decorator Annie Mathilda Nye's descendants. Miss Nye began painting at the Boston and Sandwich Glass Company in 1880. On July 31, 1880, her friend and fellow decorator Emma Wentworth Gregory wrote in her diary "Annie Nye is doing nicely." A study of this shade and other family pieces shows that Miss Nye was an extremely talented decorator. She worked side by side with Emma and Emma's sister, Mary Gregory. All three women painted winter scenes. Annie remained with the company after the official closing on January 2, 1888, to finish up the last of the decorating work in a building that had previously housed the Cape Cod Glass Company.

2200 SECOND VIEW OF ABOVE SHADE

The snowscape continues completely around the shade. Although it consists of three distinct scenes, the main house is the center of interest and the pond and barn have less importance. The pigment brushed on the shade was very thin to allow the light to glow from within. No white paint was used. The opal glass was untouched where white was needed, a characteristic of Sandwich decorated ware. Look for depth of perspective. For example, in this photo there is a tree in the foreground and, to the right of it, a point of land extending into the water. Winter scenes on cone shades in the 1874 Boston and Sandwich Glass Company catalog and on a dome shade on the Jones, McDuffee and Stratton catalog page use these devices to lend perspective. A warm weather landscape on page 66 of the Boston and Sandwich catalog was composed in the same manner.

2201 THIRD VIEW OF ABOVE SHADE

The 1874 Boston and Sandwich Glass Company catalog shows no shade larger than 12'' Dia. This example is shown in an 8'' Dia. size on page 68. We can safely date large shades after the printing of the catalog.

2202 BLOWN MOLDED OPAL DOME (LIBRARY) SHADE, GILDED AND DECORATED WITH FISH AND GAME TRANSFER PRINTS
6¼'' H. x 14'' Dia. 1875–1887

The rounded, or *dome*, style of shades came into use after the printing of the 1874 Boston and Sandwich Company catalog. This 14'' size was the largest listed by the Sandwich local of the American Flint Glass Workers Union in the early 1880's. The 1887 sloar book showed that John Louvet, who was noted for blowing very large pieces, completed a number of 14'' domes. This size is often overlooked by Sandwich collectors because they extend into a later time period. They were used in kerosene suspension lamps that could be pulled down over a table to provide bright illumination. The pheasant and hare design was a transfer print, but the shadow was hand painted to give depth. A Sandwich decorator framed the print in black. The ferns were done by hand, using gilding intermixed with green paint. *Courtesy, Sandwich Glass Museum, Sandwich Historical Society*

2203 SECOND VIEW OF ABOVE SHADE

Here again you can see the shadowing that lent depth to the fish transfer. Very seldom was the same design repeated on the same shade. They were quickly cut apart from a sheet of prints and applied in whatever order they happened to be. The background color was referred to as a *floated ground* because a thin coat was floated on with a large brush. It and the gilded ferns are faded by time and countless washings. Expect to find this kind of wear on decorated shades that are over one hundred years old. Both transfer prints can be seen on page 65 of the Boston and Sandwich catalog.

2204 BLOWN MOLDED OPAL DOME (LIBRARY) SHADE DECORATED WITH CHICKADEES AND HOUSES

6'' H. x 14'' Dia. 1875–1887

This library shade was completely hand decorated. When searching for Sandwich hand painted shades, question in your mind whether the scene is a New England one. As far back as the authors have been able to document, through written and oral record, the men in charge of the decorating department sent artists out to the woods and fields. They brought back renderings of Cape Cod and New England scenes, which were simplified for execution on glass. When a design became an established part of the decorating program, it was repeated over and over by the artists who perfected it. It is therefore possible to find all of the shades shown here. Expect minor variations, because each artist had his own technique. *Courtesy, Sandwich Glass Museum, Sandwich Historical Society*

2205 SECOND VIEW OF ABOVE SHADE

When large shades came into use, artists had more room to express their talent. Although most shades were for commercial purposes, an occasional one can be found with enough extra detail to lead us to believe it was painted to be taken home to a member of the family. Particularly on large shades, the artists painted a main subject intended to be for the front of the lamp. More detail was concentrated to please the eye. The rest of the shade was usually filled in with color to blend in with the main subject, and, in some instances such as this, small subjects with lesser detail were painted on the back. Note the depth of the design—the chickadees can almost be touched, a twig can almost be picked. One can almost walk down the paths that lead to the houses.

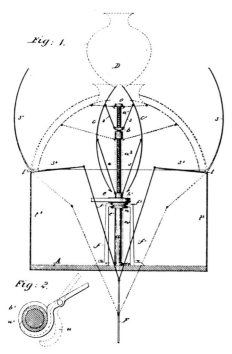

Dennis J. Lorden was a Sandwich glassworker and a member of the American Flint Glass Workers Union, Local No. 16. On November 23, 1885, he filed an application for a machine to be used ''in the manufacture of glass globes or shades of the dome class for lamps.'' We present Lorden's patent in its entirety because it describes fully how a dome shade began life as a glass tube. The *Sandwich Observer* on December 29, 1885, announced to local citizens that Lorden invented and patented a shade making machine. The patent was granted on July 20, 1886. This gives you some idea of the length of time a new design or method of manufacture could be in use prior to its patent date. By October 1887, Lorden was employed by the New England Glass Works.

Continuation follows glossary.

2206 BLOWN MOLDED OPAL GLOBE DECORATED WITH SPRIGS OF FLOWERS

4½'' H. x 4½'' Dia. 1875–1908

Production of small kerosene globes was continued into later years when fledgling companies sought to maintain glass production in Sandwich. The blank for this globe was pictured in three sizes on page 70 of the 1874 Boston and Sandwich Glass Company catalog. Designs of sprigs with more detailed flowers spaced over the surface were shown on several cone shades on page 65 and on a water bottle and tumbler set shown on page 58. Simple brush-stroke decoration was a labor-saving technique started during the closing years of the Boston and Sandwich Glass Company and continued at Charles W. Spurr's cutting shop and decorating room located at the Cape Cod Glass Company site from 1888 to 1891. The opal blank saw continuous manufacture at the Sandwich Co-operative Glass Company from 1888 until 1891, followed by other small companies at the Boston and Sandwich site. Opal globes were made and decorated by numerous glass and lamp assembly factories in the East and Midwest, but you cannot attribute them to Sandwich unless they match the designs in the 1874 catalog and you have documentation from descendants of Sandwich employees.

2207 BLOWN MOLDED OPAL GLOBE, GILDED AND DECORATED WITH SPRIGS OF FLOWERS

5⅜'' H. x 4⅝'' Dia. 1875–1887

When purchased, this globe was fitted to a Plume and Atwood burner that converted a fluid lamp to kerosene, as shown in photo 2278. This form of globe, taller than it is wide, was not shown in the reprint of the 1874 Boston and Sandwich Glass Company catalog. However, the flowers have been found on fragments dug from the site. The pink and blue flowers resemble cornflowers. The ability of Sandwich artists to adapt natural flora and fauna from the New England environment added a delicate touch to the globes when they were lighted. The flowers are geometrically spaced over the surface. There are four single flowers, with stems hanging down, placed around the upper part of the globe and four around the lower part. The four sprigs of double flowers around the center were painted in an interesting way. The lower flowers were painted in the usual manner when the globe was in an upright position, but the upper flowers were painted by placing the globe upside down.

2208 BLOWN MOLDED OPAL GLOBE CASED WITH PINK

4½'' H. x 4½'' Dia. 1880–1887

This small globe was made by covering opaque white glass with an outer layer of pink glass. The term *casing* was used to describe the placement of a layer of colored glass either on the inside or outside of a piece. When the outer layer is cut back to show the white glass beneath, it is referred to today as *Overlay*. The straight fitter tells us that the globe was meant to be fitted to a kerosene burner. The metal ring protected the rim from being chipped when the globe was lowered over a chimney. The same type of metal ring was used on small globes that were made in a variety of colors during the last years of production at the Boston and Sandwich Glass Company. Note that all globes and shades have a smooth surface. There is no indication that blown-out ''puffy'' patterns such as cherubs or flowers were ever made at Sandwich, even though this technique was used on opal vases in the 1870's.

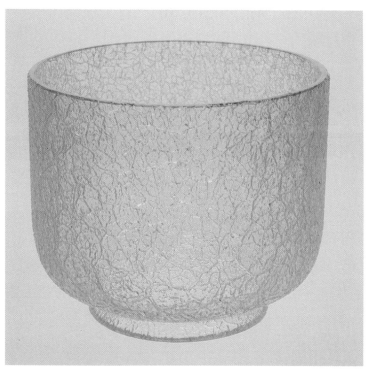

2209 OVERSHOT (FROSTED WARE) CYLINDRICAL GAS SHADE

5¼'' H. x 6'' Dia. 1880–1887

The process by which clear cullet was reduced to tiny pieces and applied to the surface of an article was perfected by the time the 1874 catalog was printed. Complete sets of Frosted Ware for the table and toilet were pictured that can be used to identify glassware found in the antiques marketplace today. Some pieces were enhanced with gilt, as seen on the rim of this piece. However, the catalog shows no lighting shades or globes in this manufacturing technique that is called "Overshot" by contemporary collectors. There were no cylindrical shades at all in the Boston and Sandwich catalog or in any of the other gas fixture catalogs we have examined that date from the 1860's and 1870's. Therefore, we conclude that the form was a late one. A detailed study of Frosted Ware is in Chapter 6 of Volume 4.

2210 THREADED CYLINDRICAL GAS SHADE ENGRAVED WITH LEAVES

5'' H. x 7'' Dia. 1880–1887

As discussed in detail in Chapter 13 of Volume 4, the method of extruding threads of glass by machine onto the surface of blown glass was perfected in England. A report in *Crockery Journal* on February 12, 1880, stated that the Boston and Sandwich Glass Company had added fine, threaded glassware to its inventory. Its acceptance by the public was instantaneous, resulting in large amounts being made in the tableware forms that can be seen in the 1874 catalog. By this time, the method of frosting glass by roughing it with sand was superseded by sandblasting and by applying hydrofluoric acid to the surface. The leaves were executed in the same manner, and the stems and berries were engraved. The frosted bands and leaf motif used here to soften the harsh gaslight was the continuation of a design often used on the earliest kerosene shades. When a gas shade had no fitter, it was held to the gas fixture by dropping it down into a metal basket-like frame that took the place of the shade ring. The glass shade became an insert, or liner, held securely by the metal straps that surrounded it.

2211 PRESSED OVAL HOBNAIL CYLINDRICAL GAS SHADE

6'' H. x 6'' Dia. 1880–1896

The number of fragments dug at the Boston and Sandwich Glass Company factory site attests to the production (and breakage) of great quantities of shades with oval hobnails. Ruby was the most predominant color and was used mostly in hallways where a soft light was needed. The reworking of all of the Oval Hobnail gas shades was extensive. Although pressed in a cylindrical mold, reheating and fire polishing blurred and flattened the pattern. The bottom rim was flared to make a fitter that could be held securely in an upright position by set screws in a metal ring that surrounded the gas jet.

2212 PRESSED OVAL HOBNAIL GAS SHADE WITH GAUFFERED RIM

4¼" H. x 8⅛" Dia. 1880–1896

This flared form was made by reheating and expanding a shade that had been formed in a cylindrical mold. The rim was then shaped, or *gauffered*, into the ten-flute configuration. This reworking flattened and elongated the hobnails, disfiguring them part way down the side. The piece was marketed as a gas shade but was sometimes fitted to the globe ring of a kerosene burner. All deep red to light pink articles were referred to as *ruby*. The differences in color were caused by the amount of coloring agent added to the batch and the thickness of the finished article. Several glass factories manufactured this shade, including Gillinder and Sons in Philadelphia, Pennsylvania. A green shade fixed to a gas lamp can be seen in photo 2214.

2213 PRESSED OVAL HOBNAIL GAS SHADE WITH GAUFFERED RIM

4¼" H. x 8" Dia. 1880–1896

Here is the same shade in green, a color that is more difficult to find today. Although this green example is the same size as the ruby one, the handwork that was necessary to reshape the upper half gave it a completely different character. The sides slope at a different angle. The ten flutes into which the rim was gauffered undulate unevenly. The ovals in the uppermost row were elongated to the point where they appear to be a molded ring just below the rim. The flared fitters of both shades are the same diameter, yet each has a different "look" when placed side by side. Characteristics such as the ones described here are clues that help us establish a manufacturing date for glass. This shade mounted on a gas lamp is shown in photo 2214.

2214 ABOVE SHADE ON GAS FIXTURE

Because gas had to be piped in, it was necessary for all of the hanging gas fixtures to be permanently attached to the ceiling. The tubes that carried the gas to the burner were incorporated into the design of the fixture. In this very simple lamp, gas flowed down the single pipe through the ceiling into both tubes that surround the shade to a shutoff cock that can be seen in the center beneath the shade. Keep in mind that the flame of the gas jet burned in an upright position, surrounded by a mantle that produced an incandescent light. This is the reason for the unusual configurations of gas fixtures. The metal smoke shade was stamped with a design that matched the ceiling canopy. Some had glass smoke bells.

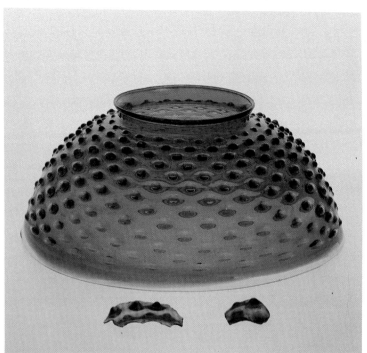

2215 PRESSED OVAL HOBNAIL DOME SHADE

5¾" H. x 14" Dia. 1880–1896

This dome-shaped shade is the large library size that was meant to be placed on a kerosene suspension lamp. The lamp was inserted into a metal fixture that hung near the ceiling from chains and could be lowered by a pulley mechanism. Note the bottom rim that shows only clear glass. The red glass is a thin layer on the inside of the dome. The blue fragments in the foreground were dug from the Boston and Sandwich Glass Company site. Red, blue and green fragments were dug in quantity. Canary is rare. Unlike the blown molded Oval Hobnail vases and colognes shown in Volume 3 of *The Glass Industry in Sandwich*, the pressed inner surface of this shade is smooth. A Gillinder and Sons catalog illustrated this dome. It was listed in three sizes and two colors, one of which was "ruby". This proves that domes of this style were not all made in Sandwich.

2216 BLOWN MOLDED GLOBE ACID-ETCHED WITH FLEUR-DE-LYS

4½" H. x 4½" Dia. 1875–1887

The Fleur-de-lys motif was incorporated into designs and patterns in glass throughout the 1800's. When translated, it means "flower of the lily", a pattern that was combined with scrolls and used extensively on Lacy toy dishes dating back to the 1830's (see photos 3336-3339 in Volume 3). When acid-etching became a popular and inexpensive way to soften the glare of a kerosene flame, the Fleur-de-lys was continued by many glass companies as one of many designs that adapted well to the rounded surface of a globe. This 4½" size globe can be seen with a wreath design on a lamp in photo 2117. It was a size that saw much use on lamps that were converted to kerosene. The example shown here has a chip that hurts its value. The *Barlow-Kaiser Sandwich Glass Price Guide* gives prices for glass in perfect condition, but also tells you how to price damaged pieces.

2217 BLOWN MOLDED KEROSENE SHADE ACID-ETCHED WITH GREEK KEY

3¾" H. x 5½" Dia. 1880–1887

This small shade is shown in photo 2272 on a tripod fitted to a Plume and Atwood Argand burner. It is not uncommon for a one-hundred year-old lamp to have had several replacement fittings. Finding an original shade in pristine condition with its original tripod is most difficult. They were often chipped from the arms of the tripod. Later replacements were more expertly produced, visibly revealing higher quality. When searching for original shades, look for certain characteristics: the thickness of the etched bands will vary; some of the Greek Key designs may be thicker than others; edges of the acid-etched portions will show brush marks. The design around the top of the shade is a variant—a cross between Greek Key and Roman Key designs. Combinations of designs can vary with each shade.

2218 ETCHING PLATE

1870–1887

This is one of several similar designs on a glass etching plate that originally belonged to the Russell family, which had two generations of members working at the glass factory. Variations of this design, sometimes combined with bands of Greek Key or Roman Key designs, were acid-etched into clear and opal cone shades. The Dietz catalog illustrated a hanging lamp globe etched with a head similar to those on the sheet of transfers shown in photo 2183, showing that this type of decoration began to gain momentum in the late 1860's. When used on opal glass and accented with black paint, the Boston and Sandwich Glass Company catalog described the designs as "black figure". See the black figure vase in photo 3064. *Courtesy, Sandwich Glass Museum, Sandwich Historical Society*

2219 BLOWN MOLDED OPAL DOME SHADE

5⅛" H. x 8" Dia. 1880–1896

Although dome shades did not appear in the 1874 Boston and Sandwich Glass Company catalog, large quantities of fragments similar to that shown in the foreground were dug in an area of the factory yard that indicated production between 1878 and 1885. Through the efforts of Dr. Jon Wetz, it has been established that most forms of opal shades manufactured at the large factory were continued by the Sandwich Co-operative Glass Company, which was in production from 1888 until 1891. The flared Tucker top first used on cone shades with plain or Vienna fitters was adapted to the new dome form. The Vienna-type fitter on this dome, smaller in diameter than the widest part of the dome, rested on an all-glass shade holder or was held in place by a metal shade ring that was supported by wire arms back to the burner. Made in several sizes, this form of shade was often combined with a student lamp. The Sandwich Co-operative Glass Company, as well as other glass companies during the 1890's, sold plain white shades and domes as blanks to decorating houses and lamp assembly companies that had decorating departments.

2220 BLOWN MOLDED DOME STUDENT SHADE

6" H. x 10" Dia. 1880–1896

Dome shades were not shown in catalogs or lamp patents much before 1880, but, once production began at many American glass factories, their use was widespread into the 1900's. The bulk of the fragments dug at the Boston and Sandwich Glass Company were made with a white inner layer and a green outer layer, a technique called *flashing*. It was perfected in the 1880's with the development of formulas for glass that melted at a much lower temperature. The previously formed blown molded white shade was flashed with a coating of green glass that had a low melting point, so the original white shade was not distorted in the process. This dome shade was also made at the Sandwich Co-operative Glass Company in the green student style and in white opal. Left plain or decorated, it was extensively used on kerosene table lamps and on "gas portables", which were table lamps that could be moved because they were fed from an outside source by flexible tubing. An interesting variety of gas table lamps was shown in Dr. Larry Freeman's *New Light on Old Lamps*. Expect to find the rim at the top and the rim on the fitter ground to smooth out the surplus glass.

2221 BLOWN MOLDED CONE STUDENT SHADE WITH RING TOP
5½'' H. x 9½'' Dia. 1880–1896

The cone form in white opal glass dates from c. 1870, but shades flashed with an outer layer of dark green were first made to compliment a very successful new style of metal kerosene device called the student, or study, lamp. Student lamps were first patented in the United States in the 1870's. By the 1880's, many patents had been issued and lamp companies marketed them with great success. They were styled after Argand burner mantle arm lamps as shown in photo 2179, streamlined to cast very little shadow. A tall, narrow, cylindrical font on one end of a horizontal tube fed kerosene through the tube to an Argand burner on the opposite end. This arrangement could slide up and down on a vertical rod connected to a weighted base. Their acceptance was such that colleges ordered them in large numbers for dormitories. The dark green prevented glare from disturbing a sleeping roommate, while the light reflecting off the white glass provided excellent downlight onto a desk, making long hours of paperwork less tedious. This shade is a high quality one that has a resonant ring.

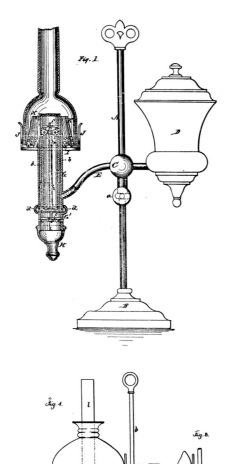

This patent for a student lamp was issued to Edward Stolpe on March 10, 1874. It was one of many styles of metal lamps patented in the 1870's and 1880's that were devised to cast very little shadow onto the work area. Some patents illustrated lamps with a fuel font mounted directly on a standard. The burner was attached to an arm that extended horizontally from the side of the font, through which the fuel was fed. They all bore a striking resemblance to the c. 1830 Argand mantle arm lamp. The font of this model patented by Stolpe and an 1889 one patented by Adolph Kleeman so closely followed the form of the Argand font that we might consider them to be "reproductions" in their time period.

The model patented by Albert Angell on January 16, 1883, is the type we most easily recognize as a student lamp. The tube that fed the fuel from the cylindrical font to the burner served as an arm that held both units. The height was adjusted by moving the device along the vertical stand that was fastened to a weighted base. Glass factories in Sandwich supplied shades for the numerous styles of lamps that were available. The principle of the shadow-free arm and slender burner was adapted to desk lamps with two burners, ceiling suspension lamps with one or two burners, and lamps that swung out from the wall on a bracket.

2222 BLOWN MOLDED OPAL GAS OR ELECTRIC SHADE

3¼'' H. x 7⅛'' Dia. 1888–1891

This shade was one of many found in a barn in the Cape Cod village of Yarmouth Port. The group of opal shades has documentation in the form of family records that ties it to the Sandwich Co-operative Glass Company, the small factory that operated for three years after the Boston and Sandwich Glass Company closed. However, unless you have unquestionable documentation, there is no way to determine origin, because this style was made over a period that began with the advent of electricity and extended well into the 1900's. The authors have seen this shade combined with opal globes on an elaborate electric chandelier that dated from the turn of the century. They can be seen today on chandeliers hanging in the restored Fort Meyers, Florida, home of Thomas Alva Edison. Glassware for electrical fixtures were manufactured all through the 1880's by the Boston and Sandwich Glass Company. Its production was a mainstay for the struggling companies that followed. The fitter is 2⅜'' Dia. Depending on the diameter of the fitter, some were used upside down on gas fixtures. The mold into which it was blown had a plain rim. The shallow flutes were hand formed after removal from the mold.

2223 BLOWN MOLDED OPAL GAS OR ELECTRIC SHADE

3¼'' H. x 5⅞'' Dia. 1888–1891

This opal shade is similar to other Sandwich Co-operative Glass Company shades with which it had been stored in a Yarmouth Port, Massachusetts, barn. All of the fitters on the Yarmouth Port group were 2⅜'' Dia. The wavy rim was formed by reheating and hand crimping after the shade had been removed from the mold. This method was also used on smoke bells. The authors were fortunate to have located Co-op glass from two family collections. See Chapter 16 in Volume 4 for documented Co-op tableware.

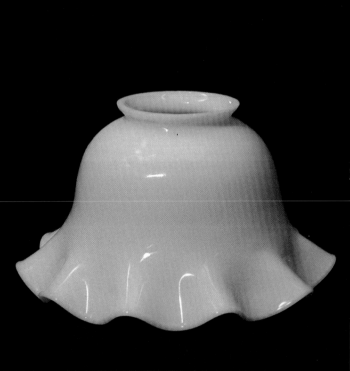

2224 PRESSED OPAL FLUTED GAS SHADE

1½'' H. x 7⅝'' Dia. 1888–1891

This shade was used on ''Solar incandescent gas lamps'', as pictured in an advertisement by the New York firm of Imperial Gas Machine Company. A mantle like one used on a present-day Coleman lantern hung over the gas jet, enclosed by a slender, cylindrical chimney. The 2⅜'' fitter suspended the shade on wire prongs that held it level with the top of the mantle. Opal shades as plain as this cannot be attributed to a specific manufacturer without documentation. The need was so great that many factories produced them. They are readily available in the antiques marketplace today.

2226 BLOWN MOLDED OPAL GAS GLOBE ON WALL FIXTURE

5'' H. x 7'' Dia. 1870–1908

The transition from gas globes with small diameter fitters to those with large diameter fitters that reduced flickering took place in the mid–1870's. The Boston and Sandwich Glass Company catalog that the authors often mention was printed at that time, so both types of fitters were pictured. The globe in this photo has a large flared fitter. It is secured by three screws to a brass fixture that would have been advertised as a "one light bracket with two joints". When gas became available, either publicly in a town or privately on a large estate, it was piped into each room. When installed through a wall, a fixture had its own valve in order to shut off the flow of gas in the same manner as we turn off an electrical light. This fixture has a shutoff cock close to the wall, the safest place on a fixture with extension arms. The jointed arms through which the fuel was fed allowed the gas jet and globe to be extended into the room when in use. When it was no longer needed, the fixture was folded back against the wall. Note that, when folded, the twists in the metal arms are centered together, even though one arm is shorter to allow space for the globe between the jet and the wall.

2225 BLOWN OPAL SHADE

1¾'' H. x 10'' Dia. 1888–1891

Clear glass flat smoke shades were made from the very beginning of Sandwich's glass industry. They were suspended above hall lights and had a much smaller opening as shown in photo 2429. This opal light shade was a continuation of the same style. There is no doubt that some of the opal fragments dug from the Boston and Sandwich Glass Company site were from flat shades, as shown in the foreground. Some flat light shades were as large as 16'' Dia. However, this 10'' Dia. shade is a documented Sandwich Co-operative Glass Company piece. The Co-op was located on Dillingham Knoll in Sandwich and operated during this three-year period. The shades were made in a variety of sizes. Some were extremely large for use in commercial establishments to reflect light from incandescent bulbs down toward the floor after electrical ceiling fixtures became popular.

2227 FREE-BLOWN KEROSENE GLOBE ENGRAVED WITH BERRIES

5¾'' H. x 6⅜'' Dia. 1855–1865

This globe was free-blown during the period when kerosene table lamps were taking the place of the metal, lard-burning solar lamps of the 1840's and 1850's. The globe was patterned after the solar globe, with a larger diameter opening at the top. The glass is ¼'' thick. The flared fitter is thicker on one side than on the other. The lower half was engraved with a design of berries and leaves. The upper half was frosted by a primitive method that was improved upon by Charles Cotesworth Pinckney Waterman in 1861. While working for John W. Jarves and Company at the Cape Cod Glass Works, Waterman patented a grinding machine that could rough the surface of a number of shades or globes at the same time. His patent No. 33,175, dated August 27, 1861, and assigned to J. W. Jarves and Company, showed twenty-three geared spindles onto which shades and globes were secured. Stationary cups surrounding each globe were filled to the desired level with "sand or other suitable material for grinding". The globes were rotated until the surface was ground to the desired roughness. If smooth rings were desired below the highest level of the sand, "bands of India-rubber or other material" were stretched over the globe to protect the surface from the grinding action. Rings can be seen in the photo delineating the two surfaces. Waterman's method of grinding with sand was superseded by sand blasting.

While working for the Cape Cod Glass Works, Charles Cotesworth Pinckney Waterman patented a machine that roughed the outside surface of shades to given them a frosted appearance. Each shade was placed in a cup, after which the cup was filled with sand. If smooth rings were wanted, rubber bands were stretched over the shade to protect that portion of the surface from the action of the sand. Waterman assigned the patent, dated August 27, 1861, to J. W. Jarves and Company, operators of the Cape Cod works.

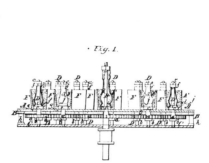

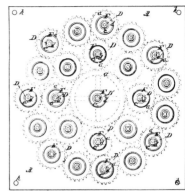

2228 BLOWN MOLDED KEROSENE GLOBE ACID-ETCHED WITH FOREST SCENE

6¾'' H. x 7½'' Dia. 1880–1908

Globes were acid-etched by first pasting paper with cut out designs onto the surface. The paper-covered globe was covered with an acid-resistant wax. The paper was removed, leaving the wax design on the glass. The globe was immersed in hydrofluoric acid, which ate into the unprotected areas. Bucolic forest and farm scenes were well suited to the broad surface of globes. Here is a herd of deer grazing and resting. The scene continues around the globe. The band and line design above and below the scene was not part of the transfers, but was added where necessary to delineate the design and adjust it to any height globe. This globe has no fitter. It may have been used on a gas newel lamp that had curved upright prongs to cup the globe. The lack of a good-sized fitter may indicate that the globe was machined to remove damage. Examine fitters and rims carefully when you are considering a purchase. A damaged globe will not add value to the lamp on which it is placed. If bumped while resting loosely on a globe ring, it may damage the chimney, the lamp, and other nearby valuable antiques that break its fall.

2229 BLOWN MOLDED KEROSENE GLOBE ACID-ETCHED WITH PASTURE SCENE AND WINDMILL

6½'' H. x 6¾'' Dia. 1880–1908

Cows at pasture was a peaceful scene often used on globes that were acid-etched in Sandwich. Note the pump and watering trough. Matching fragments dug at the factory site all had trees in the background. The double ring above the straight kerosene fitter and the single ring below the rim were made by protecting the surface of the glass from the effect of the acid. The rings were not part of the design as it was cut into the tissue that was adhered to the glass. When frosted globes with clear rings were mounted on table lamps and were put to use, each ring cast a shadow on the wall.

2230 SECOND VIEW OF ABOVE GLOBE

At first glance, one would think that this scene of a windmill and a thatch-roof cottage was a foreign one. It may very well be, because artists who drew the originals came from all over the world. However, the windmill was typical of many that dotted the landscape along the Atlantic Coast, as shown in the accompanying "View on south shore of Nantucket", a small island south of Cape Cod. As burners were improved to provide brighter light, almost the entire surface was roughed to soften the glare. Many globes were completely frosted with no etched design so that the light remained constant.

"View on south shore of Nantucket" as illustrated in *Harper's New Monthly Magazine*. The engraving dates from the early 1870's. Views of Cape Cod towns illustrated in John Warner Barber's *History and Antiquities of Every Town in Massachusetts*, published in 1839, included a number of such windmills.

2231 BLOWN MOLDED GAS GLOBE ACID-ETCHED WITH FARM SCENE

5⅜" H. x 7" Dia. 1875-1908

The most distinctive element in this farm scene is the stone water well in the foreground. A Y-post supports the dip stick that extends high into the air. A rope tied to the end holds a pail. A farmhouse is in the background, a barn and haystacks are on the left. The same scene was repeated on the other side. Set screws on a metal ring held the globe in place. *Courtesy, Sandwich Glass Museum, Sandwich Historical Society*

2232 BLOWN MOLDED KEROSENE GLOBE ACID-ETCHED WITH FLOWERS

6½" H. x 7" Dia. 1880-1908

Designs of gardens or stemmed flowers fall into the same category as the scenic designs previously shown. This globe was meant to be used with the straight fitter at the bottom; it should not be mounted upside down. Look at the bleeding hearts on the center right. They should bend toward the ground. Occasionally we find these globes incorrectly fitted to a suspension hall lamp with a pulley mechanism, as is shown in photo 2402, with no thought given to the proper direction of the design. Regardless of the design, however, a kerosene globe with only one fitter should not be used on a hall lamp. Two opal hall globes were pictured on page 71 of the 1874 Boston and Sandwich Glass Company catalog. Each had an upper and lower fitter, one that secured the globe to the upper metal ring on the lamp and one that secured it to the lower. The kerosene globe pictured here is a beautiful one. Preparation of the paper covering prior to the acid treatment was well executed. *Courtesy, Sandwich Glass Museum, Sandwich Historical Society*

2233 BLOWN MOLDED GAS GLOBE ACID-ETCHED WITH FLOWERS

4¾'' H. x 7½'' Dia. 1875–1908

Although the authors have seen squat globes with flared fitters ridiculously suspended upside down in electrical fixtures, the use is not proper. Study the design that was etched on the glass. The direction of the design determines the original use of the piece, i.e., as a globe with a fitter that rested on a metal ring, or as a shade that directed the light downward. On this example, the flowers look natural when the globe is in the position shown. The stems extend upward and outward, reaching toward the sun. If you turn the photo upside down, you will note that the flowers appear to be hanging awkwardly. The flower motif was repeated on the other side of the globe. The clear area on the right marks the edge of the design as it was stamped onto the tissue that was adhered to the glass when the acid resistant wax was applied. Globes that are light in weight were manufactured late in Sandwich glass history, after a method was perfected that allowed a piece to be thinly blown into a mold and then rotated to remove mold marks. Earlier free-blown kerosene globes, like those shown in photo 2227, were three to five times heavier.

2234 BLOWN MOLDED GAS GLOBE ACID-ETCHED WITH FLOWERS

5⅝'' H. x 7'' Dia. 1875–1908

Garden flowers were depicted on many globes acid-etched at Sandwich. Antiques dealers sometimes mention that intricate designs were more difficult to etch than simple ones and are therefore more expensive. The statement would be true only if the design was needle etched by hand onto each globe (see the oil bottle in photo 4237). Whether simple or complicated, the wax design was adhered to the clear glass globe. The paper was removed, leaving the wax, which prevented the hydrofluoric acid from eating into the glass. The only difficult step was pasting the paper on correctly. Legend states, "You could always tell when a girl worked in the etching department. She would hide her hands because the acid ate into her fingernails." The triple ring below the rim was not put on straight. This telltale sign of handwork differentiates an old globe from a modern replacement. *Courtesy, Sandwich Glass Museum, Sandwich Historical Society*

This illustration was captioned, "Preparing shades for etching". It was included in the private papers of Frederick T. Irwin, who wrote *The Story of Sandwich Glass* in 1926. The shape of the globes and the allover floral design indicates that the drawing was executed during the time period of our study. The Irwin papers have been incorporated into the Barlow-Kaiser document collection.

2235 BLOWN MOLDED GAS GLOBE
ACID-ETCHED WITH FLOWERS AND TRELLIS

5" H. x 7" Dia. 1875–1908

It was impossible to transfer the complete design from flat paper to the rounded surface of a globe in one operation. This design was combined from two paper patterns. The flowers and the trellis at the bottom appeared on the flat paper as one design. The matching trellis band that surrounds the rim was applied separately. The edge of the upper band can be seen on the right of the globe where the design does not match. Purchased designs may have provided inspiration to the decorators who painted by hand. Note the seed sprouting from the center of the flower facing forward. A similar incongruity can be seen on the decorated lamp shade in photo 2195. The blanks for globes and shades that were to be acid-etched were manufactured by many glass houses. The designs were purchased by these glass houses to be used on their own blanks. Lamp assembly companies that had etching facilities purchased the designs to use on blanks also purchased elsewhere. So, unless an etched globe has strong family ties to a glass-working family, or can be substantiated by other evidence of origin, attribution is impossible. The etched designs shown in this study all match fragments dug at the site of the Boston and Sandwich Glass Company and are designs that were retailed by merchants known to have had wholesale accounts with Sandwich glass companies. *Courtesy, Sandwich Glass Museum, Sandwich Historical Society*

2236 BLOWN MOLDED GAS GLOBE
ACID-ETCHED WITH BIRDS AND URNS

4⅝" H. x 7½" Dia. 1875–1908

Most of the gas globes that were pictured in the 1874 catalog had small diameter fitters. By the mid–1870's, it was discovered that gaslight burned more steadily if the draft was increased, so the fitters were enlarged and the metal gas fixtures were modified to accept them. When on paper, the design was flat. Close examination of the lower edge would reveal places above the fitter where the design was adjusted. Other adjustments were made at the upper edge. At first glance, the birds on pine branches alternating with flower-filled urns are attractive. But the head of the bird on the left was completely cut off to make room for the band of flowers. The globe is a good example of the speed at which glass was decorated by unhappy workers during the closing years of the glass industry. The glass itself was of poor quality. Records show that much of it annealed improperly, so breakage was high in the cutting and etching departments.

2237 BLOWN MOLDED GAS OR ELECTRIC GLOBE ACID-ETCHED WITH FLOWERS

4½" H. x 7⅛" Dia. 1880–1908

This piece has an all-over flower design that has no top or bottom. The daisies face the viewer. There are no stems and leaves to indicate that the piece must be mounted in the position shown in the photo. This form of globe was sometimes called a *tulip globe*. It was marketed in wholesale catalogs under the heading "Gas or Lamp Globes". The adjective *lamp* meant *kerosene*. But the tulip shade adapted very nicely to electrical fixtures. Electric globes were a large part of production at the Boston and Sandwich Glass Company in 1887, according to the sloar book, which was an account of the glass that was made weekly by every shop. Some elaborate electrical chandeliers combined large diameter globes, such as this one mounted with the fitter at the bottom, and smaller ones with matching patterns that were suspended as shades. After the design was etched, the wax and the acid were washed off. The globe was sent to the cutting shop. Inverted scallops were cut into the rim, which were then polished. The extra cutting "dressed" what would have been a quite ordinary gas globe. *Courtesy, Sandwich Glass Museum, Sandwich Historical Society*

2238 BLOWN MOLDED GAS OR KEROSENE GLOBE ACID-ETCHED WITH TORCHES AND WREATHS

4½" H. x 7¾" Dia. 1880–1908

Whether opened out at the top or closed in, lamp trimmings that had fitters at the bottom were called *globes*. This torch and wreath design was used on both forms of globes at Sandwich, but a variant can also be seen on a ball-shaped globe in a Gillinder and Sons catalog. Collectors sometimes try to hang this tulip-shaped globe upside down. The design itself shows that the globe was not meant to be hung. The flame of the five torches must burn upward. The ends of the ribbons that are tied around the torches and the five wreaths are blowing in the breeze. This is the only way the design looks "right". Gas pipes came up from the cellar and through the floor, even through table tops, to burn in lamps that looked very much like kerosene lamps without fonts. Globes with wide fitters that were used on gas and kerosene lamps were made in volume and are easily found today, unlike the earlier gas globes with small fitters that could not be used with kerosene. *Courtesy, Sandwich Glass Museum, Sandwich Historical Society*

INVENTORY OF SANDWICH GLASS

No.	Description	Condition	Date Purchased	Amount	Date Sold	Amount

GLOSSARY

ACID CUTBACK Cameo glass, made by treating the surface of cased glass with acid. An acid-resistant design was transferred onto the surface. Acid was applied, which "cut back", or ate through, the unprotected portions of the casing to reveal the glass beneath.

ADVENTURINE See *goldstone*.

AGENCY The office of an agent, or factor.

AGENT One entrusted with the power to negotiate the business of another, usually in a different location.

ANNEAL The gradual reheating and slow cooling of an article in a leer—an oven built for the purpose. This procedure removes any stress that may have built up in the glass during its manufacture.

APPLIED The fastening of a separate piece of glass, such as a base, handle, prunt, or stem, to an article already formed.

APPRENTICE One who was bound by indenture for a specified period to an experienced glassworker or mold maker for the purpose of instruction in the art and skill of creating glassware.

ASHERY A place where potash was made for mixing in a batch of glass.

BATCH Mixture of sand, cullet, and various raw materials that are placed in the pot to be heated into metal, or molten glass.

BLANK A finished piece of glass requiring additional work, such as decorating or engraving.

BLOWN GLASS Glass made by the use of a blowpipe and air pressure sufficient to give it form.

BLOWN MOLDED GLASS Glass made by blowing hot glass into a plain or patterned mold, and forcing it with air pressure to conform to the shape of the mold.

BOX A container of any shape and any size (e.g., it could be square, rectangular, circular or oval).

BUTTON STEM A connector between the base and the body of any article, with a button-shaped extrusion in its center.

CANE In *paperweight making*, a bundle of various colored glass rods that are arranged into a design, fused by reheating, pulled until it is long and thin, cooled and then cut into segments.

CASING A different colored layer of glass, either on the inside or outside of the main body of a blown piece, which adhered to the piece at the time it was blown.

CASTOR PLACE The location in the factory where large goods were made, such as apothecary show globes, lamp shades and decanters.

CAVE Ash pit under the furnace.

CAVE METAL Hot glass that flowed into the cave from a broken pot.

CHAIR A term used interchangeably with *shop*. Quoting Deming Jarves in a July 2, 1827, letter to William Stutson, "Do you think it advisable to form another chair for making small articles?"

CLAW FOOT An applied reeded foot resembling a scallop shell.

CLUSTER On *cut glass*, a grouping of similar designs in close proximity.

CRAQUELLE Glass that has been deliberately fractured after it has been formed, and reheated to seal the fractures, leaving the scars as a permanent design.

CROSSCUT DIAMOND On *cut glass*, a diamond that is divided into quarters.

CULLET Glass made in the factory and saved from a pot to be used in making future batches. Waste glass trimmed from rims and spouts was dropped into a cullet box. Also, glass items already annealed, either produced in the factory or purchased, and broken to be included in future batches.

CUTTING The grinding away of a portion of the surface of a blank, using wheels and wet sand to produce a design.

DECORATING The ornamenting of a blank by painting or staining it with a non-glass substance.

DESIGN The ornamentation of glass after it has been annealed, by cutting, engraving, etching or decorating.

DIP MOLD A shallow mold into which a blown gather of glass was dipped to form items such as nappies and dishes.

DONUT On *Trevaise*, the wafer-size glob of glass applied to the base. In most cases, the center of the wafer is dished out, leaving the shape of a donut.

ELECTRIC INCANDESCENT LAMP Original term for the item now called a *light bulb*. The first electric lamps were globe-shaped.

ENAMEL Colored glass made with lead. Most often, the term referred to opaque white glass. However, Deming Jarves noted in an 1867 memo, "Enamelled Glass deep color", meaning that the items listed should be made in color from glass containing lead.

ENGRAVING The process of cutting shallow designs and letters into a blank using a lathe with copper wheels and an abrasive.

ETCHING An inexpensive method of producing a design by using hydrofluoric acid to eat into the surface of a blank.

EXTINGUISHER A cone which, when placed on a burning lamp or candlestick, extinguishes the flame.

FACTOR An agent.

FILIGREE ROD A rod that has spiral or straight threads running through it. Also called *latticinio*.

FINIAL The decorative, terminal part of a newel post, writing pen, etc. The part of a cover used as a handle.

FIRE POLISHING Reheating a finished piece to remove marks left by tools or molds, leaving the article with a smooth surface.

FITTER The lower rim of a globe, shade or chimney that fits onto a metal ring or burner.

FLASHED A method developed during the 1880's of coating pressed and blown molded glass with a layer of colored glass after it was removed from the mold. The *flashed* layer was made from a formula that melted at a much lower temperature than the originally molded piece, so the original piece did not warp. On *cut glass*, a fan-like design located between the points of a fan, hobstar, or star.

FLINT A variety of quartz composed of silica with traces of iron. It is very hard, and strikes fire with steel.

FLINT GLASS Originally made from pulverized flints, it later became glass made from a batch containing lead. The term *flint* continued to be used, however. In the 1800's, it became the factory term for clear glass.

FLOATED In *decorated opal glass*, the method used to apply a solid color background.

FLUTE The hand-crimping of a rim. On *pressed* or *cut glass*, a panel rounded at the top.

FOLDED RIM A rim on either the body or base of a piece, the edge of which is doubled back onto itself, resulting in greater strength.

FRAGMENTS Broken pieces of finished glass, discarded at the time of production.

FREE-BLOWN GLASS Glass made by blowing hot glass and shaping it into its final form by the use of hand tools.

GAFFER In a group of glassworkers, called a *shop*, the most skilled artisan; the master glass blower.

GASOMETER The place where gas was generated for lighting.

GATHER The mass of hot metal that has been gathered on the end of a blowpipe.

GATHERER The assistant to the master glass blower, who gathers the hot metal on the end of the blowpipe.

GAUFFER To crimp or flute.

GILDING The application of gold for decorative purposes.

GLASS GALL Impurities skimmed from the surface of melted glass. Also called *sandever, sandiver*.

GOLDSTONE Glass combined with copper filings.

HOBSTAR On *cut glass*, a many-pointed geometrically cut star.

INDENTURE A contract binding an apprentice to his master.

KNOP A round knob, either hollow or solid, in the center of a stem.

LAMPWORK The making and assembly of leaves, petals, stems, fruit and other small parts from rods of glass that have been softened by heating them over a gas burner. Originally, oil lamps produced the open flame.

LAPIDARY STOPPER A cut, faceted stopper.

LATTICINIO A rod of glass or a paperweight background composed of threads arranged in lattice, spiral or swirl configurations. The threads are usually white. Also, an article of glass made by arranging differently colored rods in a circular configuration and fusing them to a blown gather. The gather is then manipulated into the desired form, such as a creamer or lamp font.

LEER A tunnel-shaped oven through which glass articles are drawn after formation for the purpose of annealing. Also spelled *lear, lehr*.

LIGHTING DEVICE Any wooden, metal or glass primitive or sophisticated contrivance that emits light.

LIME Oxide of calcium; the white, caustic substance obtained from limestone and shells by heat. The heat expells carbonic acid, leaving behind the lime. Documentation shows the Cape Cod Glass Company and other glass factories obtained their lime from oyster shells.

MAKE-DO A damaged item that has been repaired to ''make it do'' what was originally intended.

MANTLE A chemically treated tube of fabric that produces an incandescent glow when suspended over the flame of a gas burner.

MARBRIE In *blown glass*, a loop design made by looping and trailing threads of glass through another color, such as in paperweights and witch balls.

MARVER Iron plate on which hot glass is first shaped by rolling, in preparation for blowing into its final form.

MERESE A wafer-shaped piece of hot glass, used to connect individual units to make a complete piece, such as the base and socket of a candlestick or the bowl and standard of a footed nappie.

METAL Glass either in a molten condition in the pot, or in a cold, hardened state.

MOLD A form into which glass is blown or pressed to give it shape and pattern. Also spelled *mould*.

MOLD MARKS On glass that has been blown or pressed into a mold, the marks or seam lines left by the edges of the units of the mold.

MOVE A period of time during which a shop makes glass continuously. A glass blower is expected to make ten *moves* each week.

NAPPIE A shallow bowl of any size, whether round bottomed or flat bottomed, which can be on a standard. Also spelled *nappy*.

NEEDLE ETCHING Done by coating a blank with an acid-resisting substance, then inscribing a design into the resist with a sharp needle. The blank is then dipped into hydrofluoric acid, which etches the glass where the design was inscribed.

NIB The writing point of a pen.

OVERFILL On pieces that have been blown or pressed into a mold, the excess hot glass that seeps into the seams of the mold.

PANEL A section with raised margins and square corners.

PATTERN (ON GLASS) The specific ornamentation into which *hot* glass is formed.

PATTERN (WOODEN) Wooden model carved in detail that is sent to the foundry, used as a guide to shape a mold.

PEG On a *lamp*, the unit that holds the oil and is attached to the base with a metal connector.

PICKWICK A pointed instrument used for raising, or "picking", the wick of a whale oil lamp.

PILLAR-MOLDED GLASS Glass made by first blowing a hot gather of glass into a mold with vertical ridges (pillars). A second cooler gather is blown into the first. The hot outer layer conforms to the shape of the mold, while the cooler inner layer remains smooth.

PINWHEEL On *cut glass*, a design resembling a hobstar in motion, its points angled in a clockwise or counter-clockwise position.

PONTIL MARK Rough spot caused by breaking away the pontil rod.

PONTIL ROD A rod of iron used by glassworkers to hold the glass while it is being formed.

POT A one-piece container in which glass is melted, usually made of clay and able to withstand extreme heat.

PLINTH A square block forming the base for a standard. Also, a base and standard molded in one piece, used as the lower unit of a lamp.

PRESSED GLASS Glass made by placing hot glass into a mold and forcing it with a plunger to conform to the shape of the mold.

PRISM A pattern or design of deep parallel V-grooves that reflect the light.

PRUNT A blob of glass applied to the surface of a vessel, for the purpose of decorating or hiding a defect.

PUNTING The process of dishing out a circle with a cutting wheel, usually to remove the mark left by the pontil rod.

PUNTY A concave circle made by dishing out the glass with a cutting wheel.

QUILTING In *art glass*, an all-over diamond design, permanently molded into the piece as it was being blown.

RIBBON ROD A rod that has twisted flat ribbons of glass running through it.

RIGAREE A heavy thread of glass applied to the surface of a piece, giving a decorative rippled or fluted effect.

ROD A straight shaft of glass that will be reheated to form other things. Thin rods are fused together to make canes, and are also softened to supply glass for lampwork. Thick rods are formed into arms for epergne units. Reeded rods are used to form handles and claw feet on Late Blown Ware, as well as nibs for glass writing pens.

SERVITOR The first assistant to the gaffer in a group of glassworkers called a *shop*.

SHEDDING The flaking of the surface of finished glass, sometimes caused by minute particles of fire clay in the sand. Too much alkali in the glass and moisture in the air drawing out the soda are also contributing factors.

SHELL FOOT See *claw foot*.

SHOP A group of workmen producing glass at the furnace, consisting of a master glass blower and his help.

SICK GLASS Discoloration of the surface of an article.

SLOAR BOOK The book in which an accounting was kept of the output of glass produced by each shop at the furnace.

SLOAR MAN The glassworker who entered the output of each shop in the sloar book.

SNUFF The part of a wick that has been charred by the flame.

SNUFFER A scissors-like instrument for trimming and catching the charred part of a wick.

SOCKET EXTENSION On a *candlestick*, the section between the socket and the wafer, molded in one piece with the socket.

SPIDER PONTIL An iron unit placed on the end of the pontil rod, consisting of several finger-like rods. The fingers gave support to items that could not be held by a single rod in the center.

STAINED GLASS A finished piece of clear glass that is colored wholly or in part by the application of a chemical dye—most commonly ruby. The article is refired, making the dye a permanent finish.

STICKER-UP BOY The boy who carries hot glass on a V-shaped stick in a group of glassworkers called a *shop*.

STRAWBERRY DIAMOND On *cut glass*, a diamond which is crosshatched. Also the name of a cut glass design that utilizes crosscut diamonds.

TAKER-IN BOY The boy who carries the hot finished product to the leer in a group of glassworkers called a *shop*. During slow periods, he assists in the removal of glass from the cold end of the leer.

TALE Articles sold by count rather than by weight. In the words of Deming Jarves, "Tale was derived from the mode of selling, the best glass being sold only by weight, while light articles were sold tale."

UNDERFILL An insufficient amount of glass blown or pressed into a mold, resulting in an incomplete product. This is a characteristic, not a defect.

VESICA On *cut glass*, a pointed oval.

WAFER A flattened piece of hot glass, sometimes called a merese, used to join separately made units into a complete piece, such as the base and socket of a candlestick or the bowl and standard of a footed nappie.

WHIMSEY Unusual, one-of-a-kind item made of glass by a worker in his spare time.

CONTINUATIONS

2062

deep cutting and shallow engraving. After annealing, they were roughed in the cutting shop to give a frosted effect and then the design of grapes and berries was cut. The light was brighter through the polished grapes and appeared to flicker intermittently, so the lamps could not be used for serious lighting purposes. Clear glasses and plain roughed glasses were more frequently used, and were inexpensive by comparison. Lamp glasses and shades with this amount of decoration are usually attributed to the New England Glass Company, but the documentation accompanying this pair attests to Sandwich manufacture. They were removed from the Wing house on Sandy Neck Road in East Sandwich when Wing family descendants sold the house. The Wing family dates back to the 1640's in Sandwich history. *Courtesy, Sandwich Glass Museum, Sandwich Historical Society*

2085

molds. On most lamps, the mold marks on the font do not line up with the mold marks on the base, and the top of the standard appears to have been forced up into the knop below the font. Note the lack of color in the upper half of the amethyst font A. The glass was blown too thinly to carry enough pigment to afford an even distribution of color. The difference between the thinly blown font and the heavy pressed base is the reason why very few of these lamps are available today. When they were placed in the wood-fired annealing leer, the thin fonts sagged in the poorly controlled heat and many lamps from each move were destroyed. Many more broke when the lamp capper attempted to cement on the collar. Those that did survive did not withstand rough handling of everyday use. They are very difficult to find in pristine condition today.

2134

the pattern. The handled lamp B was blown into a mold that carried the same pattern as lamp A. Note that the handle was applied on top of the pattern of "waffles", making it difficult to adhere and form a lasting bond. This lamp is often found with its handle missing. A New England Glass Company catalog dating c. 1869 pictures this pattern in tableware and identifies the original name as *Palace*. A Cape Cod Glass Company list of glassware, 1864–1869, lists dishes made in a *Ball and Check* pattern, which is a good description of the elements of Waffle and Thumbprint, but there is no illustration. The authors point this out as a matter of conjecture until more conclusive documentation surfaces. *Courtesy, Sandwich Glass Museum, Sandwich Historical Society*

2144

2284 and on a compote. The several styles of glass standards with "hurricane shades" examined by the authors and documented by families as Boston and Sandwich Glass Company and Falmouth Glass Company pieces were equipped with peg lamps rather than candlesticks as shown in photo 4049 in Volume 4. The paneled peg lamps shown here should have whale oil or fluid burners that were lit by either taking the lamp glass off and lifting it up over the lamps, as shown in photo 2146, or by reaching down from the top with a wand that held a match. *Courtesy, Sandwich Glass Museum, Sandwich Historical Society*

2152

be found in the triangular configuration of B or arranged in a straight line across the center of the cap. On rare occasions, as many as six tubes can be found. Most fluid burners had a cap for each tube attached by a fine chain. The caps were dropped over the tubes to extinguish the flames, keep the fuel from continuing to wick up the tubes, and eliminate odor when the lamp was not in use. The caps were also available as a separate accessory for use on burners that were not equipped with a loop or hole to attach a chain. The cap was attached to one end of a chain. A small brass cuff attached to the other end was designed to fit around the tube.

DILLAWAY PATENT

that were thought to be reproductions because they showed no signs of having been held with a pontil rod. However, if they were manufactured during the latter part of the whale oil and burning fluid era when Dillaway's patent No. 17,960 was in use, they could have been held in this device.

2170

shorter, but height was gained by using an upper unit with a font extension that terminates in a knop. The hand-formed wafer can be seen below the knop. There is greater value in lamp A because pattern glass fonts are not often found combined with Monument bases. The base on lamp B is quite common, as evidenced in other photos. *Courtesy, Sandwich Glass Museum, Sandwich Historical Society*

UNITED STATES PATENT OFFICE.

DENNIS J. LORDEN, OF SANDWICH, ASSIGNOR OF ONE HALF TO JOHN CROWLEY, OF BOSTON, MASSACHUSETTS.

MACHINE FOR MAKING GLASS GLOBES, SHADES, &c.

SPECIFICATION forming part of Letters Patent No. 345,979, dated July 20, 1886.

Application filed November 23, 1885. Serial No. 183,602. (No model.)

To all whom it may concern:

Be it known that I, DENNIS J. LORDEN, of Sandwich, county of Barnstable, and State of Massachusetts, have invented an Improvement in Machines for Making Glass Globes, Shades, &c., of which the following description, in connection with the accompanying drawings, is a specification, like letters on the drawings representing like parts.

In the manufacture of glass globes or shades of the dome class for lamps, &c., the usual glass tube for a portion of its length is first blown to an oval shape. The free open end which is to form the top of the shade is then turned outward to give to the said top an ornamental appearance. The usual "post" or "snap" is then attached to the said open end or top, and the shade is then detached from the remaining portion of the tube. The open end left by detaching the shade from the tube is then turned outward or spread to complete the shade by means of a hand-tool, the bodies being previously heated.

This invention has for its object to construct a simple apparatus which may be employed to spread the oval-shaped bodies as detached from the tube into the shape they shall ultimately assume, thereby expediting and facilitating the manufacture of glass globes or shades of this class.

The invention consists in the combination, with two or more pivotally-connected expanding devices or bows, two sleeves to which the said expanding devices are pivoted, a stationary screw-threaded rod or spindle upon which the said sleeves are mounted to rotate, and means, substantially as will be described, for rotating the sleeves upon the screw-threaded rod, whereby the bows are expanded, of two or more pivoted formers or bows arranged to be brought into contact with the exterior of the globe or shade to prevent the expanding devices from giving to the globe or shade too great dimensions at any or all parts thereof.

The expanding devices herein described consist of two or more bows pivotally connected at two points intermediate of their length by connecting-rods to two sleeves, the said sleeves being mounted to rotate upon a stationary screw-threaded rod, so that as said sleeves are rotated they will travel upward upon the screw-threaded rod, and thereby turn the bows outward. Suitable retaining devices are applied whereby one sleeve is permitted to move upward upon the screw-threaded rod in advance of the other. A suitable pulley or driving wheel surrounds one of the said sleeves and held in suitable bearings, while a projection extending inward toward the center of the pulley enters a slot or guideway in the sleeve, thereby engaging and rotating the sleeve which also permitting the said sleeve to travel upward upon its screw-threaded rod.

The formers for the exterior of the globe be shaped consist of pivotal bows and suitable means whereby the said formers may brought into operation at any time desired.

Figure 1 shows in side elevation an apparatus constructed in accordance with this invention, a portion of the frame-work being broken away to show the parts within; and Fig. 2 detail of the retaining device.

The base A has rigidly connected with it or near its center, a spindle or rod, a, which screw-threaded at its upper end, as at a², a also for a portion of its length, as at a², below the said portion a', the two portions a' a² being thereby separated by a short portion of the spindle, which is deprived of screw-threads. Two sleeves, b b', are mounted on the said spindle a to rotate freely, normally being located at the portions of the said spindle which are deprived of screw-threads. The sleeves b b' are pivoted two or more expanding devices or bows, c c', by connecting-rods 2 3 4 5, respectively.

The drive-wheel or pulley e surrounds the lowermost sleeve, b', and is provided with grooved hub, c', suitable uprights, f f', rising from the base A, and having projections f² entering the grooves in said hub c', herein retaining the pulley in suitable position.

The drive-pulley e, with its hub e', is provided with an inwardly-extended projection m, which enters a groove or slot, m', passing lengthwise of the sleeve b'.

The drive-pulley e is rotated in a horizontal plane, and as it rotates the projection m engaging the sleeve b', rotates the said sleeve and as said sleeve travels upward upon the

345,979

screw-threaded portion a of the spindle the projection m follows in the groove or slot m'.

It has been found preferable that one of the sleeves should commence to travel upon its screw-threaded portion of the spindle a in advance of the other, and to this end a retaining-device consisting of a lever pivoted to the base-plate A, and having a semicircular engaging portion, n, which enters a groove, n', in the lower end of the sleeve b', is provided, the said retaining device being moved on its pivot by any suitable means, yet herein shown as moved by the hand of the operator.

In accordance with this invention the oval-shaped body shown in dotted lines at D, and supposed to be attached to any usual post or snap, is placed upon the apparatus herein described, the bows or expanding devices c c' entering the opening formed by detaching the said body from the tube. The drive pulley e is then rotated, the sleeve b' being normally engaged by the retaining device. As the sleeve b' rotates, the sleeve b, through the intervention of the connecting-rods and bows. is also rotated, and at once commences to travel upward upon the screw-threaded portion a' of the spindle, expanding the bows and spreading the hot bodies D, placed upon them, until the said sleeve b strikes the stop o. At this time the retaining device for the sleeve b' is released, and the said sleeve b' at once travels upward upon the screw-threaded portion a² of the spindle a, thereby turning the bows c c' upon their pivotal connections into the dotted line position.

To prevent the globes or shades from assuming too great dimension at any particular point, caused by the centrifugal action of the expanding devices, suitable formers are provided, each one consisting of two or more curved arms, s s', and straight arms s² s³, pivoted at t' t' to suitable uprights, t² t², rising from the base-plate A. The arms s² s³ are connected by a suitable cord or wire to the connecting-rod F, operated by any suitable treadle or other means. These formers are normally spread outward upon their pivots when the article being operated upon is near its completion, the said formers, by the connecting-rod F, being brought into contact with the exterior of the globe or shade at such time.

It is obvious that many devices may be devised for rotating the sleeve b'; but the construction herein shown being simple is the one I prefer to use.

While it is obvious that the retaining devices herein shown fully accomplish the results sought for, yet many other devices capable of producing the same result may be employed with equally beneficial effects, and without departing from my invention.

I claim—

1. In a machine for making glass globes or shades, the combination, with two or more pivotally-connected expanding devices or bows, of two sleeves, b b', to which the expanding devices are pivotally connected, a stationary spindle or rod having screw-threaded portions a' a², upon which the sleeves respectively, travel, and means, substantially as described, for rotating the said sleeves, causing them to travel upon the screw-threaded portions of the spindle and thereby expanding the bows, as set forth.

2. The combination, with two or more expanding devices or bows, two sleeves to which the said expanding devices are pivotally connected at two points by connecting-rods 2 3 4 5, respectively, of a stationary spindle having screw-threaded portions a' a², upon which the sleeves b b' respectively travel, and means, substantially as described, for rotating the said sleeves, whereby the expanding devices are moved outward, as set forth.

3. The combination, with two or more pivotally-connected expanding devices, two sleeves to which the said expanding devices are pivoted, of the stationary spindle having screw-threaded portions a' a², upon which the two sleeves respectively travel, and means, substantially as described, for operating with the lowermost sleeve to prevent the said sleeve from traveling upon the screw-threaded portion of the spindle until permitted so to do by the operator.

4. The combination, with two or more pivotally-connected expanding devices, two sleeves, of a stationary spindle having screw-threaded portions a' a², upon which the said sleeves respectively travel, of a drive-pulley having a grooved hub, e', turning in suitable uprights or bearings f f', and the projection following in the groove or slot m' in the lowermost sleeve, all substantially as and for the purpose set forth.

5. The combination, with two or more pivotally-connected expanding devices, and means, substantially as hereinbefore set forth for rotating the same, of two or more formers, consisting of pivoted levers arranged to be brought in contact with the exterior of the article being operated upon, and means, substantially as described, for moving the said formers, as set forth.

In testimony whereof I have signed my name to this specification in the presence of two subscribing witnesses.

DENNIS J. LORDEN.

Witnesses:
  B. J. NOYES,
  C. M. CONE.

INVENTORY OF SANDWICH GLASS

No.	Description	Condition	Date Purchased	Amount	Date Sold	Amount

BIBLIOGRAPHY

UNPUBLISHED SOURCES

Account book of various activities of the Boston and Sandwich Glass Company, such as the company store, seagoing vessels, wages, and wood for construction and fuel. April 17, 1826, to July 1830. Ms. collection in the Tannahill Research Library, Henry Ford Museum, Edison Institute, Dearborn, Michigan.

Barbour, Harriot Buxton. *Sandwich The Town That Glass Built*. Ms. and related correspondence in the Boston University Library, Boston, Massachusetts.

Burbank, George E. *History of the Sandwich Glass Works*. Ms. in the Barlow collection.

Corporate records. Office of the Secretary of State, The Commonwealth of Massachusetts, Boston, Massachusetts.

Correspondence pertaining to the management of the Boston and Sandwich Glass Company and the Cape Cod Glass Company, such as glass formulas, letters, special notices and transfers. Ms. collection in the Tannahill Research Library, Henry Ford Museum, Edison Institute, Dearborn, Michigan.

Correspondence pertaining to the management of the Boston and Sandwich Glass Company, the Boston and Sandwich Glass Company II and the Cape Cod Glass Company, such as glass formulas, letters, statements, etc. Ms. collection in the Rakow Library, The Corning Museum of Glass, Corning, New York.

Correspondence to and from glass authorities and writers on the subject of glass, pertaining to the excavation of the Boston and Sandwich Glass Company site and the discussion of fragments. Ms. consisting of the Francis (Bill) Wynn papers, now in the Barlow collection.

Documentation in the form of fragments dug from factory and cutting shop sites. Private collections and the extensive Barlow collection, which includes the former Francis (Bill) Wynn collection.

Documentation of Sandwich glass items and Sandwich glassworkers, such as hand-written notebooks, letters, billheads, contracts, pictures, and oral history of Sandwich families recorded on tape by descendants. Ms. in the Barlow collection, Kaiser collection and private collections.

Documents pertaining to the genealogy of the family of Deming Jarves. Mount Auburn Cemetery, Cambridge, Massachusetts.

Documents pertaining to the Sandwich glass industry, such as letters, invoices, statements, photographs, family papers and original factory catalogs. Ms. collection in the care of the Sandwich Glass Museum, Sandwich Historical Society, Sandwich, Massachusetts.

Documents pertaining to the Sandwich glass industry and other related industries, such as statistics from Sandwich Vital Records, information from property tax records, maps, photographs, family papers and genealogy. Ms. in the care of the Town of Sandwich Massachusetts Archives and Historical Center, Sandwich, Massachusetts.

Documents pertaining to the Cheshire, Massachusetts, glass sand industry, such as statistics from vital records, information from property tax records, maps and genealogy. Ms. in the care of the Town of Cheshire, Massachusetts, and the Town of Lanesborough, Massachusetts.

Documents relating to the Cheshire, Massachusetts, glass sand industry, such as original manuscripts and newspaper articles. Ms. in the care of the Cheshire Public Library, Cheshire, Massachusetts, and the Berkshire Athenaeum, Pittsfield, Massachusetts.

Documents relating to the North Sandwich industrial area, such as photographs, account books and handwritten scrapbooks. Ms. in the private collection of Mrs. Edward "Ned" Nickerson and the Bourne Historical Society, Bourne, Massachusetts.

Documents relating to the Sandwich Co-operative Glass Company, such as account books, correspondence and glass formulas. Ms. in the private collection of Murray family descendants.

Glass formula book. "Sandwich Aug. 7, 1868, James D. Lloyd." Ms. collection in the Tannahill Research Library, Henry Ford Museum, Edison Institute, Dearborn, Michigan.

Hubbard, Howard G. *A Complete Check List of Household Lights Patented in the United States 1792–1862*. South Hadley, Massachusetts: 1935.

Irwin, Frederick T. *The Story of Sandwich Glass*. Ms. and related documents in the Barlow collection.

Lapham family documents, such as pictures and genealogy. Ms. in the private collections of Lapham family descendants.

Lutz family documents, such as pictures, handwritten

biographies and genealogy. Ms. in the private collections of Lutz family descendants.

Mary Gregory documents, such as diaries, letters and pictures. Ms. in the Barlow collection, Kaiser collection, other private collections, and included in the private papers of her family.

Minutes of annual meetings, Board of Directors meetings, special meetings and stockholders meetings of the Boston and Sandwich Glass Company. Ms. collection in the Tannahill Research Library, Henry Ford Museum, Edison Institute, Dearborn, Michigan.

Minutes of meetings of the American Flint Glass Workers Union, Local No. 16. Ms. in the Sandwich Glass Museum, Sandwich Historical Society, Sandwich, Massachusetts.

Nye family documents relating to the North Sandwich industrial area and the Electrical Glass Corporation. Ms. in the Barlow-Kaiser collection.

Oral history recorded on tape. Tales of Cape Cod, Inc. collection in the Cape Cod Community College Library, Hyannis, Massachusetts.

Patents relating to the invention of new techniques in glassmaking, improved equipment for glassmaking, new designs and styles of glass, and the invention of other items relating to the glass industry. United States Department of Commerce, Patent and Trademark Office, Washington, D. C.

Population Schedule of the Census of the United States. Ms. from National Archives Microfilm Publications, National Archives and Records Service, Washington, D. C.

Property deeds and other proofs of ownership, such as surveys, mortgage deeds, and last will and testaments. Ms. in the Barnstable County Registry of Deeds and Barnstable County Registry of Probate, Barnstable, Massachusetts.

Property deeds and other proofs of ownership relating to the Cheshire, Massachusetts, glass sand industry, such as maps. Ms. in the Berkshire County Registry of Deeds, North District, North Adams, Massachusetts.

Property deeds relating to Deming Jarves and the Boston and Sandwich Glass Company. Ms. in the Plymouth County Registry of Deeds, Plymouth, Massachusetts.

Sloar books, a weekly accounting of glass produced at the Sandwich Glass Manufactory and the Boston and Sandwich Glass Company, and the workers who produced it. July 9, 1825, to March 29, 1828. Ms. collection in the Tannahill Research Library, Henry Ford Museum, Edison Institute, Dearborn, Michigan. May 31, 1887, to December 26, 1887. Ms. in the care of the Town of Sandwich Massachusetts Archives and Historical Center, Sandwich, Massachusetts.

Spurr family documents, such as pictures, handwritten autobiographies, glass formulas and genealogy. Ms. in the private collections of Spurr family descendants.

Vessel documentation records. Ms. in the National Archives and Records Service, Washington, D.C.

Vodon family documents, such as pictures and genealogy. Ms. in the private collection of Vodon family descendants.

Waterman, Charles Cotesworth Pinckney. Notes on the Boston and Sandwich Glass Company, dated November 1876, and deposited in the Sandwich Centennial Box. Ms. in the care of the Town of Sandwich Massachusetts Archives and Historical Center, Sandwich, Massachusetts.

PRINTED SOURCES

Amic, Yolande. *L'Opaline Francaise au XIXe Siecle*. Paris, France: Library Gründ, 1952.

Anthony, T. Robert. *19th Century Fairy Lamps*. Manchester, Vermont: Forward's Color Productions, Inc., 1969.

Avila, George C. *The Pairpoint Glass Story*. New Bedford, Massachusetts: Reynolds-DeWalt Printing, Inc., 1968.

Barber, John Warner. *History and Antiquities of Every Town in Massachusetts*. Worcester, Massachusetts: Dorr, Howland & Co., 1839.

Barbour, Harriot Buxton. *Sandwich The Town That Glass Built*. Boston, Massachusetts: Houghton Mifflin Company, 1948.

Barret, Richard Carter. *A Collectors Handbook of American Art Glass*. Manchester, Vermont: Forward's Color Productions, Inc., 1971.

_____. *A Collectors Handbook of Blown and Pressed American Glass*. Manchester, Vermont: Forward's Color Productions, Inc., 1971.

_____. *Popular American Ruby-Stained Pattern Glass*. Manchester, Vermont: Forward's Color Productions, Inc., 1968.

Belden, Louise Conway. *The Festive Tradition; Table Decoration and Desserts in America, 1650–1900*. New York, New York, and London, England: W. W. Norton & Company, 1983.

Belknap, E. McCamly. *Milk Glass*. New York, New York: Crown Publishers, Inc., 1949.

Bilane, John E. *Cup Plate Discoveries Since 1948; The Cup Plate Notes of James H. Rose*. Union, New Jersey: John E. Bilane, 1971.

Bishop, Barbara. "Deming Jarves and His Glass Factories," *The Glass Club Bulletin*, Spring 1983, pp. 3-5.

Bishop, Barbara and Martha Hassell. *Your Obd^t. Servt., Deming Jarves*. Sandwich, Massachusetts: The Sandwich Historical Society, 1984.

Bredehoft, Neila M. and George A. Fogg, and Francis C. Maloney. *Early Duncan Glassware; Geo. Duncan & Sons, Pittsburgh 1874–1892*. Boston, Massachusetts, and Saint Louisville, Ohio: Published privately, 1987.

Brown, Clark W. *Salt Dishes*. Leon, Iowa: Mid-America Book Company, reprinted in 1968.

_____. *A Supplement to Salt Dishes*. Leon, Iowa: Prairie Winds Press, reprinted in 1970.

Brown, William B. *Over the Pathways of the Past*. Cheshire, Massachusetts: Cheshire Public Library, 1938.

Burbank, George E. *A Bit of Sandwich History*. Sandwich, Massachusetts: 1939.

Burgess, Bangs. *History of Sandwich Glass*. Yarmouth, Massachusetts: The Register Press, 1925.

Butterfield, Oliver. "Bewitching Witchballs," *Yankee*, July 1978, pp. 97, 172-175.

Cataldo, Louis and Dorothy Worrell. *Pictorial Tales of Cape Cod*. (Vol. I) Hyannis, Massachusetts: Tales of Cape

Cod, Inc., 1956.

_____. *Pictorial Tales of Cape Cod*. (Vol. II) Hyannis, Massachusetts: Tales of Cape Cod, Inc., 1961.

Childs, David B. "If It's Threaded...," *Yankee*, June 1960, pp. 86-89.

Chipman, Frank W. *The Romance of Old Sandwich Glass*. Sandwich, Massachusetts: Sandwich Publishing Company, Inc., 1932.

Cloak, Evelyn Campbell. *Glass Paperweights of the Bergstrom Art Center*. New York, New York: Crown Publishers, Inc., 1969.

Conat, Robert. *A Streak of Luck; The Life and Legend of Thomas Alva Edison*. New York, New York: Seaview Books, 1979.

Covill, William E., Jr. *Ink Bottles and Inkwells*. Taunton, Massachusetts: William S. Sullwold Publishing, 1971.

Culver, Willard R. "From Sand to Seer and Servant of Man," *The National Geographic Magazine*, January 1943, pp. 17-24, 41-48.

Deyo, Simeon L. *History of Barnstable County, Massachusetts*. New York, New York: H. W. Blake & Co., 1890.

DiBartolomeo, Robert E. *American Glass from the Pages of Antiques; Pressed and Cut*. (Vol. II) Princeton, New Jersey: The Pyne Press, 1974.

Dickinson, Rudolphus. *A Geographical and Statistical View of Massachusetts Proper*. 1813.

Dickinson, Samuel N. *The Boston Almanac for the Year 1847*. Boston, Massachusetts: B. B. Mussey and Thomas Groom, 1846.

Dooley, William Germain. *Old Sandwich Glass*. Pasadena, California: Esto Publishing Company, n.d.

_____. "Recollections of Sandwich Glass by a Veteran Who Worked on It," *Hobbies*, June 1951, p. 96.

Drepperd, Carl W. *The ABC's of Old Glass*. Garden City, New York: Doubleday & Company, Inc., 1949.

Dyer, Walter A. "The Pressed Glass of Old Sandwich". *Antiques*, February 1922, pp. 57-60.

Eckardt, Allison M. "Living with Antiques; A Collection of American Neoclassical Furnishings on the East Coast". *The Magazine Antiques*, April 1987, pp. 858-863.

Edison Lamp Works. *Pictorial History of the Edison Lamp*. Harrison, New Jersey: Edison Lamp Works, c. 1920.

Fauster, Carl U. *Libbey Glass Since 1818*. Toledo, Ohio: Len Beach Press, 1979.

Ferson, Regis F. and Mary F. Ferson. *Yesterday's Milk Glass Today*. Pittsburgh, Pennsylvania: Published privately, 1981.

Freeman, Frederick. *History of Cape Cod: Annals of the Thirteen Towns of Barnstable County*. Boston, Massachusetts: George C. Rand & Avery, 1862.

Freeman, Dr. Larry. *New Light on Old Lamps*. Watkins Glen, New York: American Life Foundation, reprinted in 1984.

Fritz, Florence. *Bamboo and Sailing Ships; The Story of Thomas Alva Edison and Fort Myers, Florida*. 1949.

Gaines, Edith. "Woman's Day Dictionary of American Glass," *Woman's Day*, August 1961, pp. 19-34.

_____. "Woman's Day Dictionary of Sandwich Glass," *Woman's Day*, August 1963, pp. 21-32.

_____. "Woman's Day Dictionary of Victorian Glass," *Woman's Day*, August 1964, pp. 23-34.

Gores, Stan. *1876 Centennial Collectibles and Price Guide*. Fond du Lac, Wisconsin: The Haber Printing Co., 1974.

Grover, Ray and Lee Grover. *Art Glass Nouveau*. Rutland, Vermont: Charles E. Tuttle Company, Inc., 1967.

_____. *Carved & Decorated European Art Glass*. Rutland, Vermont: Charles E. Tuttle Company, Inc., 1970.

Grow, Lawrence. *The Warner Collector's Guide to Pressed Glass*. New York, New York: Warner Books, Inc., 1982.

Hammond, Dorothy. *Confusing Collectibles*. Des Moines, Iowa: Wallace-Homestead Book Company, 1969.

_____. *More Confusing Collectibles*. Wichita, Kansas: C. B. P. Publishing Company, 1972.

Harris, Amanda B. "Down in Sandwich Town," *Wide Awake* 1, 1887, pp. 19-27.

Harris, John. *The Great Boston Fire, 1872*. Boston, Massachusetts: Boston Globe, 1972.

Hartung, Marion T. and Ione E. Hinshaw. *Patterns and Pinafores*. Des Moines, Iowa: Wallace-Homestead Book Company, 1971.

Hayes-Cavanaugh, Doris. "Early Glassmaking in East Cambridge, Mass.," *Old Time New England*, January 1929, pp. 113-122.

Haynes, E. Barrington. *Glass Through the Ages*. Baltimore, Maryland: Penguin Books, 1969.

Hayward, Arthur H. *Colonial and Early American Lighting*. New York, New York: Dover Publications, Inc., reprinted in 1962.

Hayward, John. *Gazetteer of Massachusetts*. Boston, Massachusetts: John Hayward, 1847.

Heacock, William. *Encyclopedia of Victorian Colored Pattern Glass; Book 1 Toothpick Holders from A to Z*. Jonesville, Michigan: Antique Publications, 1974.

_____. *Encyclopedia of Victorian Colored Pattern Glass; Book 2 Opalescent Glass from A to Z*. Jonesville, Michigan: Antique Publications, 1975.

_____. *Encyclopedia of Victorian Colored Pattern Glass; Book 3 Syrups, Sugar Shakers & Cruets from A to Z*. Jonesville, Michigan: Antique Publications, 1976.

_____. *Encyclopedia of Victorian Colored Pattern Glass; Book 4 Custard Glass from A to Z*. Marietta, Ohio: Antique Publications, 1976.

_____. *Encyclopedia of Victorian Colored Pattern Glass; Book 5 U. S. Glass from A to Z*. Marietta, Ohio: Antique Publications, 1978.

_____. *Encyclopedia of Victorian Colored Pattern Glass; Book 6 Oil Cruets from A to Z*. Marietta, Ohio: Antique Publications, 1981.

_____. *1000 Toothpick Holders; A Collector's Guide*. Marietta, Ohio: Antique Publications, 1977.

Heacock, William and Patricia Johnson. *5000 Open Salts; A Collector's Guide*. Marietta, Ohio: Richardson Printing Corporation, 1982.

Hebard, Helen Brigham. *Early Lighting in New England*. Rutland, Vermont: Charles E. Tuttle Company, 1964.

Heckler, Norman. *American Bottles in the Charles B. Gardner Collection*. Bolton, Massachusetts: Robert W. Skinner, Inc., 1975.

Hildebrand, J. R. "Glass Goes To Town," *The National Geographic Magazine*, January 1943, pp. 1-16, 25-40.

Hollister, Paul, Jr. *The Encyclopedia of Glass Paperweights.* New York, New York: Clarkson N. Potter, Inc., 1969.

Hough, Walter. *Collection of Heating and Lighting Utensils in the United States National Museum.* Washington, District of Columbia: United States Government Printing Office, 1928.

Hunter, Frederick William. *Stiegel Glass.* Dover Publications, Inc.: New York, New York, 1950.

Ingold, Gerard. *The Art of the Paperweight; Saint Louis.* Santa Cruz, California: Paperweight Press, 1981.

Innes, Lowell. *Pittsburgh Glass 1797–1891.* Boston, Massachusetts: Houghton Mifflin Company, 1976.

Irwin, Frederick T. *The Story of Sandwich Glass.* Manchester, New Hampshire: Granite State Press, 1926.

Jarves, Deming. *Reminiscences of Glass-making.* Great Neck, New York: Beatrice C. Weinstock, reprinted in 1968.

Jarves, James Jackson. *Why and What Am I?.* Boston, Massachusetts: Phillips, Sampson and Company, 1857.

Jones, Olive R. and E. Ann Smith. *Glass of the British Military 1755–1820.* Hull, Quebec, Canada: Parks Canada, 1985.

Jones, Olive and Catherine Sullivan. *The Parks Canada Glass Glossary.* Hull, Quebec, Canada: Parks Canada, 1985.

Kamm, Minnie W. and Serry Wood. *The Kamm-Wood Encyclopedia of Pattern Glass.* (II vols.) Watkins Glen, New York: Century House, 1961.

Keene, Betsey D. *History of Bourne 1622–1937.* Yarmouthport, Massachusetts: Charles W. Swift, 1937.

Knittle, Rhea Mansfield. *Early American Glass.* New York, New York: The Century Co., 1927.

Lane, Lyman and Sally Lane, and Joan Pappas. *A Rare Collection of Keene & Stoddard Glass.* Manchester, Vermont: Forward's Color Productions, Inc., 1970.

Lanmon, Dwight P. "Russian Paperweights and Letter Seals?" *The Magazine Antiques,* October 1984, pp. 900-903.

_____. "Unmasking an American Glass Fraud," *The Magazine Antiques,* January 1983, pp. 226-236.

Lardner, Rev. Dionysius. *The Cabinet Cyclopedia; Useful Arts.* Philadelphia, Pennsylvania: Carey and Lea, 1832.

Lechler, Doris Anderson. *Children's Glass Dishes, China, and Furniture.* Paducah, Kentucky: Collector Books, 1983.

Lechler, Doris and Virginia O'Neill. *Children's Glass Dishes.* Nashville, Tennessee, and New York, New York: Thomas Nelson, Inc., Publishers, 1976.

Lee, Ruth Webb. *Antique Fakes & Reproductions.* Wellesley Hills, Massachusetts: Lee Publications, 1966.

_____. *Early American Pressed Glass.* Wellesley Hills, Massachusetts: Lee Publications, 1960.

_____. *Nineteenth-Century Art Glass.* New York, New York: M. Barrows & Company, Inc., 1952.

_____. *Sandwich Glass.* Wellesley Hills, Massachusetts: Lee Publications, 1939.

_____. *Victorian Glass.* Wellesley Hills, Massachusetts: Lee Publications, 1944.

Lee, Ruth Webb and James H. Rose. *American Glass Cup Plates.* Wellesley Hills, Massachusetts: Lee Publications, 1948.

Lindsey, Bessie M. *American Historical Glass.* Rutland, Vermont: Charles E. Tuttle Co., 1967.

Lovell, Russell A., Jr. *The Cape Cod Story of Thornton W. Burgess.* Taunton, Massachusetts: Thornton W. Burgess Society, Inc., and William S. Sullwold Publishing, 1974.

_____. *Sandwich; A Cape Cod Town.* Sandwich, Massachusetts: Town of Sandwich Massachusetts Archives and Historical Center, 1984.

Mackay, James. *Glass Paperweights.* New York, New York: The Viking Press, Inc., 1973.

Manheim, Frank J. *A Garland of Weights.* New York, New York: Farrar, Straus and Giroux, 1967.

Manley, C. C. *British Glass.* Des Moines, Iowa: Wallace-Homestead Book Co., 1968.

Manley, Cyril. *Decorative Victorian Glass.* New York, New York: Van Nostrand Reinhold Company, 1981.

Mannoni, Edith. *Opalines.* Paris, France: Editions Ch. Massin, n.d.

McKearin, George S. and Helen McKearin. *American Glass.* New York, New York: Crown Publishers, Inc., 1941.

McKearin, Helen and George S. McKearin. *Two Hundred Years of American Blown Glass.* New York, New York: Bonanza Books, 1949.

McKearin, Helen and Kenneth M. Wilson. *American Bottles & Flasks and Their Ancestry.* New York, New York: Crown Publishers, Inc., 1978.

Measell, James. *Greentown Glass; The Indiana Tumbler and Goblet Company.* Grand Rapids, Michigan: The Grand Rapids Public Museum with the Grand Rapids Museum Association, 1979.

Metz, Alice Hulett. *Early American Pattern Glass.* Columbus, Ohio: Spencer-Walker Press, 1965.

_____. *Much More Early American Pattern Glass.* Columbus, Ohio: Spencer-Walker Press, 1970.

Millard, S. T. *Goblets II.* Holton, Kansas: Gossip Printers and Publishers, 1940.

Miller, Robert W. *Mary Gregory and Her Glass.* Des Moines, Iowa: Wallace-Homestead Book Co., 1972.

Moore, N. Hudson. *Old Glass.* New York, New York: Tudor Publishing Co., 1924.

Mulch, Dwight. "John D. Larkin and Company: From Factory to Family," *The Antique Trader Weekly,* June 24, 1984, pp. 92-94.

Neal, L. W. and D. B. Neal. *Pressed Glass Salt Dishes of the Lacy Period 1825–1850.* Philadelphia, Pennsylvania: L. W. and D. B. Neal, 1962.

Padgett, Leonard. *Pairpoint Glass.* Des Moines, Iowa: Wallace-Homestead Book Company, 1979.

Pearson, J. Michael and Dorothy T. Pearson. *American Cut Glass Collections.* Miami, Florida: The Franklin Press, Inc., 1969.

Pearson, J. Michael and Dorothy T. Pearson. *American Cut Glass for the Discriminating Collector.* Miami, Florida: The Franklin Press, Inc., 1965.

Pellatt, Apsley. *Curiosities of Glass Making.* Newport, England: The Ceramic Book Company, reprinted in 1968.

Pepper, Adeline. *The Glass Gaffers of New Jersey.* New York, New York: Charles Scribner's Sons, 1971.

Perry, Josephine. *The Glass Industry.* New York, New York, and Toronto, Ontario: Longmans, Green and

Co., 1945.

Peterson, Arthur G. *Glass Patents and Patterns*. Sanford, Florida: Celery City Printing Co., 1973.

_____. *Glass Salt Shakers: 1,000 Patterns*. Des Moines, Iowa: Wallace-Homestead Book Co., 1960.

Raycraft, Don and Carol Raycraft. *Early American Lighting*. Des Moines, Iowa: Wallace-Homestead Book Co., n.d.

Raynor, Ellen M. and Emma L. Petitclerc. *History of the Town of Cheshire, Berkshire County, Massachusetts*. Holyoke, Massachusetts, and New York, New York: Clark W. Bryan & Company, 1885.

Revi, Albert Christian. *American Art Nouveau Glass*. Exton, Pennsylvania: Schiffer Publishing, Ltd., 1981.

_____. *American Cut and Engraved Glass*. Nashville, Tennessee: Thomas Nelson Inc., 1972.

_____. *American Pressed Glass and Figure Bottles*. Nashville, Tennessee: Thomas Nelson Inc., 1972.

_____. *Nineteenth Century Glass*. Exton, Pennsylvania: Schiffer Publishing, Ltd., revised 1967.

Righter, Miriam. *Iowa City Glass*. Des Moines, Iowa: Wallace-Homestead Book Co., 1966.

Robertson, Frank E. "New Evidence from Sandwich Glass Fragments," *The Magazine Antiques*, October 1982, pp. 818-823.

Robertson, R. A. *Chats on Old Glass*. New York, New York: Dover Publications, Inc., 1969. Revised and enlarged by Kenneth M. Wilson.

Rose, James H. *The Story of American Pressed Glass of the Lacy Period 1825-1850*. Corning, New York: The Corning Museum of Glass, 1954.

Rushlight Club. *Early Lighting; A Pictorial Guide*. Talcottville, Connecticut: 1972.

Sandwich Glass Museum. *The Sandwich Glass Museum Collection*. Sandwich, Massachusetts: Sandwich Glass Museum, 1969.

Sauzay, A. *Wonders of Art and Archaeology; Wonders of Glass Making*. New York, New York: Charles Scribner's Sons, 1885.

Schwartz, Marvin D. *American Glass from the Pages of Antiques; Blown and Moulded*. (Vol. I) Princeton, New Jersey: The Pyne Press, 1974.

Smith, Allan B. and Helen B. Smith. *One Thousand Individual Open Salts Illustrated*. Litchfield, Maine: The Country House, 1972.

_____. *650 More Individual Open Salts Illustrated*. Litchfield, Maine: The Country House, 1973.

_____. *The Third Book of Individual Open Salts Illustrated*. Litchfield, Maine: The Country House, 1976.

_____. *Individual Open Salts Illustrated*. Litchfield, Maine: The Country House, n.d.

_____. *Individual Open Salts Illustrated; 1977 Annual*. Litchfield, Maine: The Country House, 1977.

Smith, Frank R. and Ruth E. Smith. *Miniature Lamps*. New York, New York: Thomas Nelson Inc., 1968.

Smith, Ruth. *Miniature Lamps II*. Exton, Pennsylvania: Schiffer Publishing Ltd., 1982.

Spillman, Jane Shadel. *American and European Pressed Glass in The Corning Museum of Glass*. Corning, New York: The Corning Museum of Glass, 1981.

_____. *Glass Bottles, Lamps & Other Objects*. New York, New York: Alfred A. Knopf, Inc., 1983.

_____. *Glass Tableware, Bowls & Vases*. New York, New York: Alfred A. Knopf, Inc., 1982.

_____. "Pressed-Glass Designs in the United States and Europe," *The Magazine Antiques*, July 1983, pp. 130-139.

Spillman, Jane Shadel and Estelle Sinclaire Farrar. *The Cut and Engraved Glass of Corning 1868-1940*. Corning, New York: The Corning Museum of Glass, 1977.

Stanley, Mary Louise. *A Century of Glass Toys*. Manchester, Vermont: Forward's Color Productions, Inc., n.d.

Stetson, Nelson M. *Booklet No. 6; Stetson Kindred of America*. Campbello, Massachusetts: 1923.

Stow, Charles Messer. *The Deming Jarves Book of Designs*. Yarmouth, Massachusetts: The Register Press, 1925.

Swan, Frank H. *Portland Glass*. Des Moines, Iowa: Wallace-Homestead Book Company, 1949. Revised and enlarged by Marion Dana.

_____. *Portland Glass Company*. Providence, Rhode Island: The Roger Williams Press, 1939.

Taylor, Katrina V. H. "Russian Glass in the Hillwood Museum." *The Magazine Antiques*, July 1983, pp. 140-145.

Teleki, Gloria Roth. *The Baskets of Rural America*. New York, New York: E. P. Dutton & Co., Inc., 1975.

The Toledo Museum of Art. *American Glass*. Toledo, Ohio: The Toledo Museum of Art, n.d.

_____. *Art in Glass*. Toledo, Ohio: The Toledo Museum of Art, 1969.

_____. *The New England Glass Company 1818-1888*. Toledo, Ohio: The Toledo Museum of Art, 1963.

Thuro, Catherine M. V. *Oil Lamps; The Kerosene Era in North America*. Des Moines, Iowa: Wallace-Homestead Book Co., 1976.

_____. *Oil Lamps II; Glass Kerosene Lamps*. Paducah, Kentucky, and Des Moines, Iowa: Collector Books and Wallace-Homestead Book Co., 1983.

Thwing, Leroy. *Flickering Flames*. Rutland, Vermont: Charles E. Tuttle Company, 1974.

_____. "Lamp Oils and Other Illuminants". *Old Time New England*, October 1932, pp. 56-69.

Towne, Sumner. "Mike Grady's Last Pot," *Yankee*, March 1968, pp. 84, 85, 136-139.

VanRensselaer, Stephen. *Early American Bottles & Flasks*. Stratford, Connecticut: J. Edmund Edwards, 1971.

Van Tassel, Valentine. *American Glass*. New York, New York: Gramercy Publishing Company, 1950.

Vuilleumier, Marion. *Cape Cod; a Pictorial History*. Norfolk, Virginia, 1982.

Walsh, Lavinia. "The Romance of Sandwich Glass," *The Cape Cod Magazine*, July 1926, pp. 9, 26.

_____. "Old Boston and Sandwich Glassworks....," *Ceramic Age*, December 1950, pp. 16, 17, 34.

Warner, Oliver. *Statistical Information Relating to Certain Branches of Industry in Massachusetts for the Year Ending May 1, 1865*. Boston, Massachusetts: Wright & Potter, 1866.

Watkins, Lura Woodside. *American Glass and Glassmaking*. New York, New York: Chanticleer Press, 1950.

_____. *Cambridge Glass 1818 to 1888*. New York, New York: Bramhall House, 1930.

Webber, Norman W. *Collecting Glass*. New York, New York: Arco Publishing Company, Inc., 1973.

Webster, Noah. *An American Dictionary of the English Lan-*

guage. Springfield, Massachusetts: George and Charles Merriam, 1847. Revised.

_____. *An American Dictionary of the English Language.* Springfield, Massachusetts: George and Charles Merriam, 1859. Revised and enlarged by Chauncey A. Goodrich.

_____. *An American Dictionary of the English Language.* Springfield, Massachusetts: G. & C. Merriam, 1872. Revised and enlarged by Chauncey A. Goodrich and Noah Porter.

Wetz, Jon and Jacqueline Wetz. *The Co-operative Glass Company Sandwich, Massachusetts: 1888-1891.* Sandwich, Massachusetts: Barn Lantern Publishing, 1976.

Williams, Lenore Wheeler. *Sandwich Glass.* Bridgeport, Connecticut: The Park City Eng. Co., 1922.

Wilson, Kenneth M. *New England Glass & Glassmaking.* New York, New York: Thomas Y. Crowell Company, 1972.

(no author). "Cape Cod, Nantucket, and the Vineyard". *Harper's New Monthly Magazine* LI (c. 1870), pp. 52-66.

CATALOGS

A. L. Blackmer Co. Rich Cut Glass 1906-1907. Shreveport, Louisiana: The American Cut Glass Association, reprinted in 1982.

Amberina; 1884 New England Glass Works; 1917 Libbey Glass Company. Toledo, Ohio: Antique & Historical Glass Foundation, reprinted in 1970.

Averbeck Rich Cut Glass Catalog No. 104, The. Berkeley, California: Cembura & Avery Publishers, reprinted in 1973.

Boston & Sandwich Glass Co., Boston. Wellesley Hills, Massachusetts: Lee Publications, reprinted in 1968.

Boston & Sandwich Glass Co. Price List. Collection of the Sandwich Glass Museum, Sandwich Historical Society, Sandwich, Massachusetts, n.d.

Catalog of 700 Packages Flint Glass Ware Manufactured by the Cape Cod Glass Works, to be Sold at the New England Trade Sale, Wednesday, July 14, 1859 at 9½ O'clock. Collection of The Corning Museum of Glass Library, Corning, New York, 1859.

C. Dorflinger & Sons Cut Glass Catalog. Silver Spring, Maryland: Christian Dorflinger Glass Study Group, reprinted in 1981.

Collector's Paperweights; Price Guide and Catalog. Santa Cruz, California: Paperweight Press, 1983.

Cut Glass Produced by the Laurel Cut Glass Company. Shreveport, Louisiana: The American Cut Glass Association, reprinted, n.d.

Dietz & Company Illustrated Catalog. Watkins Glen, New York: American Life Books, reprinted in 1982.

Egginton's Celebrated Cut Glass. Shreveport, Louisiana: The American Cut Glass Association, reprinted in 1982.

Elsholz Collection of Early American Glass (III vols.) Hyannis, Massachusetts: Richard A. Bourne Co., Inc., 1986-1987.

Empire Cut Glass Company, The. Shreveport, Louisiana: American Cut Glass Association, reprinted in 1980.

F. X. Parsche & Son Co. Shreveport, Louisiana: American Cut Glass Association, reprinted in 1981.

Glassware Catalogue No. 25 Gillinder & Sons, Inc. Spring

City, Tennessee: Hillcrest Books, reprinted in 1974.

Higgins and Seiter Fine China and Cut Glass Catalog No. 13. New York, New York: Higgins and Seiter, n.d.

Illustrated Catalog of American Hardware of the Russell and Erwin Manufacturing Company 1865. Association for Preservation Technology, reprinted in 1980.

J. D. Bergen Co., The; Manufacturers of Rich Cut Glassware 1904-1905. Berkeley, California: Cembura & Avery Publishers, reprinted in 1973.

Lackawanna Cut Glass Co. Shreveport, Louisiana: The American Cut Glass Association, reprinted, n.d.

Launay Hautin & Cie. Collection de dessins representant... Collection of The Corning Museum of Glass Library, Corning, New York, n.d.

Launay Hautin & Cie. Des Fabriques de Baccarat, St. Louis, Choisey et Bercy. Collection of The Corning Museum of Glass Library, Corning, New York, n.d.

Launay Hautin & Cie. Repertoire des Articles compris dans la Collection... Collection of The Corning Museum of Glass Library, Corning, New York, 1844.

Launay Hautin & Cie. Usages principaux pour services de table... Collection of The Corning Museum of Glass Library, Corning, New York, n.d.

Libbey Glass Co., The; Cut Glass June 1st, 1896. Toledo, Ohio: Antique & Historical Glass Foundation, reprinted in 1968.

List of Glass Ware Manufactured by Cape Cod Glass Company. Collection of the Sandwich Glass Museum, Sandwich Historical Society, Sandwich, Massachusetts, n.d.

M'Kee Victorian Glass; Five Complete Glass Catalogs from 1859/60 to 1871. New York, New York: Dover Publications, Inc., reprinted in 1981.

Monroe Cut Glass. Shreveport, Louisiana: American Cut Glass Association, reprinted, n.d.

Morey, Churchill & Morey Pocket Guide to 1880 Table Settings. Watkins Glen, New York: Century House, reprinted, n.d.

Mt. Washington Glass Co. Clinton, Maryland: Leonard E. Padgett, reprinted in 1976.

Mt. Washington Glass Company (cut glassware). Collection of The Corning Museum of Glass Library, Corning, New York, n.d.

Mt. Washington Glass Company; Crystal Gas Fixtures. Collection of The Corning Museum of Glass Library, Corning, New York, n.d.

Mt. Washington Glass Works (glass prisms and beads). Collection of The Corning Museum of Glass Library, Corning, New York, n.d.

Mt. Washington Glass Works Price List. Collection of The Corning Museum of Glass Library, Corning, New York, n.d.

New England Glass Company. Collection of The Corning Museum of Glass Library, Corning, New York, n.d.

New England Glass Company (list of glassware). Collection of The Corning Museum of Glass Library, Corning, New York, n.d.

Picture Book of Authentic Mid-Victorian Gas Lighting Fixtures; A Reprint of the Historic Mitchell, Vance & Co. Catalog, ca. 1876, with Over 1000 Illustrations.

Mineola, New York: Dover Publications, Inc., reprinted in 1984.

Plume & Atwood Manufacturing Company, The. Simpson, Illinois: J. W. Courter Enterprises, reprinted in 1975.

Public Auction Richard A. Bourne Company, Inc. Boston, Massachusetts: The Nimrod Press, Inc., 1970–1985.

Quaker City Cut Glass Co. Shreveport, Louisiana: American Cut Glass Association, n.d.

Rich Cut Glass Pitkin & Brooks. Berkeley, California: Cembura & Avery Publishers, reprinted in 1973.

Sandwich Glass Patterns. West Englewood, New Jersey: Bernadine Forgett, c. 1960.

Taylor Bros. & Company, Inc., Manufacturers of Cut Glass. Shreveport, Louisiana: American Cut Glass Association, n.d.

BUSINESS DIRECTORIES

Boston City Directories. 1789–1891.

Resident and Business Directory of Bourne, Falmouth and Sandwich, Massachusetts. Hopkinton, Massachusetts: A. E. Foss & Co., 1900

NEWSPAPERS AND TRADE PAPERS

Academy Breezes. 1884–1886.

Acorn, The. Sandwich, Massachusetts: The Sandwich Historical Society, 1967–1987.

American Collector. New York, New York: Educational Publishing Corporation, 1933–1946.

Barnstable County Gazette. 1826.

Barnstable Patriot. 1846–1869.

Barnstable Patriot and Commercial Advertiser. 1830–1846.

Barnstable Patriot, The. 1869–1905, 1912–1916, 1918–1923.

Berkshire Evening Eagle. Pittsfield, Massachusetts: Eagle Publishing Company, 1948.

Berkshire Hills, The. Pittsfield, Massachusetts: 1904.

Bourne Pioneer, The. 1906–1907.

Brockton Searchlight, The. 1909.

Cape Cod Advocate, and Nautical Intelligencer. 1851–1864.

Cape Cod Gazette. 1870–1872.

Casino Bulletin. 1884–1885.

Chronicle of the Early American Industries Association, The. Flushing, New York: Leon S. Case, January 1938.

Crockery & Glass Journal. New York, New York: George Whittemore & Company, 1885–1890.

Crockery Journal. New York, New York: George Whittemore & Company, 1874–1884.

Glass Club Bulletin, The. The National Early American Glass Club, 1938–1987.

Hyannis Patriot, The. 1908–1909, 1916–1918, 1923–1925.

Illuminator, The. Toronto, Ontario, Canada: The Historical Lighting Society of Canada, 1987–1988.

Independent, The. 1895–1908.

Nautical Intelligencer, and Barnstable County Gazette. 1824.

Nautical Intelligencer and Falmouth and Holmes'-Hole Journal. 1823–1824.

Old Colony Memorial & Plymouth County Advertiser. 1822–1832.

Sandwich Collector, The. East Sandwich, Massachusetts: McCue Publications, 1984–1985.

Sandwich Independent. 1920–1921.

Sandwich Independent, The. 1908–1909.

Sandwich Mechanic and Family Visitor. 1851.

Sandwich Observer. 1846–1851.

Sandwich Observer, The. 1884–1895, 1910–1911.

Sandwich Review, The. 1889–1890.

Seaside Press, The. 1873–1880.

Village Broadsider, The. 1978–1985.

Weekly Review, The. 1881–1882.

Yarmouth Register and Barnstable County Advertiser. 1836–1839.

Yarmouth Register and Barnstable County Weekly Advertiser. 1839–1846.

Yarmouth Register. 1849–1906.

INVENTORY OF SANDWICH GLASS

No.	Description	Condition	Date Purchased	Amount	Date Sold	Amount

INTRODUCTION TO PRICE GUIDE

It is most important to determine the condition of a glass item before you purchase it. We are often so fascinated by a good "find" that we miss its obvious condition. The prices in this guide are for items that are in perfect, or *mint*, condition. *Mint condition* is an article of glass that is pristine. It has no defects. If there is roughage only in places where there are mold marks, it is still considered to be mint, because if the item was good enough to pass inspection at the time of production, it is good enough to be called mint today. Shear marks (often called "straw marks"), caused by cutting through a glob of glass while it was hot, do not detract from value. They are a fact of construction procedure. Manufacturing errors, such as annealing marks, bent or twisted pieces, off-center pieces, underfilled or overfilled molds, and overheating, add character to a piece of glass. However, the mint condition status of the glass is not affected. Rapid reductions in pricing are caused by damage after the time of manufacture in the following order, using the 100% value of a mint item as a base.

An unusually rare article, even though broken, must be considered for purchase regardless of price, if the serious collector is to have an example of that article.

Glass cannot be repaired without removing additional glass to smooth out or eliminate a chip. The "repair" rarely adds to value because the form of the article is altered. A goblet that has been machined down to eliminate a rim chip will not match its undamaged counterparts.

CONDITION	MAXIMUM VALUE OF MINT
CHIPPED Damage serious enough to penetrate into the body of an article, but small or shallow enough so that it cannot be glued back or replaced.	80%
BRUISED When an article has been struck with enough force to send cracks in several directions, penetrating the surface at the center.	60%
CRACKED When the glass is split through one or more layers, caused by a blow, a change in temperature, or stress in the glass at the time of manufacture. This is the first stage of deterioration, leading to eventual destruction. Value is seriously affected.	50%
BROKEN An article is broken when it is in two pieces, even though one of the pieces may only be the tip of a scallop, or the corner of a base, or the peg of a lamp font. If one piece must be glued back in order to make the article whole, the article is broken and its value must be reduced accordingly.	25%

LIGHTING DEVICES

Most early whale oil lamps were clear, so expect the price of colored lamps to be extremely high. Many early lighting devices will be priced in clear glass only. Expect to pay more for pieces accompanied by documentation.

Photo No.	Clear	Clambroth (Alabaster)	Opaque White	Canary	Amber	Blue	Amethyst	Green	Unusual Color
2001	235 ea.								
2002	450 ea.								
2003	575 ea.								
2004	800 ea.								
2005	900 ea.								
2006	900 ea.								
2007	1400 ea.								
2008	800 ea.								
2009	450 ea.								
2010	450 ea.					950 ea.			
2011	500 ea.					1000 ea.			
2012 a	25 ea.					60 ea.			
b	650 ea.					2000 ea.			
2013	575 ea.								
2014	1500 ea.								
2015	700 ea.								
2016	650 ea.								
2017 a	750 ea.								
b	650 ea.								
2018	650 ea.								
2019	190 ea.								
2020	900 pr.					7500 pr.			
2021 a	185 ea.								
b	185 ea.								
c	225 ea.								
2022	325 ea.								
2023	475 pr.								
2024	475 pr.								
2025	575 ea.								
2026	700 ea.								
2027	—								
2028	600 ea.								
2029	600 ea.								
2030	1500 pr.								
2031	700 ea.								
2032	575 ea.					1350 ea.			
2033	1000 ea.								
2034 a	175 ea.								
b	700 ea.								
2035	900 ea.								
2036	875 ea.					2750 ea.		4000 ea.	
2037 a	175 ea.								
b	700 ea.								
2038	1600 pr.					6500 pr.			
2039 a	575 ea.								
b	500 ea.								
c	—								
2040	1000 pr.								
2041	360 ea.								
2042	—								
2043	700 ea.								

Photo No.	Clear	Clambroth (Alabaster)	Opaque White	Canary	Amber	Blue	Amethyst	Green	Unusual Color
2044 a	2000 ea.								
b	1500 ea.								
2045 a	400 ea.								
b	450 ea.								
2046 a	550 ea.								
b	400 ea.		700 ea.			1800 ea. opaque			
2047	550 ea.								
2048	450 ea.				1800 ea.	1400 ea. blue and clear		1600 ea. green and clear	
2049	450 ea.								
2050	40 ea.								
2051	450 ea.								
2052	575 pr.								
2053	650 pr.								
2054	190 ea.								
2055	300 ea.								
2056	175 pr.								
2057	185 ea.								
2058	200 ea.								
2059	700 pr.								
2060	800 pr.								
2061	900 pr.								
2062	1500 pr.								
2063	450 ea.								
2064	600 pr.								
2065	750 pr.								
2066	900 pr.								
2067	400 ea.								
2068	900 pr.								
2069	800 pr.								
2070	2000 pr.								
2071	—								
2072	300 ea.			900 ea.					
2073	—								
2074	—								
2075	—								
2076	350 ea.		750 ea.						
2077						1500 opaque			
2078	100 ea.								
2079	700 pr.		800 pr.						
2080 a	90 ea.								
b	—								
2081	425 ea.								
2082	—								
2083	575 ea.								
2084	225 ea.								
2085 a			800 ea.				1200 ea.		
b			800 ea.				1200 ea.		
2086 a							4000 ea. in box		
b			800 ea.				1200 ea.		
2087	110 ea.								
2088	350 ea.					700 ea.			

Photo No.	Clear	Clambroth (Alabaster)	Opaque White	Canary	Amber	Blue	Amethyst	Green	Unusual Color
2089	50 ea.								
2090 a	110 ea.								
b	135 ea.								
2091	135 ea.								
2092	400 pr.			900 pr.	3200 pr.	2200 pr.	1800 pr.	2600 pr.	
2093 a	190 ea.			375 ea.	1300 ea.	1000 ea.	800 ea.	1200 ea.	
b	140 ea.			350 ea.		900 ea.			
2094	180 ea.			700 ea.		1400 ea.	1500 ea.	1600 ea.	
2095	5000 ea.								
2096	—								
2097 a	180 ea.			700 ea.		1400 ea.	1500 ea.	1600 ea.	
b	180 ea.			700 ea.		1400 ea.	1500 ea.	1600 ea.	
2098	235 ea.			900 ea.		1600 ea.	1750 ea.	1800 ea.	
2099	—								
2100	190 ea.			750 ea.		900 ea.	900 ea.	1000 ea.	
2101	450 pr.			1300 pr.	6500 pr.	3600 pr.	3600 pr.	6500 pr.	
2102 a	225 ea.			550 ea.	3000 ea.	1800 ea.	1500 ea.	2800 pr.	
b							1000 ea.		
2103	225 ea.			550 ea.	3000 ea.	1800 ea.	1500 ea.	2800 ea.	
2104 a	250 ea.			950 ea.		2200 ea.	1800 ea.	3000 ea.	
b				140 ea.					
2105	250 ea.			950 ea.		2200 ea.	1800 ea.	3000 ea.	
2106	235 ea.					800 ea.	900 ea.	1000 ea.	
2107	200 ea.	400 ea.	550 ea.			900 ea.	800 ea.	1000 ea.	
2108	200 ea.								
2109 a	550 ea.								
b	190 ea.			550 ea.	3000 ea.	1500 ea.	1500 ea.	2800 ea.	
2110	450 pr.			1300 pr.	6500 pr.	3600 pr.	3600 pr.	6500 pr.	
2111 a, b	450 pr.			2000 pr.		3600 pr.	3600 pr.	6500	
c	200 ea.			900 ea.		1600 ea.	1600 pr.	3000 ea.	
2112	—								
2113 a	140 ea.			650 ea.		900 ea.	900 ea.	1000 ea.	
b	140 ea.			650 ea.		900 ea.	900 ea.	1000 ea.	
2114	300 pr.			1400 pr.		2000 pr.	2000 pr.	2200 pr.	
2115									6500 + pr. peacock green
2116	100 ea.	1600 ea. fiery opalescent		950 ea.		1500 ea.	1200 ea.	1800 ea.	
2117	200 ea.	1700 ea. fiery opalescent		1050 ea.		1600 ea.	1300	1900 ea.	
2118	300 ea.	1200 ea.	950 ea.	1200 ea.		1500 ea.	1500 ea.	2800 ea.	
2119 a	300 ea.	1200 ea.	950 ea.	1200 ea.		1500 ea.	1500 ea.	2800 ea.	
b						1200 ea.			
2120	300 ea.	1200 ea.	950 ea.	1200 ea.		1500 ea.	1500 ea.	2800 ea.	
2121	650 pr.	2500 pr.	2200 pr.	2500 pr.		4000 pr.	3500 pr.	6000 pr.	
2122	60 ea. burner								
2123						4000 ea. blue and white			
2124	—								
2125	2 ea.								
2126 a	200 ea.								

Photo No.	Clear	Clambroth (Alabaster)	Opaque White	Canary	Amber	Blue	Amethyst	Green	Unusual Color
b	90 ea.					1200 ea.			
2127 a	180 ea.								
b	55 ea.								
2128	1000 ea.					3500 ea.			
2129	200 ea.								
2130	2200 ea.								
2131	—								
2132	5000 pr.								
2133	200 ea.								
2134 a	190 ea.			750 ea.				900 ea.	
b	150 ea.			450 ea.				575 ea.	
c	190 ea.								
2135 a	350 ea. pickwick								
b	75 ea. pickwick								
2136	250 ea. pickwick								
2137	160 ea.			550 ea.					
2138 a	175 ea.								
b	190 ea.								
2139	235 ea.								
	250 ea.								
2140	350 ea.								
2141	40 ea.								
2142	150 ea.								
2143	235 ea.								
2144			6000 pr.	9000 pr.		10,000 pr.	10,000 pr.	12,000 pr.	
2145		2200 ea.	2200 ea.	3500 ea.		4500 ea.	4500 ea.	5000 ea.	
2146	—								
2147	575 pr.	1200 pr.		1600 pr.					
2148 a	275 ea.								
b	225 ea.	500 ea.		650 ea.					
2149	—								
2150 a	375 ea.								
b	275 ea.	500 ea.				1200 ea. blue and white		1500 ea. green and white	
2151 a	275 ea.	500 ea.				1200 ea. blue and white		1500 ea. green and white	
b	275 ea.								
2152 a	25 ea. burner								
b	40 ea. burner								
c	60 ea. burner								
2153	100 ea. burner								
2154 a	100 ea. burner								
b	60 ea. burner								
2155	80 ea. burner								

Photo No.	Clear	Clambroth (Alabaster)	Opaque White	Canary	Amber	Blue	Amethyst	Green	Unusual Color
2156	40 ea. hook								
2157	90 ea.	200 ea.				330 ea.		575 ea.	
2158	—								
2159		1000 the set				1500 the set		1800 the set	
2160	475 pr. with burners					2250 pr. with burners blue and white			
2161	150 ea.	900 ea. fiery opalescent				575 ea. blue and clear			
2162 a	450 ea.								
b	40 ea.								
2163 a	125 ea.								
b	—								
2164	125 ea.								
2165	150 ea.								
2166	—								
2167 a	175 ea.								
b	185 ea.								
2168	375 pr.								
2169		1600 pr.							
2170 a	200 ea.								
b	185 ea.								
2171	285 ea.								
2172	175 ea.								
2173	200 ea.								
2174	240 ea.								
2175	350 ea. with teapot								
2176	100 ea. teapot with burner								
2177	250 ea.								

LAMP SHADES AND GLOBES

The shape of a shade or globe is not as important as the design that may be cut, engraved, painted or transferred onto it. The price is determined by the intricacy of the design. Prices do not reflect family documentation. Expect to pay three times these prices for pieces accompanied by family documentation.

Photo No.		Photo No.		Photo No.	
2178	75 ea.	2183	—	2191	185
2179	400 the set	2184	—	2192	—
	4200 with lamps	2185	40	2193	40
2180	180 pr.	2186	175	2194	75
2181	1800	2187	175	2195	185
	20,000 with lamps	2188	—	2196	200
	and prisms	2189	165	2197	135
2182	—	2190	—	2198	185

Photo No.		Photo No.		Photo No.	
2199	450	2214	325 with fixture	2228	80
2200	—	2215	185	2229	110
2201	—	2216	40	2230	80
2202	350	2217	60	2231	80
2203	—	2218	—	2232	55
2204	400	2219	40	2233	55
2205	—	2220	95	2234	55
2206	90	2221	85	2235	55
2207	90	2222	15	2236	65
2208	135	2223	15	2237	55
2209	60	2224	20	2238	50
2210	110	2225	20		
2211	150	2226	45 the globe		
2212	110		145 with fixture		
2213	125	2227	45		

LIGHTING DEVICES

Multiple combinations are possible when lamps are assembled by joining fonts to bases with metal connectors. Therefore the price will reflect only the lamp that is pictured. Expect to pay more for items accompanied by documentation.

Photo No.		Photo No.		Photo No.	
2239 a	550		14,000 with blue	2289	40
b	450		opal globe	2290	20
2240 a	325		16,000 with lilac	2291	15
b	165		opal globe	2292 a	285
2241	265	2267	—	b	285
2242	475	2268	125	2293	210
2243	90	2269	40	2294	235
2244	—	2270 a	125	2295	525
2245	8000	b	235	2296	525
2246	475	2271 a	140	2297	575
2247	450	b	150	2298	600
2248 a	300	2272	250	2299	—
b	—	2273 a	25	2300	575
2249	165	b	8	2301	7500
2250	110	c	40	2302	495
2251	2200	2274 a	125	2303 a	475
2252	135	b	175	b	525
2253	900	2275	—	2304	235
2254	195	2276	185	2305	575
2255	110	2277	235	2306	525
2256	110	2278	300	2307	350
2257	165	2279	190	2308	425
2258 a	135	2280	40	2309	—
b	145	2281	185	2310	425
2259	195 complete	2282	—	2311	110
2260 a	3750	2283	400 pr.	2312	850
b	6500	2284	2000	2313 a	95 pr.
2261	7500	2285	450	b	40 ea.
2262	—	2286 a	265	2314	360
2263	4000	b	210	2315	100
2264	235 peg lamp	2287 a	185	2316	—
2265	—	b	225	2317	100
2266	12,000 with white	c	160	2318	—
	opal globe	2288	265	2319	75

Photo No.		Photo No.	
2320	250 pr.	2323	160
2321 a	360	2324	450
b	160	2325	—
2322	450		

OVERLAY (PLATED) LIGHTING DEVICES

The workmanship on Sandwich Overlay lamps can be crude. The layers of glass can vary in thickness and the cut designs can vary in size on the same piece. These manufacturing inconsistencies do not deter from value. Expect to pay more for items accompanied by documentation.

Photo No.		Photo No.		Photo No.	
2326 a	400	2345	3200	2372	3000
b	375	2346	7000	2373	1200
2327	600	2347	3800	2374	1600
2328 a	60	2348	5000	2375	2200
b	125	2349	475	2376	2400
c	125	2350	1200	2377 a	375 lamp
d	150	2351	1100	b	375 lamp
2329	750	2352	1150	a	250 pickwick
2330	1000	2353	6500	b	250 pickwick
2331	—	2354	1500	2378	3800
2332	1200	2355	2000	2379	2400
2333	—	2356	7500	2380	1400
2334	40	2357	6500	2381	1600
2335	125	2358	1800	2382	8000 pr.
2336 a	90	2359	235	2383	3500
b	90	2360 a	750	2384	1800
c	75	b	800	2385	7000 pr.
d	80	2361	175	2386	1400
2337	75	2362	1200	2387	800 pr.
2338	40	2363	2250	2388	1200
2339	475	2364	2000	2389	1800
2340	900	2365	12,000	2390	1600
2341 a	360	2366	1400	2391	375 font only
b	350	2367	900	2392	1200
2342 a	275	2368	900	2393	1400
b	300	2369	1100	2394	6000
c	325	2370 a	1200	2395	2000
2343	1200	b	2500	2396	1400
2344	8000	2371	7500	2397	1800

SUSPENSION LAMPS AND LANTERNS

Lanterns are priced as if the name appearing on the globe cannot be identified. Expect to pay more for documented pieces.

Photo No.		Photo No.		Photo No.	
2398	600	2405	110	2412	75
2399	—	2406	200	2413	140
2400	600	2407	200	2414	—
2401	—	2408	110	2415	—
2402	1000	2409	40	2416	2000
2403	—	2410	250	2417	—
2404	65	2411	40	2418	—

Photo No.		Photo No.		Photo No.	
2419	—	2423	—	2427	100
2420	400	2424	600	2428	125
2421	400	2425	—		
2422	300	2426	300		

SMOKE SHADES AND BELLS

Most smoke shades and bells have an applied glass ring by which they are hung. If the hanging ring is damaged in any way, the value of the item is lost. Small bells have metal hanging rings. Do not purchase small bells that are missing their metal rings. It is impossible to find replacement metal fittings.

Photo No.		Photo No.		Photo No.	
2429	22	2442	135	2455	100
2430	60 with chain	2443	90	2456	20
2431	50	2444	100	2457	35
2432	50	2445	150	2458	85
2433	45	2446	150	2459	75
2434	65 with hanger	2447	55	2460	75
2435	55	2448	125	2461	85
2436	90	2449	125	2462	60
2437	35 with chain	2450	125	2463	115
2438	20	2451	115	2464	—
2439	25	2452	90	2465	125
2440	85	2453	90	2466	—
2441	125	2454	110		

ELECTRIC LIGHTING

Photo No.	
2467 a	15
b	—
2468 a	15
b	25